Equity by Design

Mirko's Dedication

For the Putnam Avenue Upper School Community, your passion, dedication, and courage.

For Dr. Carolyn Turk for believing in me and this work, when so many others did not.

Katie's Dedication

As always, for my sweet babies, Torin, Aylin, Brecan, and Boden.

Equity by Design

Delivering on the Power and Promise of UDL

Mirko Chardin

Katie Novak

CORWIN
A SAGE Publishing Company

A SAGE Publishing Company

FOR INFORMATION:

Corwin

A SAGE Companyy

2455 Teller Road

Thousand Oaks, California 91320

(800) 233-9936

www.corwin.com

SAGE Publications Ltd.

1 Oliver's Yard

55 City Road

London, EC1Y 1SP

United Kingdom

SAGE Publications India Pvt. Ltd.

B 1/I 1 Mohan Cooperative Industrial Area

Mathura Road, New Delhi 110 044

India

SAGE Publications Asia-Pacific Pte. Ltd.

18 Cross Street #10-10/11/12

China Square Central

Singapore 048423

Program Director and Publisher: Dan Alpert

Senior Content Development Editor: Lucas Schleicher

Associate Content Development Editor: Mia Rodriguez

Production Editor: Vishwajeet Mehra

Copy Editor: Lynne Curry

Typesetter: Hurix Digital

Proofreader: Tricia Currie-Knight

Indexer: Integra

Cover Designer: Candice Harman

Graphic Designer: Scott Van Atta

Marketing Manager: Maura Sullivan

Printed in the United States of America

Library of Congress Cataloging-in-Publication Data

Names: Chardin, Mirko, author. | Novak, Katie, author.

Title: Equity by Design : delivering on the power and promise of UDL / Katie Novak, Mirko Chardin.

Description: Thousand Oaks, California: Corwin Press, Inc, [2021] | Includes bibliographical references.

Identifiers: LCCN 2020022952 | ISBN 9781544380247 (paperback) | ISBN 9781544394435 (epub) | ISBN 9781544394442 (epub) | ISBN 9781544394459 (ebook)

Subjects: LCSH: Social justice and education. | Universal design. | Educational change. | Educational equalization.

Classification: LCC LC192.2 .N68 2021 | DDC 370.11/5—dc23

LC record available at https://lccn.loc.gov/2020022952

This book is printed on acid-free paper.

SUSTAINABLE FORESTRY INITIATIVE

Certified Chain of Custody
At Least 10% Certified Forest Content
www.sfiprogram.org
SFI-01028

20 21 22 23 24 10 9 8 7 6 5 4 3 2 1

DISCLAIMER: This book may direct you to access third-party content via Web links, QR codes, or other scannable technologies, which are provided for your reference by the author(s). Corwin makes no guarantee that such third-party content will be available for your use and encourages you to review the terms and conditions of such third-party content. Corwin takes no responsibility and assumes no liability for your use of any third-party content, nor does Corwin approve, sponsor, endorse, verify, or certify such third-party content.

CONTENTS

PROLOGUE

"The function, the very serious function of racism is distraction. It keeps you from doing your work. It keeps you explaining, over and over again, your reason for being. Somebody says you have no language and you spend twenty years proving that you do. Somebody says your head isn't shaped properly so you have scientists working on the fact that it is. Somebody says you have no art, so you dredge that up. Somebody says you have no kingdoms, so you dredge that up. None of this is necessary. There will always be one more thing."

—Toni Morrison

When we think about the work of deconstructing our school systems, it is clear that none of us can do this important work alone. We are called to find partners to carry the weight of this work because our students who are historically marginalized deserve an army. And this is our fight.

Since the inception of public education, countless individuals and institutions have contributed to and maintained the current status quo of inequitable systems, structures, practices, norms, and expectations. None of us can change the system alone. Social justice in education will only manifest through teams and partners working together to ensure that all students have equal opportunities to succeed. Professional collaboration and connection among educators called to this work are critical to dismantle the systems that have been built over the course of centuries.

Maya Angelou was an American poet, storyteller, and civil rights activist. Her work was grounded in triumph over tragedy and an unrelenting belief that she could meet any challenge head on. In the poem "Alone," Maya Angelou (1994) writes,

> *Now if you listen closely*
>
> *I'll tell you what I know*
>
> *Storm clouds are gathering*
>
> *The wind is gonna blow*
>
> *The race of man is suffering*
>
> *And I can hear the moan,*

'Cause nobody,

But nobody

Can make it out here alone.

We are writing this book together because we know that none of us can do this work alone, and yet, sometimes it feels isolating to be called to this work. When we finally cross paths with educators, policy makers, and thinkers who believe in all students and are willing to speak on their behalf, the mission to deconstruct the privilege in our educational system becomes a little more real.

As authors of this text, our professional paths intersected at a conference focused on building equity through the principles of Universal Design for Learning (UDL). Although our backgrounds are different—a black man and a white woman—we arrived at a place where we are both invested and committed to fighting for students for whom the system was not built.

We, like Maya Angelou, believe that with the right support system, every student can become the person they want to be, they deserve to be, and that success knows no bounds. In an interview for *Smithsonian Magazine*, Angelou shares that our system is often "crippling" to children as we tell them what they are supposed to be as though there is a single path to success (Moore, 2003). She writes,

> *So, yes, we cripple our children, we cripple each other with those designations that if you're a brick mason you shouldn't love the ballet. Who made that rule? You ever see a person lay bricks? [She moves her hands in a precise bricklaying manner.] Because of the eye and the hands, of course he or she would like to see ballet. It is that precise, that established, that organized, that sort of development from the bottom to the top.*

Our systems cripple many children because they were designed so that students who have been historically marginalized cannot be successful. The data speaks for itself, and yet, if you're reading this, you, like us, know we can do better. Know students deserve better. In this text, we share research and concrete strategies to help you to transform systems so that they are centered on the students we serve, not the privileged populations for whom the systems were built. And we believe, without a doubt, that this transformation is possible.

As much as we can look around the world and curse the injustices and hate that surround us, one would hope that the great promise of education, the great equalizer, as they say, would help to even the playing ground for all students and provide them with opportunities to become wildly successful in whatever life they choose to live. The purpose of education in this country, set forth by Horace Mann, was to provide all students with a free, non-selective, academically challenging, fair, and morally just system of schooling (Baines, 2006). Clearly this hasn't come to fruition, which has led to the need for universally designed, social justice education or an education focused on disrupting cycles of inequality so that every student has an opportunity to be successful regardless of their zip code, the color of their skin, the language they speak, their sexual and/or gender identity, and whether or not they have a disability.

Lawrence Baines (2006), an associate dean at the University of Oklahoma, notes, "One of the obstacles to implementing Mann's philosophy has always been that the wealthy have little incentive to abandon their privately run, well-appointed institutions, within which they wield significant power, for the motley vibrancy of the democratically controlled public school." The power and privilege of the elite has resulted in students who are segregated by race, ability, and wealth. In order to deconstruct this system, we, as educators, have to get uncomfortable and recognize the brilliance of the scholars who sit in front of us as they strive to be both bricklayers and ballerinas if those are the lives they choose.

In our partnership and friendship, we have pushed each other to grow, embrace discomfort, become aware of blind spots, and develop a richer sense of expertise and precision in regards to this work. We are incredibly grateful for the opportunity to invite you on this journey.

We wrote this book for PK–12 teachers who have the amazing privilege to alter the outcomes of students by designing equal opportunities for them to learn and succeed. Although we are both administrators—an acting principal and an assistant superintendent of schools—we argue that teachers, who have the autonomy to design learning, to create relationships, and to change the trajectory of students' lives, are in an amazing position to lead this work. Throughout the text we offer theory, practice, and implementation spotlights to inspire teachers to design more equitable learning through the principles of UDL. Let's join together and face this challenge head on "'Cause nobody, But nobody Can make it out here alone."

ACKNOWLEDGMENTS

FROM MIRKO

To Katie—it has been such an honor to be able to get to know you, learn for you, and partner with you. You motivate and inspire me to push myself more each and every day. I am excited at how much we have been able to accomplish in such a short period of time and am looking forward to continuing to expand our impact. This is only the beginning of our journey together, and I am thrilled to see what happens next.

To all our colleagues who have trusted Katie and me with your voices, work, and wisdom. This text would not exist without you. Continue to let your light shine by continuing to inspire those you work with as well as the hearts and minds of the youth and community that you are impacting in dynamic ways.

To our team at Corwin—Dan, Lucas, and Mia. Thank you for making the dream of creating a manuscript that will support educators in being agents of change through embracing UDL, social justice, and equity a reality.

To Odeline and Uncle Lami—if the two of you had not been educators and role models for me, I am not certain what direction my life may have gone in. Thank you for your love, care, guidance, and continual words of wisdom.

To Hayley—thank you for your love, support, partnership, and faith in me. You lend me strength when I am not certain that I can continue upon the path that I have chosen, and I am thankful for your willingness to be such a large part of my journey, for always having my back, for keeping me grounded, and for keeping a smile on my face.

FROM KATIE

Writing this book has been an honor, a privilege, and a challenge. I recognize the power I have in being able to share my voice, and I don't take that lightly. That being said, I couldn't have written this book without Mirko Chardin. Mirko, you have become a dear friend, colleague, and guide in this work. Your friendship, inspiration, and light have changed me more than you know. For all the late-night calls, laughs, matching outfits, and heartbreaking losses in Taboo, I love the work we are doing. And we're only getting started. Thank you.

To all our colleagues who allowed us to elevate and celebrate their voices, I am in awe of the work you are doing. Allowing Mirko and me a peek into your practice and journey, and allowing us to share it with the larger professional community has made our work so much stronger. We are nothing if we are not propelled by the stories of others. All of you have helped to carry us through this journey.

To our team at Corwin—Dan, Lucas, and Mia. Our work was merely clay, and you helped us to set it again and again to the wheel to create a polished piece to share with the world. This work is braided with your feedback, encouragement, and support.

To Mom and Dad—you raised me in a world that gave me everything, but the most important gift you gave me was the realization that what I had was just that, a gift. It wasn't something I deserved as much as something I was blessed and privileged to have. And, most importantly, that everyone should have the same. I promise you, I will always fight so everyone has the opportunities in life that you were able to give to me.

Torin, Aylin, Brecan, and Boden. I know you love to see your names in books, but what you don't know if that thoughts of you drive every word I write on every page. You have helped me to know that EVERY child is somebody's baby. And I will fight for all of them as much as I fight for you.

And to Lon, the love of my life. Even though our friends made fun of us when we got our wedding rings engraved with, "There is only one," and thought we were making an allusion to Lord of the Rings, I believe that with my whole heart.

PUBLISHER'S ACKNOWLEDGEMENTS

Corwin gratefully acknowledges the contributions of the following reviewers:

Andrea Honigsfeld, EdD
Associate Dean, EdD Program Director
Molloy College
Rockville Centre, NY

Becki Cohn-Vargas, EdD
Educator and Author
Independent Consultant
El Sobrante, CA

Kelsey Pretzer
English Teacher
East Kentwood High School
Kentwood, MI

Lisa Graham
Director, Early Childhood Education
Douglas County School District
Lone Tree, CO

Melanie Sitzer Hedges
NBCT Art Teacher
West Gate Elementary School
West Palm Beach, FL

Melissa Miller
Science Instructor
Randall G. Lynch Middle School
Farmington, AR

Natalie Bernasconi, EdD
Educator
UC Santa Cruz and Rancho San Juan High School
Santa Cruz, CA

Patricia Baker
Retired Educator/School Board Member
Culpeper County Public Schools
Culpeper, VA

Paul Forbes
Executive Director
NYC Department of Education
New York, NY

Rui Gomes
Assistant Principal of Operations & Instruction
Paul A. Dever Elementary School, BPS
Cleveland, OH

Sydney Chaffee
Teacher, Instructional Coach; 2017 National Teacher of the Year
Codman Academy Charter Public School
Dorchester, MA

Wendy Murawski
Eisner Endowed Chair & Executive Director, Center for
    Teaching & Learning
California State University Northridge
Northridge, CA

ABOUT THE AUTHORS

Mirko Chardin is the Founding Head of School of the Putnam Avenue Upper School in Cambridge, MA. Mirko's work has involved all areas of school management and student support. His greatest experience and passion revolves around culturally connected teaching and learning, recruiting and retaining educators of color, restorative practice, and school culture. He delivers keynotes across the nation on equity, social justice, and personal narrative. He is also a race, diversity, and cultural proficiency facilitator and leadership coach for the Aspire Institute at Boston University's New Wheelock College of Human Development. He is a principal mentor for the Perone-Sizer Creative Leadership Institute, a Trustee at Wheaton College, and an active hip-hop artist.

Katie Novak, EdD is an internationally renowned education consultant as well as a practicing leader in education in Massachusetts. With 17 years of experience in teaching and administration, an earned doctorate in curriculum and teaching, and seven published books, Katie designs and presents workshops both nationally and internationally focusing on implementation of Universal Design for Learning (UDL) and universally designed leadership.

UNIVERSAL DESIGN AS AN INSTRUMENT OF CHANGE

"Education either functions as an instrument which is used to facilitate integration of the younger generation into the logic of the present system and bring about conformity or it becomes the praxis of freedom, the means by which men and women deal critically and creatively with reality and discover how to participate in the transformation of their world."

—Paulo Freire

SETTING THE STAGE

This chapter is split into three sections. In the first section, we introduce the Universal Design for Learning (UDL) framework, a powerful framework that was created to eliminate inequalities, and discuss how the implementation of the framework helps to build equity in our schools and classrooms. Next, we define the concept of social justice education and make the connection between UDL and social justice explicit. Lastly, we provide concrete examples and case studies to help educators see the connection between UDL and social justice and to take first steps in deconstructing systems that don't work for all students.

THE POWER AND PROMISE OF UNIVERSAL DESIGN FOR LEARNING

Privilege: an invisible package of unearned assets that I can count on cashing in each day, but about which I was "meant" to remain "oblivious."

—Peggy McIntosh

Privilege is a funny thing. As McIntosh (1988) shares, it's an invisible package—those who carry it often have trouble seeing it. When carrying privilege, you don't have to follow the same rules. You can get in anywhere, and then once you're there, it's easy to chalk up the journey to hard work, discipline, and innate talent. Increasing segregation and widening wealth inequality are startlingly harsh realities playing out amid mythic claims that we live in a world where everyone has equal opportunities to succeed (Swalwell, 2016).

We are all born with equal potential in an unequal world that stacks against us quickly. The parents who bore us, the city we live in, how we identify, and the milieu around us make the deck loaded quickly in a multitude of different directions. The hand you're dealt is the hand you play, and when you're carrying around a full house, it's easy to say it's a fair game. At the same time, if you are dealt an inequitable hand, you can't play that round. That is the reality of many of our best and brightest young scholars due to no fault of their own.

As educators, we are expected to implement a personalized, educational framework built on the belief that "all means all," but we are faced with very political and public rhetoric that sends a different message. This corroborates the fact that we have a very shallow understanding of "all means all" and a lack of understanding of the level of complexity that is involved in supporting growth, learning, and the development of young minds. Recent breakthroughs in research on neurology and brain science have provided insights into how complex, challenging, and possible this work is.

Zaretta Hammond (2015), a renowned teacher educator, shares a growing body of research focused on how building brain power is the missing link to closing the achievement gap for underperforming culturally and linguistically diverse students. She argues that productive struggle grows brain power and can build habits of mind, intellectual capacity, and cognitive processes and structures that will prepare them for independence, complex thinking, and academic success.

Students do not have equal opportunities to reach for high expectations, grapple with complex thinking, and learn how to learn when teachers design curriculum and instruction using "one-size-fits-all" approaches to teaching and learning. You know the ones. Every student is expected to read the same books at the same pace, listen to the same lectures, and complete the same math problems using the same materials. These "one-size-fits-all" solutions expect nothing more than compliance and favor those students who don't face significant barriers to learning. Many of the "tried and true" techniques and curricula perpetuate privilege and compliance rather than focusing on the power of learning, productive struggle, and empowerment. Luckily, there is a framework that rejects these "one-size-fits-all" solutions and empowers educators to proactively design curriculum and instruction so all learners can increase their brain power and accelerate their learning. The framework is Universal Design for Learning (UDL).

What Is Universal Design for Learning?

In December 2015, the Every Student Succeeds Act (ESSA) replaced No Child Left Behind and endorsed Universal Design for Learning (UDL) numerous times as the framework to ensure that all students experience success. UDL calls explicitly for expert learning or teaching students how to learn, how to set goals, and how to share what they know to reach those goals in authentic, meaningful ways. Because students come to us with a unique mix of strengths and weaknesses, the UDL framework calls for educators to transfer power to students so they have options and choices for how to learn and how to share what they have learned.

UDL, which is built on decades of research in neuroscience, is grounded on a foundation of three principles, all of which remind educators to provide students with options for personalizing their education:

> **Universal Design for Learning (UDL):** The Every Student Succeeds Act (ESSA) of 2015 (2020) appropriates the UDL definition found in the Higher Education Opportunity Act of 2008 as a scientifically valid framework for guiding educational practice that (A) provides flexibility in the ways information is presented, in the ways students respond or demonstrate knowledge and skills, and in the ways students are engaged; and (B) reduces barriers in instruction, provides appropriate accommodations, supports, and challenges, and maintains high achievement expectations for all students, including students with disabilities and students who have limited English proficiency.

1. Multiple means of engagement

2. Multiple means of representation

3. Multiple means of action and expression

> **Multiple means of engagement:** Affect represents a crucial element to learning, and learners differ markedly in the ways in which they can be engaged or motivated to learn. There are a variety of sources that can influence individual variation in affect including neurology, culture, personal relevance, subjectivity, and background knowledge, along with a variety of other factors. Some learners are highly engaged by spontaneity and novelty while others are disengaged, even frightened, by those aspects, preferring strict routine. Some learners might like to work alone, while others prefer to work with their peers. In reality, there is not one means of engagement that will be optimal for all learners in all contexts; providing multiple options for engagement is essential.
>
> **Multiple means of representation:** Learners differ in the ways that they perceive and comprehend information that is presented to them. For example, those with sensory disabilities (e.g., blindness or deafness), learning disabilities (e.g., dyslexia), language or cultural differences,

and so forth may all require different ways of approaching content. Others may simply grasp information quicker or more efficiently through visual or auditory means rather than printed text. Learning and transfer of learning also occur when multiple representations are used, because they allow students to make connections within, as well as between, concepts. In short, there is not one means of representation that will be optimal for all learners; providing options for representation is essential.

Multiple means of action and expression: Learners differ in the ways that they can navigate a learning environment and express what they know. For example, individuals with significant movement impairments (e.g., cerebral palsy), those who struggle with strategic and organizational abilities (executive function disorders), those who have language barriers, and so forth approach learning tasks very differently. Some may be able to express themselves well in written text but not speech, and vice versa. It should also be recognized that action and expression require a great deal of strategy, practice, and organization, and this is another area in which learners can differ. In reality, there is not one means of action and expression that will be optimal for all learners; providing options for action and expression is essential.

Source: CAST UDL Guidelines, 2018. www.cast.org

The UDL foundation serves to eliminate barriers to learning. In contrast, when teachers design curriculum to be "one-size-fits-all", students in a classroom are expected to have the same learning experience each day. This results in barriers for many students. These barriers can be categorized into barriers to access and barriers to engagement.

The purpose of education for centuries was the acquisition of knowledge, and even that was secured for the most privileged students. Teachers were hired as subject-matter experts, and it was their calling to transfer this knowledge to the next generation. You probably remember the classrooms of our childhood: a middle-class white woman as teacher, worn brown or grey desks, heavy textbooks, worksheets, multiple-choice tests, no mention of race, class, gender, religion, or sexual identity, and teacher-directed lectures while we feverishly took notes in composition books. Without Siri and Alexa, we had to [gasp] memorize information because unless we had access to a college library and encyclopedias, we may never have the opportunity to learn it again. And many teachers assured us, usually without providing context and/or relevance, "You will need this later."

Now this knowledge is at the fingertips of our students, so we need to transform classrooms to teach students how to use all this information in meaningful ways and how to think critically at high levels. Because knowing how to apply knowledge and resources to accomplish something is far more important than acing a multiple-choice test.

If teachers require all students to read the same text to build knowledge, they are not recognizing that the text may not be accessible to many students. In inclusive classrooms, some students may not decode at that level yet, are English language learners, are visually impaired, struggle with fine motor skills, struggle with executive function, and/or may face cultural barriers. A traditional novel or textbook is not the best tool for these students. When using the principles of UDL, teachers are reminded to provide options for representation so texts are accessible. For example, students can be encouraged to access the traditional text or access the same content in audio or video or in an e-book so they can customize the display of information. Providing these options for all students embraces diversity, values all learners, and provides students with access to rigorous curriculum.

Making learning accessible, however, is only the beginning. Educators must also provide options and choices so students are engaged with content that is relevant, authentic, and meaningful. In the example above, not only would educators be challenged to encourage students to choose text representations that are accessible, but they would also allow students to choose resources that are engaging and culturally sustaining. In UDL, student voices are critical. When providing options, we can share our standards with students and then ask them, "What do you already know about this and what else do you need to learn?" "What is the most accessible way for you to learn it?" And finally, "How are you going to express what you learned so we both know that you met the standard?" This allows for both linguistically appropriate and culturally sustaining options for all learners, and most importantly, the learning is student-directed and learner voice is optimized.

When teachers align the design of learning experiences to the three UDL principles, all learners personalize their journey to the same destination, and this celebrates every student as they drive the learning that is taking place. The two words that drive UDL are "choice" and "voice." How often, in your learning environment, do all students truly have choice and voice?

Where to Begin? Reflecting on Ourselves, Our Students, and Our Systems

To implement UDL, the beginning of every learning journey is paved with self-reflection and self-assessment. In order to set meaningful goals for your journey to eliminate inequities, you have to understand where you are starting from. Before diving deeper into UDL and its connection to privilege, equity, and social justice, ask yourself some tough questions. One teacher suggests simply asking the following questions to students, but we believe these questions must also be turned on ourselves. When you think about teaching and learning, the questions can be framed as a starting point to examine systemic inequality in your school or district (Blake, 2015).

- When decisions are being made, how is "who has a voice and who is left out" represented?

- How are who benefits and who suffers reflected across race, class, gender, and religious lines?

- Who determines if and why a given practice is fair or unfair, and what is their identity and background?

- What is required to create change, and who is responsible?

- What alternatives can we imagine if we reimagine our system? What would change and why?

These questions allow us to grapple with our own contributions to the systems we inhabit. Whether we are in a place of privilege or not, we own this problem, and we have the potential and power to address it through actions that communicate positive change.

Many students do not have access to learning opportunities that support their cognitive development or their personalized journey. To fight against this injustice, educators should examine their own implicit bias (see callout box for definitions of "bias") and beliefs, their power and privilege, and create classrooms and schools where all students have equal opportunities to learn, share their voice, speak their truth, and work toward meaningful, authentic, and relevant goals.

Bias is a tendency to believe that some people, ideas, and so forth are better than others, which often results in treating some people unfairly.

Explicit bias refers to attitudes and beliefs (positive or negative) that we consciously or deliberately hold and express about a person or group. Explicit and implicit biases can sometimes contradict each other.

Implicit bias includes attitudes and beliefs (positive or negative) about other people, ideas, issues, or institutions that occur outside of our conscious awareness and control, which affect our opinions

Once we ask ourselves tough questions, we have to acknowledge that our students witness and experience hate, discrimination, marginalization, and apathy based on race, sexual and gender identity, homelessness, religion, socioeconomic status, immigration. language, and disability both inside and outside our schools. These experiences affect their readiness to learn when we implement traditional, one-size-fits-all curriculum and pedagogy.

Educators hold incredible power: power to design learning experiences, power to set expectations for students, power to elevate and celebrate student voices, power to inspire and motivate students, power to create consequences, and power to allow for choice and personalization. We have to understand that all of us carry that power and privilege and we must use it as a tool to confront and dismantle inequities so all students have equal opportunities to learn.

There are times of tragedy where student voices are amplified to the nation. As one example, consider what occurred at Marjory Stoneman Douglas High School in Parkland, Florida. In February 2018, a gunman opened fire with a semiautomatic weapon at his former high school, murdering 17 classmates. In the aftermath of the event, students Cameron Kasky and David Hogg founded Never Again MSD and became leading voices in the nation's debate on school safety. A tragedy thrust them onto the stage of advocacy where suddenly the power of rhetoric, ideas, and words became relevant, authentic, and meaningful. But why should other students have to wait for tragedy to strike to have their voices heard? They don't.

and behavior. Everyone has implicit biases—even people who try to remain objective (e.g., judges and journalists)—that they have developed over a lifetime. However, people can work to combat and change these biases.

Confirmation bias, or the selective collection of evidence, is our subconscious tendency to seek and interpret information and other evidence in ways that affirm our existing beliefs, ideas, expectations, and/or hypotheses. Therefore, confirmation bias is both affected by and feeds our implicit biases. It can be most entrenched around beliefs and ideas that we are strongly attached to or that provoke a strong emotional response.

Source: Facing History and Ourselves (2020)

Education today should be designed to elevate and celebrate the voices of students. A focus on teaching advocacy and channeling student passions in our classrooms needs to replace our focus on depositing knowledge to students sitting passively in rows. These boys and their peers aren't inserting themselves into national politics because they learned to diagram sentences, analyze Shakespeare, and complete worksheets of quadratic equations. They have a voice because someone taught them how to be motivated, self-directed, purposeful, and resourceful.

We don't know the GPAs of Kasky and Hogg, and in truth, we don't care. Those grades don't matter because these kids are speaking out to make a difference, in spite of critics, hate, and politics. All students should have the same opportunity to have their voices heard.

In a meeting between Parkland students and the "Peace Warriors," a group of predominantly black high school students from Chicago who have been fighting gun violence for 10 years without garnering much attention from the outside world, Sarah Chadwick, a Parkland survivor stated, "I acknowledge my white privilege. . . . I said it because it's true. White privilege does exist, and a lot of us have it. . . . . If we could use our white privilege to amplify the voices . . . then we're going to use it, the more we ignore it, the worse it gets" (Chan, 2018).

She is acknowledging that Parkland, a wealthy suburb of Broward County, had been named one of the safest communities in Florida before a gunman killed 17 students and faculty in a mass shooting—while more than 3,400 people were shot in Chicago in 2017 alone, according to police. Arieyanna Williams, a 17-year-old Peace Warriors member, shares, "We felt like we weren't alone in this situation and we finally can use our voices on a bigger scale." The meeting reaffirmed her belief that she had to stop accepting gun violence as normal. She goes on to add, "Parkland is one of the safest cities in Florida. . . . It's a different moment for them to realize that just because they had that title that it wouldn't happen to them. We see it every day. The difference is the amount of violence going on, the similarity is the hurt. They thought for so long they'd never see the violence and we thought for so long that we couldn't see it stopped." Through the sharing and acknowledging of voice and difference, the two student groups realized they had a lot in common; they are "fighting for the same thing." (Chan, 2018)

The tragedy at Parkland and the public acknowledgment of privilege have provided students around the country with an opportunity to see the power of voice, of motivation, and of passion. And this is why we teach our kids. Students need to know that education is about creating a better world and making changes where changes need to be made. As Cameron Kasky tweeted (3/10/2018), "Guys I just heard a crazy wild ridiculous bonkers rumor that amendments can be amended. . . ."

By implementing UDL, we are focused on providing more students with the type of education that will prepare them to identify problems and create strategies to solve them and make a new and better world.

Next Steps

Take time independently or with colleagues to journal your answers or foster courageous conversations in a professional learning community or faculty meeting using the following questions.

- What is our desired impact?
- Who do we want our students to become?
- What world, society, and/or time period are we preparing them for?
- What does it look, feel, and sound like when we are successful?
- What role do we play in student success?
- How have we engaged in courageous conversations?
- How do we acknowledge and celebrate differences?
- Do all members of our school community feel safe, seen, and heard?
- Does our work validate the lives and experiences of folks from different backgrounds and/or identities?

CONNECTING UDL AND SOCIAL JUSTICE

How can we, as educators, align our practice to UDL so all students learn how to sustain effort and persistence, to know they matter, to question everything, to think critically, to be resourceful, to collaborate, to be global citizens, and to set meaningful goals to change our world for the better? The following steps are critical signposts in the journey.

Identify the Barriers

To start, we need to identify and acknowledge all of the potential barriers that stand in the way of teaching and learning being universally accessible and engaging, so that we can design environments, lessons, units, curricula, and learning experiences that ensure that all of the learners in our classrooms have authentic access despite ability and/or language. Then, we must take this a step further by going beyond access through acknowledging that the barriers that must be addressed and removed cannot be limited solely to ability and/or language but must include race, class, gender, religion, and sexual identity.

Embrace Variability

UDL is critical for educators to design and deliver an education that meets the needs of all students and empowers them to personalize their pathways. UDL isn't a one-size-fits-all framework, which means if all students in your class are expected

> Variability is the dynamic and ever-changing mix of strengths and challenges that make up each individual. Often, lessons are designed based on perceived ability, but ability is only a single variable in the mix of strengths and challenges, and it varies widely depending on the task.

to be doing the same exact thing, it's not UDL. Given their variability and their different needs, one curriculum, without embedded flexible options using the principles of UDL, cannot possibly build equity within the classroom. Instead, educators need to embrace a framework that acknowledges and celebrates the unique identities of students and provides all students with whatever they need to be successful.

Reflect on Our Biases

Next, we need to examine our practices, tools, and resources to ensure that they are not biased, therefore limiting access to students based on identity and/or culture, so that all students have authentic, engaging opportunities to learn. We often have the tendency to believe that some people, ideas, and so forth are better than others, which often results in treating some people unfairly. This can manifest implicitly as well as explicitly with the former perhaps being the most dangerous. Again, we must consider race, class, gender, religion, and sexual identity to confront whether or not our practices and materials reflect all of our learners by treating their respective identities with respect and dignity.

Expect Discomfort

We need to normalize discussing and addressing issues that typically make us uncomfortable: privilege, race, class, gender identity, religion, sexual identity, and ability. We must embrace the fact that our classrooms and school need to be brave spaces in order to truly be transformative. Brave spaces are ones in which we have the courage to lean into discomfort for the sake of authentic conversation, dialogue, and practice. The desire to maintain a sense of comfort, while addressing issues of inequity, reflects privilege, which can easily be surfaced by asking whose level of comfort we are concerned with: Is it that of our students who have been disabled by the system and our practices, or is it that of our own?

Amplify Student Voice

As educators, we need to empower all learners. To create a world that is socially just and equitable, we need to arm these kids with powerful weapons—their voices. To do this, we need to transform our schools and ensure that students and all stakeholders learn to embrace their own identity, appreciate, value, and respect diversity, and take action against hate and injustice by participating in courageous conversations and sharing their stories using multiple means of representation. We need to ensure that the culture of our system, schools, and classrooms are welcoming to all and we truly elevate and celebrate the voices of all students and provide them with a platform to share their voices, all while ensuring that the notion of difference is both thoroughly embraced and celebrated and kept at the center.

Take Action

Most importantly, we have to take action. We need to have the courage to examine our thinking, practices, traditions, and culture to ensure that despite whatever we believe our intentions to be, we don't get in the way. We must acknowledge that the impact of our action or lack of action, in and through the lives of our students, matters more than our intentions. Therefore, we must value impact over intention to make changes in our classrooms, learning, and schools.

Our goal as educators is clear. We must create learning environments that give all students equal opportunities to personalize their education, share their voices, and create their own paths to success while embracing their own identities. This is not to say that we don't have academic goals for students—we do, but those goals and objectives must fit into a larger context/journey for our students—one that leads them to academic and social growth, empowers them as agents of change, and builds positive identity development.

Too often, schools are focused on the power of a packaged curriculum in changing the outcomes of students. Among practitioners of UDL there is a saying that gets to the heart of this—"kids over content." Standards and curriculum are important, but they are only the beginning. If empowering young minds is what our work as educators is about, then we need to keep our students, their humanity, their lives, and their experiences at the center of our work and decision-making; a UDL approach and a social justice lens work in tandem to make this possible.

Social Justice as Moral Imperative

A socially just approach to education is rooted in the core belief that our systems are broken and that all educators, despite their role and/or title, must do more than what has been prescribed to them to positively impact the lives of the students and families that they serve. In an education system that purports to value inclusion, many students have been excluded from the same opportunities bestowed on their peers, and this must be fixed. We, as educators, cannot remain silent. As Elie Wiesel, a Holocaust survivor penned, we cannot remain neutral.

As educators, we must examine the dispositions that are needed to build a foundation for a socially just education in all of our schools and fight until these systems are in place. Recent research on the importance of social justice education argued that educators must have a moral commitment and courage to make changes that will transform education for all students—especially those who have traditionally been underserved by our schools (Allen, Harper, & Koschoreck, 2017). We must summon such moral commitment to acknowledge and address the harsh truth that our systems do not work for all students. Instead, they function as if they are rigged to serve a small number of privileged students, while sacrificing all too many. Only by continuously examining our own assumptions, beliefs, and practices can we begin to ensure that we are not contributing to the inequities that the system propagates.

Without this moral imperative, we may provide students with implicit messages about their worth by delivering a hidden curriculum that isn't focused on equality or equity but the perpetuation of the status quo. In short, we have made many of our students the victims of their own education by not acknowledging how varied their identities and experiences of our system and society are.

> **Hidden Curriculum** was coined by Jean Anyon (1980) to explain the phenomenon where teachers share their expectations of students implicitly through their instruction and how they define student success.

As Jonathon Kozol (1991) notes in *Savage Inequalities*, "But what is now encompassed by the one word ("school") are two very different kinds of institutions that, in function, finance and intention, serve entirely different roles. Both are needed for our nation's governance. But children in one set of schools are educated to be governors; children in the other set of schools are trained for being governed. The former are given the imaginative range to mobilize ideas for economic growth; the latter are provided with the discipline to do the narrow tasks the first group will prescribe."

Social Justice as Hidden Curriculum

If students are only ever taught how to follow directions, take orders, and follow along, they will never be creators and thinkers, makers, and writers. They will never learn the power of their own identity, their own thinking, and their own voice. They will be governed by those who continue to have power and privilege and make the rules. They will never have an opportunity to speak their truth, create their own path, chart their own course, and impact our society.

To do this, educators have to be aware of both their explicit curriculum and their hidden curriculum. For example, if teachers are focused solely on classroom management, following directions, not asking questions of authority, and completing traditional assessments using traditional curriculum materials, they are sending a message that it does not matter whether you feel seen or heard and that success is doing what you're told. Think about the message that is sent to those students—compliance, routine, and subservience are the goal.

We often measure the level of compliance through grading. In the text *Grading for Equity*, Feldman (2018) highlights the truth that as much as we have worked to change policies and procedures to address inequity and disproportionality, teachers have "one remaining island of autonomy" in their grading procedures. Whether we choose to acknowledge it or not, teacher grading practices reflect their own identity and values. Awarding points for being on time, meeting assignment deadlines, and participating in class reflect a teacher's belief that those skills are important. These traditional grading practices may have helped to perpetuate inequities in the classroom implicitly.

On the other hand, when teachers focus on embracing identity, voice, diversity, problem-solving, creativity, and personalization through the UDL framework, they are sending a very different type of message on what it takes to be successful. If students don't have these opportunities to personalize their education so it's relevant, authentic, and meaningful, they will become what Zaretta Hammond has coined as "dependent learners," meaning that they will be overly reliant on the teacher to carry the load of the cognitive task, will be unsure of how to tackle new tasks, will not be able to complete tasks without scaffolds, will sit passively and wait until the teacher intervenes, and will not retain information well (Hammond, 2015). In other words, they will be taught a form of learned helplessness.

On the contrary, in a social justice curriculum, teachers work hard to be transparent about their privilege, their practices, and why they have structured things the way they have. There are numerous options and choices for students to share their voices and their feedback about the design of instruction. When we universally design curriculum and elevate student experiences and their voices, our "hidden curriculum" is transparent and empowering.

Social Justice as Equity

In order to ensure that hidden curriculum is socially just, it's important that educators understand the distinction between equality and equity. Boris Kabanoff (1991), a professor at the University of New South Wales, wrote a compelling article titled "Equality, Equity, Power, and Conflict." This piece provides a foundation for differentiating the two constructs.

Equality is the belief that all people have equal value as individuals and should therefore have equal inputs and outcomes. In short, equality is equal distribution where everyone gets the same thing, distributed evenly among them because everyone has the same worth. Sounds warm and fuzzy, doesn't it? Equality, through an education lens, generally translates into an argument of high expectations using one-size-fits-all practices. When focused on equality, we, as educators, have the same high expectations for all students and provide them with the same instruction, curriculum materials, and assessments as if providing students with the same high quality of education will result in equal outputs. Equality of outcomes, according to

Kabanoff, emphasizes a "common fate" and cohesion, thus, in theory, promoting solidarity. The problem with this is that no educator could possibly argue that what we have been doing has resulted in "common fates" for any of our students. There's a reason for that. In organizations that focus on equality, according to Kabanoff, the main function of equality is to maintain and preserve the arrangement of roles or relationships created by the system. That's clearly what has happened in education.

Equity, in comparison, is focused on productivity, or ensuring that everyone has what they need in order to be successful. This "fair distributive principle" means that marginalized individuals will need significantly more inputs to have the same, or similar, outputs than individuals with privilege and power. The conflict here is that often people in power perceive equity as unjust because they feel they deserve an equal share. People in power and privilege often want equality when what we need to transform education is equity if our goal is to provide access to all learners. The UDL framework was designed to eliminate inequities, not perpetuate equality.

This is the reality we face. This is not about blame, shame, or judgment, but embracing the reality that our educational system does not take into account the condition of learners when they walk through our doors. Learners who are brown, broke, and have emotional, behavioral, and learning and/or physical disabilities, are English language learners or are LGBTQ individuals and have not been the beneficiaries of the best that we have to offer, because they have been systemic afterthoughts. In short, the best we have to offer is equally distributed, and those who need it the most simply get "their share" at best, while those with power and privilege continue to flourish.

Kozol (1991) explores this concept further when he notes, "Unless we have the wealth to pay for private education, we are compelled by law to go to public school—and to the public school in our district. Thus the state, by requiring attendance but refusing to require equity, effectively requires inequality. Compulsory inequity, perpetuated by state law, too frequently condemns our children to unequal lives."

Social justice is about the belief that every person deserves an equal opportunity to succeed—or, as Kozol would say, an equitable life. The truth is this: If we believed that, we would create public schools where all students have equal access to high-quality teaching and curricula that allow them to feel safe, seen, and heard while providing them with the skills they need to overcome inequity. We would all invest our best resources into public schools, and we would fight like hell.

Social Justice as Impact Over Intentions

A socially just education is not solely about what we say or what we aspire to; it's about what we do. It's about how we measure impact.

It's about being morally courageous enough to acknowledge publicly that what we are both currently doing and expected to do isn't working for all students. It's about acknowledging and owning the fact that it never worked—that being well intentioned is not good enough. Systems must acknowledge that the work is not just about our presence but what specifically we are doing and how we measure impact in and through the lives of our students.

In a recent article, "Equity in Our Schools: A Pretty Little Lie," the concept of "good enough" was examined for its incredible hypocrisy in an educational landscape where teachers are evaluated in teaching all students (Fritzgerald & Novak, 2019).

> *The answer to improving our schools is not to settle for "pretty good" or to create newer and "better" options. Instead, we need to invest in our current schools and deconstruct the systems we have established that do not meet the needs of teachers and marginalized students. We need to create opportunities where every single student is treated with dignity and respect, held to high expectations, and supported academically, behaviorally, and social-emotionally. This change does not require new buildings or new frameworks but instead involves an acknowledgment of and alignment to the evidence-based ideas about equity and race that are endorsed today that are being ignored.*

As the world, through daily technological advances such as the widespread usage of social media, becomes a smaller and smaller place, the acknowledgment of difference has become more commonplace. Fortune 500 corporations know that to turn a profit and stay competitive in the world of today, they must embrace diversity and expand their knowledge of cultural intelligence, however imperfectly. Schools are one of the few structures that exist in our world that purport to recognize and embrace diversity; however, our systems clearly have not adapted to the point that such a claim can possibly be substantiated. We are rooted in traditional ideals of how students should be taught and how they should behave—norms that are relics of a time in which our society openly oppressed any who did not fit into the typical upper-middle-class, white, male prototype.

Through engaging with this work, you will be inspired to stand up and challenge the status quo through your actions and decision-making. You will learn from the examples and strategies that we present you with as well as implementation examples from our colleagues that social justice is about action. To be socially just is to do work that leads to powerful impact. It is to make change. We have written this text as a guidepost, one with multiple entry points. You don't need to be an expert to believe in and do this work; you just have to be open, humble, and committed. We do not profess to have all of the answers, but we have concrete strategies to share—strategies that work.

Our work as social justice educators is fluid, and a commitment to engaging in such work requires us to forever be open to learning new methods, strategies, and approaches. We believe in this vision, and if you're reading this, it's because you do too. So, game on.

Next Steps

Sanjin (2009) notes that "during his or her stay in school, the student experiences three types of education: useful, unnecessary and negative" and made an explicit connection to these three types of education and hidden curriculum. Take a moment and consider your own education. What strikes you as being the most useful thing you learned in school? The most unnecessary? The most negative?

Useful	Unnecessary	Negative

Once you are done, consider how the negative education you received may have been underpinned by a hidden curriculum, such as a teacher's teaching style, the system of punishments and rewards, the climate and culture of the classroom, and the educational space (Safta, 2017).

Reflection Questions

- What is a socially just education, and how does it align with the principles of UDL?
- How can a socially just education address some of the disparities that your students have or may encounter?
- What are the key differences between "equality" and "equity"?
- What is a "hidden curriculum"? What hidden curriculums exist in your institution, practice, and/or classroom?
- What does "impact over intentions" mean to you?
- How do UDL and social justice complement each other?

Additional Resources

- To learn more about UDL and the concept of variability, access UDL Theory and Practice, which is free online at http://udltheorypractice.cast.org/
- To learn more about Jonathon Kozol's work, visit his web site at https://www.jonathankozol.com/

CONCRETE EXAMPLES AND STRATEGIES

Many educators have taken on this fight, and you will hear from them throughout the book. We also empower you, as a reader, to begin to change your own system, regardless of where you teach. Every educator can be a social justice educator. To provide an example, we'd love to introduce you to the work of three of our colleagues, Dr. Linda Nathan, Carmen Torres, and Ian Wilkins.

Teacher as Artist, Educator, and Community-Based Leader

Linda Nathan, EdD, is executive director of the Center for Artistry and Scholarship (CAS). As an experienced leader in education, she actively mentors teachers and principals and consults nationally and internationally on issues of educational reform, leadership, teaching with a commitment to racial justice and equity, and the critical role of arts and creativity in schools.

Carmen Torres, co-founder of the Perrone-Sizer Institute for Creative Leadership, is a veteran urban school educator and school founder. Carmen facilitates workshops and trainings focused on issues of race, equity, and culturally proficient pedagogy.

Carmen and Linda are committed to distributed leadership where educators take on leadership roles within their schools and districts. Their advice for anyone trying to change the status quo? "Leadership is about adapting and evolving with a sense of humility and a sense of humor. Listening is a much underrated element of leadership."

One critical aspect of UDL is to empower student voices as you design learning experiences that impact them. As you develop your leadership potential, don't forget to foster collaboration and community with the students you serve by providing them with options and choices to be co-designers and to make them an integral part of the decision-making process. As educators, as you consider stepping into your school community or department as a social justice leader, consider how the following implementation spotlight can support you on your journey to optimize voices of students as you eliminate barriers to authentic, rigorous learning.

IMPLEMENTATION SPOTLIGHT

BY DR. LINDA NATHAN AND CARMEN TORRES

We deeply believe that the schools we have today should not be the schools we have tomorrow. If we are going to speak seriously about delivering culturally responsive and equitable education for all students, we must acknowledge the scope of the

(Continued)

transformation required, the vision, self-reflection, creativity, social capital, technical expertise, and raw talent we will need from every individual involved.

Any great change requires great leadership, of course, but so much "school reform" today seems to rely on what we like to call the Superman or Superwoman mentality—that we need a hero to swoop in to save us, who through the use of data or a new reading strategy will "fix" all that is wrong. And too often, the professional development provided for emerging leaders perpetuates this superhero myth and the never-ending quest for the quick fix.

So, a few years ago, we asked ourselves, what would be a revolutionary approach to educational leadership development that would foster equally revolutionary change? We knew we wanted to cultivate leaders who build and depend upon networks and partnerships, who walk beside rather than in front of the communities they serve, and who take an artist's or designer's approach to experimentation and creative problem solving. We wanted to nurture creative, community-focused leaders who would motivate their colleagues, communities, and students to try, fail, and try again until we begin to close the gap between today's reality and what we believe is possible.

The Perrone-Sizer Institute for Creative Leadership (PSi) develops creative, innovative, equity-focused leaders of both schools and youth-focused nonprofits, who apply the perspective of three lenses to the challenges they face:

- The Artist – accessing inspiration and utilizing creativity, design, risk-taking, and experimentation to solve complex problems; artists persist and consider, refine, and illuminate many different approaches.

- The Educator – committed to racial justice and equity, and informed and driven by research; drawing upon a deep knowledge of child and adolescent development; and applying a profound understanding of the learning process to prepare students for academic and personal success.

- The Community-Based Leader – employing a culturally proficient understanding of the needs of youth and families in a given community to engage effectively in a dynamic collaborative process of community growth, development, and networking.

At the center of PSi is the Capstone Leadership Project, which the program builds toward throughout the year. It is participant driven and independently designed to suit the professional goals and interests of each individual in the cohort. The Capstone Leadership Project must: 1) address an opportunity for growth in the participant's learning community, and 2) leverage a partnership between a community-based organization and the home organization. Participants are expected to develop a project that improves outcomes for youth and their families.

The following vignette written by a PSi student about her Capstone project illustrates the potential of a network of colleagues and of organizational partnerships both to solve common challenges and to challenge and change beliefs that stand in the way of culturally responsive teaching and leading.

A shift to the students' perspective

When I started my Capstone project, I thought it was a technical fix to class size overage. We started "Leadership Elective" because there weren't enough specialists to cover the middle school planning block. We selected older students with behavior problems with their grade level peers and placed them in a "leadership" role in a younger classroom. We observed that many behavioral problems disappeared. This led us to expand the program school-wide, opening the opportunity for all middle school students to participate in leadership roles throughout the building. Discussions then turned toward creating a community service component by partnering with a local elder care facility. I took on the role of liaison between the community partner and the school.

Going into this partnership program, I had the mentality that my students were the only ones who stood to gain from the experience. I was going to teach them how to care about others and how to show social responsibility—how to act for the benefit of the community at large rather than just for themselves. What I learned, through the reflections and questioning of my cohort members, instructors, and guests who came to speak with us at PSi, was that my students already had a strong sense of who they were and how to act in authentic community situations. The experience and insights of fellow educators helped me recognize that my students already brought a wealth of kindness, consideration, and compassion that teachers often didn't have the opportunity to see within the confines of the regular school day. What I discovered was a bigger issue that needed to be addressed: how to fix the cultural value mismatch that sometimes presents itself when students enter an artificial community, such as that of a school. How do we help students feel representation and agency within a school?

With a new lens, I was able to shift my work to help both students and teachers better visualize how student voice and agency could be valued. The adaptive challenge at hand was how to shift the traditional school structure so that students could see their assets honored. I'll never forget a student at the beginning of the program who responded angrily when reminded of how he was expected to conduct himself on our first community service trip because he was representing the school. "Yah, but does the school represent me?" he challenged. It was then that I realized we didn't have a behavior problem at my school but a deeply seated cultural problem. If students don't feel empowered and embraced by their school community, they will not engage. I believe that by trying to repair that broken connection, we can take steps towards helping students have a vision of what social justice can mean within a school. And that, in turn, has become the new focus of my Capstone project.

—Amy Wedge

This emerging leader, through conversations and work with colleagues who challenged her assumptions, and through her ever-improving ability to listen to colleagues and collaborators in this work, has deepened her own self-knowledge and her ability to see and build upon the assets of their learning communities. And she has embraced not the heroic, but the *collective* effort that is required to ensure that we don't "allow cultural bias and access gaps to continue to flourish within new structures." As Zaretta Hammond suggests—and our students understand—*we* are the strategy

Next Steps

- Identify, if any currently exist, or develop opportunities for students who are currently considered as disengaged to positively contribute to the school community in nonpunitive ways, for example community service, as mentioned above.
- Create a list of potential community service opportunities and resources for students.

(Continued)

- During a faculty meeting, discuss the following questions:
  - What are we allowing our students to teach us?
  - Are we explicitly valuing their funds of knowledge or treating them like empty vessels to be filled?
- How are we helping students to feel representation, agency, and self-efficacy?

Additional Resources

- Learn more about the Center for Artistry and Scholarship's Perrone-Sizer Institute for Creative Leadership at www.artistryandscholarship.org/psi

- Linda Nathan blogs regularly at www.lindanathan.com.

Finding the Social Justice Key

Ian Wilkins is a quiet force in the classroom. Standing at over six feet tall, he is as foreboding as a linebacker, but speaks in a soft voice, knows how to craft a guitar from raw wood, and spent his summers studying literature at the Bread Loaf School in Vermont. He started his career as a musician and embraced the grunge scene in Seattle at its height. He wears a rust-covered cardigan from which his knuckles peek out, tattooed with "Rock" on the fingers of one hand, and "Roll" on the other.

Ian Wilkins is a high school English language arts teacher. After many years of pursuing a career in music and working blue-collar jobs to make ends meet, he had an epiphany that ultimately led him to obtain a BA in English/secondary education. "Teaching is in my family, and I always had it in the back of my mind. My time playing in bands had run its course, and I wanted to do something that mattered. I've always been an agent for change, even when working in the most trivial jobs, and I thought, 'Maybe I can bring this into a classroom, a school, a community, and see if I can make a difference.'"

Ian approaches his teaching and role in the school community with a focus on authenticity. All of the real-world experience he gained prior to returning to school helps to add important perspective to the learning and training he has received and puts into focus for him what his responsibilities are as an educator. When he considers the power of design, he looks for opportunities to make dynamics of power and privilege more visible to students so they can begin to work to eliminate the status quo. The concepts of "voice" and "choice" go far beyond any benefit of personalized learning. UDL is focused on distributing privilege and empowering diverse voices. This is important in every district and in every classroom.

IMPLEMENTATION SPOTLIGHT

BY IAN WILKINS

"I work in a school district that is based in a couple of middle-class to upper-middle-class towns, with a student body that is demographically very non-diverse—mostly white, mostly secure socioeconomically. We have great resources and a very comfortable working and learning environment. The challenge here is that the students and the community don't necessarily feel the realities of social injustice in their daily lives; they live in a bubble.

"I've struggled since coming here to figure out how to pop that bubble and bring a dose of reality to these students. And I've struggled to feel like I'm doing something meaningful by teaching in a place like this, where you don't necessarily see the difference you're making in individual lives, definitely not in the same way as when you work with underserved students in communities that face many more hardships."

The problem of how to have an effect as a social justice–oriented educator in a privileged community has been at the forefront of Wilkins's mind ever since he transitioned from his student teaching in a low socioeconomic, highly diverse school district to his current job, although some of the roots of it can be traced back to his own school and life experiences. It can seem daunting, yet he never doubted its importance and has come to some deep realizations about it.

"Almost all of my students are coming from a place of privilege. These are kids who will get great educations, and will go out into the world and be influencers and wielders of power. It's one thing to empower marginalized groups in society's hierarchies; the crucial importance of this is obvious. But eventually they will come up against others who hold the power to make decisions—about things like employment, housing, finance, politics. Where are those in power coming from? What kinds of perspectives do they have? Unless someone with influence along the way has purposefully challenged them to consider the world they live in from a social justice standpoint, I don't feel confident that they will use their power and privilege in just ways. It seems like a huge challenge, but I have a sense of responsibility to it that motivates me. I could easily ignore the outside world and go about my business here in a culturally myopic way and nobody would ever really challenge me on that. Which, I think, makes it more imperative that I work hard to bring as much awareness as I can to issues of social justice.

"Yet, what kind of difference can I really make as one person? I have a metaphor that I find very useful in seeking an answer to this question: There is a castle, heavily fortified, gates shut. Outside the walls, disease, hunger, war, and all manner of other problems plague those who live there. Of course, things are very comfortable and safe inside. There are people outside who work hard to make those people's lives better, in the trenches with them. Some of these altruists even grew up inside the castle and, having peered over the walls by some twist of fate or influence, chose to leave the comfort and venture out to make a difference. But mostly the castle-dwellers are content and inward-looking. What if the castle were to open its gates? What if there was one person on the inside, one person with influence and drive, who convinced the castle-dwellers that it is their responsibility to allow access to their resources, to open the gates and create a free flow between the inside and outside? Maybe they could make space in their castle. Maybe they could help build other castles. Maybe they can't afford to ignore what's going on outside the walls

(Continued)

(Continued)

anymore. That one person, if she is successful, could have an incredibly outsized influence on the state of the kingdom, as it were."

While Wilkins is still in his early years of teaching, he has had some successes in having an effect on his students and on the culture of his school. He sees what he is doing as a step-by-step process, one that requires equal parts passion, practice, and persistence, which Singleton and Linton (2006), editors of *Courageous Conversations About Race: A Field Guide for Achieving Equity in Schools*, consider the three critical factors or the three Ps of courageous conversations.

Next Steps

BY IAN WILKINS

Start Small, Be Observant. Metaphors can be useful in understanding the general philosophical underpinnings of an idea, but every school community is different and therefore requires a different approach for the educator who seeks change. For example, saying that a school district is nondiverse and privileged actually tells you very little about it. It's important to fully understand all of the complexity at play: Who are your students? What kinds of families do they come from? What do they think about and care about? How do they self- identify? What are their hopes and dreams? Who are the administrators and leaders in your school? Who are your colleagues in teaching, guidance, and so forth? What are the historical events in the district and school that have shaped the attitudes and perspectives there?

As a teacher, you have multiple avenues for finding answers to these kinds of questions. Design lessons in your classroom that prompt students to think critically and to be self-reflective. Engage your students in discussions about themselves and their lives. And introduce them to concepts of social justice through your curriculum (e.g., choosing texts to work with that give them perspectives they don't normally get, discussing the history of the subject matter you teach with a focus on diverse groups, and encouraging them to question their own ideas and beliefs).

Look for the Key: Now that you've taken the time to get a full sense of what it is you are working with (and up against), try to find the key to the gate, to return to the castle metaphor. You can't try to change everything all at once, but if you can find one thing, one issue or way of thinking that you identify as fundamental to how the community operates, you can focus your attention and efforts. For example, Wilkins found that while it's important to bring diversity to his students by introducing other perspectives, other lives, and so forth, they fundamentally remain concerned with what's right in front of them. This means that, when he teaches something like the history of how African Americans have faced individual and systemic racism, or the origins and fallout of the Iran-Iraq war, or issues facing the post–Duvalier Haitian diaspora, his students can be engaged on an academic level but tend to stay emotionally and psychologically removed. What he realized was that when he prompted them to look at an issue from a gender-equity perspective, they were engaged on a much more personal level. Why? Because for all of the homogeneity in the student population in terms of socioeconomics and race, gender diversity is present in their immediate experience, which means it is unavoidable for them. Based on proximity and/or acknowledged connection to an issue, we respond to it either emotionally, intellectually, morally, and/or relationally

(Singleton & Linton, 2006), and the more he thought about it, the more he saw the ways that his school is locked into gender stereotypes. A look at gender issues appears to be the key to the gate.

Take Your Ideas and Run With Them: Now that you've been observant and patient, and the key has been identified, the next step is to go big! Look for ways that you can take what you've found to the whole community. Wilkins, once he had identified gender as the key, immediately began reworking some of his lessons to take on a feminist critical lens. He also took the opportunity to volunteer to design and lead a professional development series titled "Gender Stereotyping in Our School Community." This had several positive effects: He was able to collaborate with colleagues on this key issue, getting their perspectives and creating allies simultaneously; it identified him as a leader, someone who is looking to have those difficult but important conversations; and it let the rest of the school community know that this issue was being looked at in a serious way. He then was given the chance to learn more about how other schools approach gender issues by attending a conference where he identified a gender violence awareness program that he plans to bring to his school in the next couple of years. And he is now leading a group whose purpose is to investigate the causes of gender-based gaps in standardized testing throughout the district, an opportunity that all of his previous work had set him up for perfectly. He believes that altering the way the school community thinks about gender will establish a framework for other social justice issues to be thought about in a more authentic way

Reflection Question

Regardless of where you teach, what is your "key"? To ask a different way, what inequalities exist in your learning environment that you can explicitly name and use as a foundation to discuss more implicit inequities?

Additional Resources

- www.jacksonkatz.com – Jackson Katz is an educator, speaker, filmmaker, and public intellectual who challenges his audiences to see that while gender issues have traditionally been seen as women's issues, they are equally men's issues.

- www.mvpstrat.com – Mentors in Violence Prevention is an organization, started by Jackson Katz, that provides training and curriculum in professional and educational settings on how to understand, recognize, and prevent gender-based violence.

- Follow Ian on Twitter – @IanPWilkins – to see how all of his efforts are going!

CHAPTER TWO

LAYING THE GROUNDWORK FOR SOCIAL JUSTICE IN OUR CLASSROOMS AND LEARNING COMMUNITIES

"Justice will not be served until those who are unaffected are as outraged as those who are."

—Benjamin Franklin

SETTING THE STAGE

This chapter introduces five steps for beginning social justice and equity work in our classrooms and learning communities: concept stabilization, concept calibration, identity development, equity audit, and taking action. Each of these steps is critical in building the foundation of a more equitable school and aligns to the principles of Universal Design for Learning (UDL). Concrete strategies, steps, and protocols are offered in each step.

Just as you can't reap fabulous produce without hard work and healthy soil, you also can't begin to transform your learning environment without taking concrete action steps to prepare an academic and social environment for the growth that will occur. When our vegetables don't grow, we don't blame the soil. We have to work to determine how to change the soil so it better supports growth. Similarly, to transform our classrooms and learning communities, our approach must be grounded in diagnostics and not deficits.

Our "soil" must be nourished with the notion that all learners, with no exceptions, can and will succeed. To some, these are lofty ideas, but to those who are committed to being agents of change, who have dedicated themselves to transforming the experience and life of the learners who our system has forgotten, these ideas are our truth and way of life and will result in fabulous growth for all students. This foundational work, as we call it, will ensure that your classroom, learning community, school, or district is primed and ready to implement the strategies that follow.

Universal Design for Learning (UDL) is a framework that can transcend classroom instruction. Systemic barriers prevent students from accessing and engaging with high-quality instruction. Just as UDL can be used as a framework for lesson planning, it can also be used for reflective professional learning and designing classrooms and systems that work for students academically, behaviorally, socially, emotionally, and culturally.

To offer a universally designed framework for beginning social justice work in your school, we have outlined a series of five steps that are critical in creating foundations for social justice and equity. These five steps address potential barriers that have the potential to derail social justice work. These potential barriers include but are not limited to the following:

- **Step 1: Concept Stabilization.** Critical to build a shared understanding of what social justice is and/or why it is necessary

- **Step 2: Concept Calibration.** Helps to build agreement and define what socially just, universally designed practice looks like in practice

- **Step 3: Identity Development.** Provides an opportunity for all teachers to embrace their own identity and recognize bias, including but not limited to implicit bias

- **Step 4: Equity Audits.** Provides evidence on the differences in student experience as a result of race, class, gender, sexual and gender identity, ability, language, and/or religion.

- **Step 5: Taking Action.** Empowers educators to take action against inequity, oppression, and discrimination

The steps that follow address some of these barriers by providing options and choices for you, as educators, to help to "fertilize the soil," where equity can grow.

CONCEPT STABILIZATION: DEFINING SOCIAL JUSTICE IN YOUR CONTEXT

Educators at the Putnam Avenue Upper School in Cambridge, Massachusetts, value diversity and have collectively defined "social justice" as recognizing the different experiences that come with race, class, gender, sexual identity, ability, language, and religion. On their website, they state, "We believe it is our responsibility to use this knowledge to better the world we live in."

We share this as an example of the first condition of a social justice education. You must be able to define "social justice" for your classroom, team, and school, then create a shared vision of what social justice is in order to build a foundation for growth. After reading Chapter 1, take an opportunity to define "social justice" for yourself in the space that follows. If you have the opportunity to share your definition with a professional learning community or colleagues, please do. We have to normalize conversations about social justice, and that begins with our ability to name what social justice is.

Define "social justice" in the space below:

_____

_____

_____

_____

Every classroom, school, and district is different so the implementation of strategies and practices to support the pursuit of social justice will vary based on the context. At the same time, regardless of context, if a commitment to social justice cannot be explicitly named, then there is no real commitment to being socially just.

We truly believe that you have to start somewhere, and it's never too late to name *for your students* what social justice is and what you are doing about it. It doesn't matter if it's during the first quarter, term, semester, or your final class of the year. Our challenge to you is to explicitly name and introduce social justice to your students and/ or team, and engage them in creating or renewing a commitment to a shared vision for your work.

We suggest sharing a snapshot of what to expect from an introduction to social justice so you heighten the salience of goals and objectives and highlight that social justice is on the map and is important. Here is a sample lesson that you can use or adapt for this first and crucial step. Although the lesson is designed for middle to high school students, it can be adapted to elementary students by providing more scaffolding and initial exposure to concepts of social justice through read-alouds, short videos, and/or explicit vocabulary instruction on what "fair" and "unfair" mean, and how they relate to the concept of social justice.

The Time for Equity Is Now! Protocol

Objectives:

- Reflect on our current understanding of social justice, as well as the impact of power and privilege on academic success.
- Create a shared definition of "social justice."

Warm-Up:

Entrance Ticket: as students enter the classroom, have an entrance ticket where they have to complete a sentence like, "If I had to define "social justice," I would define it as. . . ." You can provide the option to fill out a hard copy of the ticket or contribute on a Padlet or Google Doc. Arrange all the tickets on the wall and project electronic submissions. This is a great opportunity to model reflection live and begin a conversation about the importance of creating one definition as a learning community. Be bold and share the definition you created with your students.

The Why:

If you have technology available, have a QR code or bit.ly waiting for students that brings them to the Google Doc with multiple options for them to explore resources about social justice. Instead of "Now we're all going to read an article," lead them to a page that notes "You will have 10 minutes to explore a resource to build background knowledge on why a renewed emphasis on social justice is critical. You can watch a video, read an article, and so forth."

If you don't have technology available, you may want to create stations where students can explore books, and articles, talk to a guest speaker, or watch a short video on a single device. The options are endless! This not only helps them explore concepts of justice in engaging ways but also may be your first step into implementing Universal Design for Learning (UDL) in your classroom to optimize choice.

The What:

- We stole this idea from a rock star teacher/friend, Tara Trainor. The activity is called "Pass the Plate." After exploring resources and seeing everyone's initial definitions of "social justice," provide students with a prompt, as in, "What are all the words that come to mind when you think of social justice?" Then, put them in groups of four or five students and give every person in the group a marker and one cheap paper plate per group. Set a timer for two minutes and have groups feverishly write their ideas as they pass their plate around. Activities like this ensure participation from all group members and provide the option for physical activity. When the two minutes are done, collect and display the plates. Allow everyone to take a quick learning walk to view everyone's answers before coming back and beginning a discussion.

This is a great way to build background knowledge, optimize reflection, and build community—in only a couple of minutes.

- 10 minutes: Working in dyads or groups of three, participants share their updated definitions of "social justice" using the resources they have explored as well as the products of the Pass-the-Plate activity and combine them into a single (collective) definition. They then write their definition on large chart paper or use a digital platform.

- 10 minutes: As a whole group, participants review all posted statements and highlight critical concepts, words, and ideas that resonated from each group's contribution.

Wrap-Up:

As a ticket out, have each learner share how their understanding of social justice changed throughout the class. Consider providing them with options to share their perspective: Create a Twitter hashtag, post a Padlet, and provide a hard copy of the ticket or a link to the Google form. This allows for multiple means of action and expression.

We can't emphasize enough the importance of an entire school community engaging in Concept Stabilization as well as the remaining four steps. The previous protocol can also lend itself to a variety of professional learning settings including but not limited to PLCs, faculty meetings, and school or district leadership teams. Consider how you can introduce or facilitate the protocol with your team to get the conversation going. If your school is already committed to social justice, the activity can still be a great review activity to reflect on the work you have done. The following chapter will provide an in-depth exploration of how you can apply an equity/social justice lens to the work of your PLCs.

CONCEPT CALIBRATION: NOW THAT WE'VE DEFINED IT, WHAT DOES IT LOOK LIKE?

In addition to naming a commitment to social justice and defining the term, it's imperative that classroom communities as well as the wider school community calibrate their understanding. Calibration is the second foundational condition for social justice and perhaps the easiest one to overlook or take for granted.

By "calibration" we mean providing an opportunity for stakeholders to be made aware of the definition as well as to develop a shared understanding or interpretation of the common definition and what it looks like in practice. If there is no calibration, then it is very likely that efforts to act on your definition of "social justice" will be inconsistent or, even worse, counterproductive.

Calibration, in many research studies, focuses on interrater reliability, which is the degree of agreement among raters or the consensus they have when interpreting a concept. A common example of this is studying the scores assigned by evaluators when asked to respond to whether a particular student (or educator) came close to meeting a designated standard.

All stakeholders in a socially just system must have strong inter-rater reliability when it comes to unpacking and aligning practice to the district or school's definition of "social justice." To put it simply, all members of the community should agree on what a socially just education looks like and understand the concrete actions and strategies that ensure more equitable outcomes for all students. This is incredibly important because a "firm goal" of social justice ensures that all learning is designed in order to provide pathways to the goal. Since UDL is all about "firm goals, flexible means," different educators may provide variable learning experiences, but all of them lead to equitable opportunities for all students to learn.

One great way to begin this work at the classroom level is to watch videos and ask students to make a list of teaching strategies and actions that they believe promote social justice, while also noting those that would create barriers through the lens of Universal Design for Learning (UDL).

Similarly, the adults in the school community should take the time to engage in calibration activities. As an example, the Massachusetts Department of Elementary and Secondary Education website has a tool for educators and administrators called the Calibration Video Library. The videos, which represent a range of teacher practices, are not meant to be exemplars. Rather, they serve a developmental purpose in that they allow educators to collaboratively analyze the videos and compare notes on the effectiveness of the teaching practices depicted in the clips, using an Educator Evaluation rubric. We argue that these videos can also be used to calibrate a shared understanding of social justice. [Note: anyone can access these videos at http://www.doe.mass.edu/edeval/resources/calibration/]

After watching short videos, whether you are working with your students or with colleagues, all should review their notes and begin to create a "look-fors" tool in a shared document that could then be shared with teachers as they implement instructional rounds to see evidence of effective social justice practice throughout the school.

As an example, consider the complexities of understanding what it means to create a foundation for social justice by fostering trauma-informed practice. Oftentimes, when learning about pedagogical practice, seeing the practice in action helps to provide a visual representation.

Given that so many students experience trauma, it is important that educators be aware of the impact of trauma as they design learning experiences for students. When teachers are trauma-informed, they can play a major role in improving

> Trauma-informed practice is focused on approaching the teaching and learning process with an informed understanding of the impact trauma can have on learners (Cavanaugh, 2016).

educational outcomes for the more than 25% of students who encounter physically, sexually, or emotionally abusive experiences that are perceived as traumatizing (Crosby, 2015).

Stress and trauma are both barriers that need to be named and taken into consideration to ensure that all students can be fully present. Recent breakthroughs in neuroscience have taught us that stress and/or trauma can potentially manifest as physiological barriers to learning by triggering a fight-or-flight response. It is key to note what actually happens in the brain once this natural protective response is invoked—the brain is flooded with the chemical cortisol, which cuts off access to the neocortex (the part of the brain where thinking and the processing of new thoughts takes place) as well as to long-term memory. It takes on average three full hours before the cortisol is gone. As social justice educators, we need to ensure that our actions and practices are not unintentionally triggering this response in our students, by proactively using UDL lens to removing things from our practice that may manifest as barriers due to insensitivity to stress and/or trauma.

Using the UDL lens, trauma-informed practices are designed to minimize barriers for students who experience trauma and stress. A colleague who is an expert in trauma-informed practice is Alice Cohen. Cohen had been a theatre teacher for 20 years when she transitioned to children's residential treatment programs. Her years with these young people taught her how to shape the environment and intervention to create the conditions for success. Alice has tremendous respect for these young strivers, and in her current role as the Lead Teacher for Social Emotional Learning for the Cambridge Public Schools, she continues to help schools build the capacity of the adults to understand and respond to traumatized and stressed learners and to create classroom environments that are informed by the current research of the neurobiology of trauma.

IMPLEMENTATION SPOTLIGHT

BY ALICE COHEN

We cannot minimize the impact of trauma and toxic stress on learning. Marginalized populations affected by poverty and violence come to school with additional burdens: The growing brain can be hijacked by the intensity of this stress. These students are more likely to use behavior as the method for emotional communication. These behaviors can be impulsive and intense. Traumatized students are more likely to be suspended for what appears to be egregious behavior but is, in reality, emotional communication related to help-seeking behavior.

(Continued)

(Continued)

A school can implement best practices for learners who experience trauma in the following ways:

- Providing professional development to all of the adults in the learning setting. This training describes the impact of trauma on the developing brain, tools, and strategies for understanding and intervention, particularly in the area of teaching self-regulation and relationship-building.

- Providing opportunities for adults to check in frequently about the experience of students. Is there time in the schedule for this? How is it monitored?

- Creating systems of support for young people both in and out of the classroom. What supports are available for all students academically, behaviorally, and socio-emotionally?

- Creating conditions in the classroom to increase a sense of soothing and containment. Are there conditions of nurture?

- Building systems of restorative practice for young people.

Next Steps

- Again, these practices shouldn't be limited to actions of adults in the school community. Consider sharing the practices with students as you ask them the following questions to help calibrate their understanding of socially just education and optimize their voices so you ensure that you design options and choices that work for them. Each question aligns with one of the best practices noted by Cohen.

- The following calibration protocol can be used in your classrooms to help refine teacher and student understanding of socially just curriculum and instructional practices. The activity, which requires access to videotaped lessons such as the aforementioned Massachusetts calibration video collection, can also be adopted for use in your professional learning communities or team meetings. Alternatively, individual teachers are encouraged to share the results of the student activity with their PLCs as a way of further honing the staff understanding of teaching practices that promote social justice.

Reflection Questions

- What are the best ways for teachers to check in on students academically? Behaviorally? Social emotionally? For example, do you prefer informal check-ins every day, check-ins via technology, scheduled meetings, and so forth?

- What supports in class help you to feel successful and a part of the community?

- What practices help you to feel cared for in the classroom?

- If you do something that requires discipline, what are the most effective ways to help you to not repeat the behaviors?

Additional Resource

- The School Justice Partnership, which provides an overview of the impact of trauma on students, offers strategies for creating trauma-informed classrooms. You can download this guide at https://safesupportivelearning.ed.gov/resources/trauma-informed-classrooms

Calibrating Our Understanding Social Justice Protocol

Objectives:

- Translate our "social justice" definition into a list of "look-fors."
- Calibrate our understanding of our social justice "look-fors."

Warm-Up:

Display the "social justice" definition that was created in a previous class or team meeting. Line a table with chart paper and ask everyone to list practices or draw pictures that help to align to the definition of "social justice." You may want to start by providing exemplars also. For example, you may identify such practices as allowing students to choose to study books written by authors who look like them or offering students the opportunity to share their knowledge through multiple means of expression.

The Why:

Once everyone sits down, ask them to review their brainstormed list of "look-fors" and then share that everyone is going to have an opportunity to view the practice of a classroom teacher to determine the teacher's effectiveness in creating a socially just classroom. It's important to note that one cannot rate a teacher in such a short amount of time, but it does provide a foundation to discuss what practices provide students with equal opportunities to learn.

The How:

1. Before watching the video, ask students to discuss what they hope to see. For example, what type of teaching would provide students with equal opportunities to succeed? This discussion will minimize errors based on the interactions between raters and the task. For example, "What would a socially just middle school math class look like?" "How can teachers empower students to embrace their identity and foster collaboration?"

2. Once everyone has discussed what to look for, play the video for 5 minutes. After viewing the video, ask students, "How would you feel about being in that class? Did you see anything that would make you feel like the teacher valued social justice?" Alternatively, you can ask, "Did you see anything that would make you feel like the teacher didn't value social justice? Why and how could he or she have used different practices?"

IDENTITY DEVELOPMENT: WHO ARE WE, AND WHAT DO WE BELIEVE?

As a classroom community or a professional learning community, you have created a shared vision for social justice and have begun to unpack what social justice could look like in practice. As a next step, you, as a teacher, need to begin to explore and acknowledge the barriers that may get in the way of creating an environment that is culturally responsive and socially just, including the presence of implicit bias. Begin this process by reflecting on your own identity as well as the intersectional identities of your students. One example of how to foster reflection about bias and identity development was contributed by Dr. Brian Wright.

Brian L. Wright, PhD, is program coordinator and assistant professor of early childhood education at the University of Memphis in Texas. Brian's research focuses on high-achieving African American boys/males in urban schools, pre-K–12, racial-ethnic identity development of boys and young men of color, African American males as early childhood teachers, and teacher identity development. Brian is the author of *The Brilliance of Black Boys: Cultivating School Success in the Early Grades* (Wright, 2018).

Wright's "Photo-Cultural-Ecological Self-Study Paper" (PCESSP) is a very effective assignment that promotes identity development and awareness. We encourage you to apply this concept to your individual work as a teacher. We have adapted this prompt to be a brief written reflection, journal entry, composition of a series of social media posts, or rich discussions with your colleagues in a professional learning community. You can learn more about the assignment and the theory and practices that build a foundation in the Implementation Spotlight below.

IMPLEMENTATION SPOTLIGHT

BY BRIAN WRIGHT

Culturally Competent Teachers

Culturally proficient teachers of students of color and those living in poverty have an awareness of the social construction of their identities and those of their students and what those identities represent in broader social contexts. Teachers need to be aware that identity is shaped by cultural experiences and that both the individual and the cultures they represent have an impact on teaching and learning. This becomes especially poignant in the case of white, middle- and upper-class teachers where there is a need for them to recognize what they symbolize: their whiteness, along with the power and privilege it embodies. It is important to note that while student diversity has continued to increase, teacher diversity has not. Some 52% of students are non-white, but some 85% of teachers are white (Kena et al., 2016). Although a teacher may share many cultural aspects with his or her students, including racial and ethnic background, other differences, such as socioeconomic status, can create challenges for teachers. Moreover, matching in terms of race and ethnicity does not equal consciousness. Hence all teachers need to become aware of the many cultures they are a part of as well as the impact of structural inequalities and how these factors might affect their teaching and their students' learning.

Photo-Cultural-Ecological Self-Study Paper

This assignment is grounded in three theoretical frameworks. They include sociocultural theory, bioecological systems theory, and positionality theory. For more information on these theories, please see Appendix A. This assignment broadly conceived aims to sustain and advance the profession of teaching guided by the "affirmation that all students deserve a high-quality educational experience, with a fully prepared teacher in every classroom" (AACTE, 2018, p. 1).

This assignment aims to expose educators to the world critically and their position in it. This focus is primarily because teachers must be "prepared to understand, respect, and address" (AACTE, 2018, p. 3) the unequal distribution of resources that limit access and opportunity for students from historically marginalized populations. Moreover, this assignment is designed to help educators understand and value the legitimacy of cultural heritages as legacies that affect students' dispositions, attitudes, and approaches to learning as well as their own.

Using This Assignment to Optimize Social Justice and Eliminate Inequities in a Learning Environment

The Photo-Cultural-Ecological Self-Study paper was created as an initial assignment to elicit personal reflections and responses through photographs of cultural artifacts (e.g., rosary beads, rainbow/LGBT pride flag) in order for them to undertake a critical self-study of their own cultural/ethnic identity development. Educators use photographs to illustrate a succinct and compelling narrative that pays explicit attention to multiple identities that have shaped and informed their attitudes, beliefs, values, and practices in and outside of the classroom. Examples of these

(Continued)

(Continued)

identities include but are not limited to "race, ethnicity, gender, gender expression, age, appearance, ability, national origin, language, spiritual beliefs, size [height and/or weight], sexual orientation, social class, economic circumstance, environment, ecology, culture . . ." (Conference on English Education Commission on Social Justice, 2009).

This assignment is important to optimize social justice and eliminate inequities in a learning environment in part because educators must reflect on how issues of access and opportunity are granted or denied on the basis of one or more of their identities. More importantly, this assignment encourages teachers to teach all students more fairly and equitably because they understand every student in their respective classrooms is entitled to the same opportunities for academic achievement regardless of background or unearned privilege.

How to Replicate This Assignment for Your Own Reflection

What follows is an outline of the requirements and expectations for replicating the Photo-Cultural-Ecological Self-Study paper assignment as one way to develop cultural proficiency in teachers. This assignment can be adapted for use with middle and high school students as well. The requirements are as follows:

1. Include a total of five photographs. The first four should be recent photographs, and the final photograph should be an older one (possibility from childhood). The purpose of including an old photograph is to document/describe a sociohistorical moment. All photographs should illustrate participation in various cultural communities.

2. Photographs should reflect and represent some aspect of the author's culture (e.g., ethnic/racial identity, region of country s/he is from, neighborhood, socioeconomic background, gender, sexual orientation, language, religion, lifestyle, past experiences). For example, authors may include photos of food, celebrations, natural places, and images that represent memories. NOTE: Photographs should not include buildings, people, or Internet pictures.

3. Decide whether to document aspects of early childhood, adolescence, and/or adulthood, OR all three.

4. Evidence of critical thinking and examples of learning, unlearning, and relearning should be explicit in the narrative (Wink, 2010). By this I mean educators are encouraged to reflect on critically how the "who" and the "what" they are has contributed to where they are i.e., access and opportunity). Educators are encouraged to reflect on how their access and opportunities might have been limited based on a different set of identities e.g., race, sexual orientation, disability, etc.

5. In a brief paper, journal entry, or series of social media posts, take the reader and/or audience on a "Photo-Cultural-Ecological Self-Study Journey" of their cultural/ethnic identity formation specifically indicating the impact of this introspection in shaping their attitudes, beliefs, values, and practices.

6. Finally, educators are encouraged to share at least one photograph and its significance and what they actually learned, unlearned, and relearned with their peers.

Critical to this assignment is a personal interrogation of your ethos, beliefs, cultural practices, and the impact of American culture/ideologies in terms of race, class, gender, economic, and social divisions that remain in our society. This interrogation should result in consideration of "temporal experiences"—past, present, and future—of the learner's narrative toward a deeper introspection of what these revelations may mean for their work with students and families. What follows are quotes taken from papers written by a diverse group of teacher candidates.

Voices of Teacher Candidates

Lisa, Chuck, and Ming-Lee (all names are pseudonyms) come from very different cultural, socioeconomic, and linguistic backgrounds. All three share the discomfort, disbelief, and alternative views to ponder as a result of their own reflections on what sociocultural experiences make them the teachers they are. Lisa, a middle-aged white female, undergoes a life-altering experience when she suddenly finds herself outside of the comfort zone of her previously unexamined whiteness.

When My Bubble Burst

Lisa's examination and reconstruction of her experiences growing up emphasize living a sheltered life and then having to come to terms with all that she had assumed about the opportunity structure that she believed worked the same for all Americans irrespective of race, class, and gender. She explains: "I have lived a sheltered life and a sheltered white life at that. Now at the age of 25 years old, I am being made aware of what the world is really like and being forced to see and acknowledge my whiteness as it represents not only the color of my skin but the language I speak, the biases I will never have to encounter, and the everyday experiences which I take for granted."

Lisa furthered explains that having to reflect upon her sheltered life became an immense source of anxiety and discomfort whenever she found herself engaged in conversations about race and racism: "It is this sheltered life that I will need to overcome in order to effectively teach students who haven't lived the same life as me. It is this sheltered life that leaves me feeling helpless when the issues of race come up in a classroom [urban university] setting among students because this is something that was never discussed or acknowledged in my classes [previous rural university]."

On the one hand, Lisa worries about the reality of the effect that having lived a sheltered life might have on her work as a teacher. However, on the other hand, she appears ready to confront her fears: "It is my sheltered life that I need to break away from to benefit not only for myself as a person but for the sake of my students so that the same disservice I feel was done to me is not done to them."

To Be Black American or Nigerian Is the Question

Chuck's dilemma comes as a contrast to Lisa's. A recent college graduate, he quickly learned what it means to self-identify as either black American and/or Nigerian in U.S. society where the identification as black American was considered a negative label. He explained: "As I moved up in the grades, I started identifying less with being black and more with being Nigerian. When you say you're a Nigerian, people—that is, teachers and administrators— equate that with being an immigrant. And it is perceived by people in this society that immigrants strive for educational advancements. So, identifying more with being Nigerian, a black immigrant, opens up more opportunities in some instances and less in other cases but more importantly set me apart from the less positive classification of

(Continued)

(Continued)

being a black American. From this experience, I feel it is my duty to introduce my students to the notion of Pan-Africanism to understand the contributions of black Americans within the Diaspora."

Despite the urgency on Chuck's part not to be associated with what he had come to understand as negativity with respect to black Americans, he (though not reflected in his quote) learned that whether being black American or Nigerian, his experience with both overt and subtle forms of racism abound, resulting in his desire as a teacher to teach his students about the African Diaspora developing students' ethnic pride individually and as a group. Moreover, he comes to learn that respectability politics—the idea that if black people alter their behavior to attempt to appease some arbitrary standard of mainstream decorum, their humanity will command more respect—is similar to the myth of meritocracy.

Who Am I?

Ming-Lee, just like Chuck, is in search of her identity as an Asian American of Vietnamese ancestry. She is also a recent college graduate. She explores what it was like as she was in search of her identity: "I went through a time where I wanted to change my name to an 'American name' and eat only 'American food.' that period lasted for a while until I realized how beautiful my culture was: My language, my family, and my values. These are innately who I was and am—this assignment led me to examine the ways in which society (i.e., Dominant Culture) forces non-white groups to reject their racial/ethnic/cultural identity in order to be a true 'AMERICAN,' and I can't risk this happening to my students."

The evidence suggests that teachers' multicultural consciousness may be raised through such an assignment. Specifically, their recognition of the ethnic, racial, socioeconomic, or linguistic divisions that remain in society heightens and leads to their desire to work to transform the culture of schools in order to be effective teachers of students from diverse backgrounds and complex environments.

Conclusion

Research that focuses on race, culture, and positionality emphasizes the contextual nature of class, race, and gender and how these social position variables socially, institutionally, and historically structured opportunities to learn for some, while prohibiting others. Moreover, engaging educators around issues of class, race, and gender plays up the importance for teachers to pay careful attention to their own and others' racialized and cultural systems of coming to know, knowing, and experiencing the world. In addition to developing racial and cultural consciousness, this assignment aims to help:

- examine and address their own ideological assumptions;
- learn about and examine solutions generated from current research that could assist them in designing curricula and implementing lessons that eliminate or minimize the barriers to learning that exist for students from culturally, linguistically, and economically diverse backgrounds;
- listen astutely and hear the social and academic experiences of their students in order to create, design, and implement curriculum and instruction that both maintains academic rigor and is also culturally responsive; and
- challenge the dominant discourse on class, race, and gender as it relates to education by examining how educational theory and practice are used to subordinate certain racial and ethnic groups.

- After learning about the Photo-Cultural-Ecological Self-Study Paper, how can you examine your own ideological assumptions by adapting the paper into your own reflection?

Another way to help to foster identity development is to facilitate deep reflections on our beliefs about teaching our students. UDL requires us to have high expectations for all students, regardless of variability. In *Universal Design for Learning: Theory and Practice*, Meyer, Rose, and Gordon (2014) share, "Continual improvement, engagement, and growth are available to and expected of everyone" (p. 15).

This technique has been facilitated by Robert Porter. Robert Porter is an educator at an alternative high school. He has worked at all grade levels in the alternative setting for most of his career. In the following Implementation Spotlight, Porter shares a process for having conversations with colleagues about individual and shared belief systems.

IMPLEMENTATION SPOTLIGHT

BY ROBERT PORTER

Rita Pierson, in her TED talk (2013), shared that students don't learn from people they do not like. The mantra in the school district that I work in, is every student, every day, in every class. That means that we as educators must plan for every student, every day in every class.

You may be asking, "Isn't that what we do? Or isn't that our job?" We may believe that in theory, but it doesn't always translate into action. In order for intentionality to take place, educators, like us, must acknowledge and care more about the students than the content. The mantra, as it is on #UDL twitter chats, must be "kids over content." As educators we must invest time and energy into getting to know our own students in authentic manners and confront our own bias.

As an educator at an alternative school that serves a population that is 100% of students with learning disabilities, this has been the focus of my work. I am continuously wrestling with the question, "What will spark the practice of authentically teaching all students while addressing implicit bias that may affect students?" One practice is inspired by the work of Research for Better Teachers (RBT). It is grounded in the premise that before we can address improving practice, we have to first address what we believe or don't believe about kids and their potential, and name it.

You and your colleagues can begin this work by reflecting on the following questions:

- What do you believe about teaching students at our school?
- What do you believe about the relationships you wish to form with your students?
- What do you believe about students at our school?

(Continued)

(Continued)

The purpose of these questions is to prompt educators to explicitly express their thoughts about students in writing, then to share these thoughts with colleagues who teach the same group of students. The next step is for the team to discuss the similarities and differences across these responses with each other and to commit to developing a shared system of beliefs. Ideally, colleagues should have an opportunity to discuss what these beliefs look like when lived/enacted in our classrooms (i.e., hidden curriculum).

Other great prompts include:

- How would your students' parents feel if they observed your class?
- What types of feedback would parents offer you to better engage their child?

When we believe in all students, we intentionally design learning that is relevant and authentic. As a classroom teacher, I worked with students who were expelled from other schools. They worked on understanding Pythagoras as a person in order to better understand his theorem. Students worked on the art of public speaking by mastering and owning the words of Emily Dickinson's poem, "I'm Nobody! Who Are You?" After visiting over 100 classrooms in multiple schools in urban and suburban areas, it was evident to me that what makes for a rich learning environment is that the educators must believe that all their students can and will learn and that it's the educators' responsibility to make that happen.

To begin to help colleagues understand their identity, implicit bias, and beliefs about students, it is important that we have the courage to engage them in conversation about these issues and to ask hard questions that challenge beliefs that do not result in teaching that meets the needs of every child, every class, every day. This extends beyond our classrooms and individual practice. We also cannot sit by and wait for administrators to have these conversations or hope that they come up in a professional development or training session. If we really and truly believe in our students, then we need to have the courage to talk to our colleagues about social justice issues and push the boundaries of our collective efficacy.

Additional Resources

- Rita Pierson: https://www.ted.com/talks/rita_pierson_every_kid_needs_a_champion
- Research for Better Teaching: http://www.rbteach.com/about-rbt
- Research for Better Teaching: *The Skillful Teacher: The Comprehensive Resource for Improving Teaching and Learning* (7th ed.)
- Developmental Designs: https://www.originsonline.org/developmental-designs
- National Center on Time and Learning: https://timeandlearning.org

EQUITY AUDIT

After thinking about your own identity, personality, and beliefs, it is critical that you objectively examine what the data says about the experience of marginalized groups in your classroom.

- Which groups have been historically and/or are currently being marginalized in your setting?

- What does it mean to acknowledge that a group has been and/or is currently being marginalized in your setting?

- How do both quantitative and qualitative forms of data support this? How have we, as educators, contributed to this?

- How have our beliefs and actions contributed to this?

There are a number of equity audits that are readily available that you can use for this work. Teaching Tolerance, a project of the Southern Poverty Law Center to prevent the growth of hate, recommends the equity audits designed by the Mid-Atlantic Equity Consortium (MAEC) (2020). MAEC, in partnership with the Department of Education, developed Criteria for an Equitable School, Criteria for an Equitable Classroom, and Teacher Behaviors that Encourage Student Persistence. These tools are available, in their entirety, at maec.org/resource/equity-audit-materials/.

When looking at the Criteria for an Equitable School, for example, the audit encourages educators to examine school policy, school administration, school climate, staff, assessment/placement, professional learning, and standards and curriculum development by asking targeted reflection questions. These questions will likely lead to research, discussion, and action planning. To share the depth and weight of the questions, imagine addressing the first five questions for curriculum development. If your answer is yes, what data do you have to support your stance? If the answer is no, how will you address the disproportionality?

When examining curriculum development, for example, the first ten questions are as follows:

1. Are all teachers involved in curriculum development to meet standards?

2. Are all students held to the same standards?

3. Are the policy and instructional modifications put in place when students are unable to meet the standards?

4. Does the curriculum utilize print and non-print materials that represent diverse groups?

5. Do recommended textbooks and other instructional materials reflect, as much as possible, the experiences and perspectives of diversity among racial, ethnic, language, religious, and gender groups?

6. Are the teachers' classroom activities and examples multicultural according to race, ethnicity, language, gender, and disability?

7. Does the teacher use classroom lessons to increase awareness and counter the past effects of bias and discrimination?

8. Do the curricula infuse culturally responsive information into instructional approaches and prepare students for a diverse society and workplace?

9. Are people with disabilities shown in the curriculum actively interacting with people both with and without disabilities?

10. Is language used that does not stereotype people or groups?

It is also important to maximize student feedback and capture the experiences of students in your classroom, as optimizing voice and choice is critical in universally designing relevant, authentic, and meaningful learning experiences. Students can improve our teaching. The main reason that we teach is to make a difference for our students. By eliciting feedback from students before we finalize our answers to these questions, we can improve our teaching practices to give our students better opportunities to learn. Because this process helps to highlight inequities across the learning environment, equity audits are a critical step in the process of becoming a more equitable school, as once you identify the problem or barrier, you can begin to eliminate it.

TAKE ACTION AND NEXT STEPS

A socially just and universally designed learning environment is one where all teachers are committed to fostering equity, providing choices, and elevating and celebrating student voices. This can be accomplished by throwing away assumptions and judgments of what an individual's capacity is or should be. Just because folks say that they believe in or are passionate about social justice does not mean that they know what it is or what to do about it. The disconnect between outward social justice beliefs and inward racist and/or deficit-based thinking is a reality that must be addressed through consistent action. Good intentions are not enough; we must focus on impact. Specifically, what are the impacts of our actions, or lack thereof, in and through the lives of the students we serve?

Let's face it head on—one of the most challenging aspects of this work is that it revolves around belief and value systems.

Therefore, we must be bold in naming the fact that the work is not primarily about technical fixes and solutions. If we are truly committed to this work, then we must acknowledge that a lion's share of it lives in the adaptive and not technical domain.

One great example of adaptive change was contributed by Michael S. Martin, EdD, the director of learning for South Burlington School District in Vermont and senior associate with the Rowland Foundation. Martin has written over 100 commentaries for Vermont Public Radio and his doctoral dissertation, *Vermont's Sacred Cow: A Case Study of Local Control of Schools*, examines local school governance as a social construct. He is the author of *Dewey's Ghost* and a chapter in *The Full Vermonty: Vermont in the Age of Trump* (Mares & Danzinger, 2017).

Martin knows what it means to stand for all students. One example was the flying of the Black Lives Matter flag in Montpelier, Vermont. He shares the work of the educators in his district as an example for all of us to reflect on the power of action.

IMPLEMENTATION SPOTLIGHT

BY MICHAEL S. MARTIN

Raising the Black Lives Matter Flag: A Community Takes Action Together

On February 1, 2018, Montpelier High School raised a Black Lives Matter (BLM) flag on its Vermont campus, flying prominently below the flag of the United States. In recent years, many high schools have seen the BLM flag brandished at student protests, but Montpelier is believed to be the first high school to display the flag at the direction of its school board. With its unanimous resolution to raise a BLM flag, the Montpelier School Board issued the following statement, "We echo our students in saying that we make this decision to fly the Black Lives Matter flag with love in our hearts and courage in our voices, and we reject any purported connections to violence or hate. We believe that our students are not motivated by hostility toward others; only by a desire for respect for every student in our community, and the Board shares this desire."

The simplicity of this single, powerful gesture to raise the flag was belied by the extensive work that led up to the event. In fact, student leaders from the Racial Justice Alliance had been in discussions with school administrators and school board commissioners for over a year before the flag-raising. The school board chair, superintendent, and Principal Mike McRaith took the time to work through the ramifications of the decision and to enlist teachers, parents, and the wider community in the initiative. McRaith contacted the local chapter of Veterans of Foreign Wars (VFW) to explain why a BLM flag deserved a place under the Stars & Stripes. He also sat down with local law enforcement officials, both to let them know that the message was in no way anti-police and also to ask for help with security concerns stemming from the flag.

(Continued)

(Continued)

The Racial Justice Alliance issued a statement that showed that students understood that the flag was part of a concerted effort to address structural racism in school and society. The students wrote, "Raising this flag is a part of a wider campaign to grow awareness and make changes in our curriculum, climate, and shared understanding of the need for racial justice. Over the past year there have been many steps forward in our community including some direct curricular choices, administrative trainings, faculty in-service, a schoolwide assembly and the Race-Against-Racism. And yet, we need to do more to raise our predominantly white community's collective consciousness to better recognize white privilege and implicit bias. The Racial Justice Alliance believes putting up a Black Lives Matter flag is imperative for both demonstrating our school's fight for equitable education for our Black Students and modeling a brave and appropriate challenge to the status quo impeding public institutions across the country."

The controversy sparked by the BLM Flag was, in fact, an incredible catalyst for learning. There was no shying away from such a bold statement, and each student, teacher, and parent would be asked by their friends and neighbors why the Montpelier community supported taking this step. Montpelier teachers and administrators leaned into the challenge. There were schoolwide screenings of Ava DuVernay's *13th*, followed by facilitated discussions in advisory groups.

Teacher advisors led Quote of the Day discussions unpacking great ideas from Maya Angelou, Barack Obama, bell hooks, Alice Walker, and Dave Chappelle. Teachers increasingly placed books like *Between the World and Me*, *The New Jim Crow*, and *Waking Up White* at the heart of their curriculum. James Baldwin and Langston Hughes began to get referenced more often, outside of Black History Month. Teacher PLC Leaders underwent training to stop microaggressions, and teachers won grants from the Rowland Foundation and the Vermont NEA to pay for expert facilitators to lead professional development in equity literacy. The Montpelier School Board also pointed out that this work was in line with the district action plan priorities of Equity, Personalization, and Proficiency-Based Learning.

Above all, Principal Mike McRaith learned that this work really teaches empathy. "We need to look past our own personal challenges, struggles, discomforts, and rationalizations, and do the work needed to see and feel the world through the lens of someone besides ourselves. In so doing, we improve our empathy skills, which will hopefully transfer across a wide range of privileges needing empathetic perspectives including but not limited to race, gender, ability, sexual orientation, financial status, education, and citizenship," McRaith (2018) wrote in a recent blog post. He also pointed out that empathy is one of the Six Facets of Understanding (Wiggins & McTighe, 2011) and that the ability to adopt multiple perspectives is a hallmark of deeper learning. Seen in this light, racial justice work does not detract from the curriculum, but in fact ensures that there is room for students to tackle real-world issues that matter to them, or as one African American student eloquently stated "I want to see myself in the curriculum."

Finally, the types of discussions that the BLM Flag engendered constituted a step in the direction of a Critical Pedagogy (Freire, 1972), where students began to learn how to identify social structures that reproduce injustice in our institutions across generations, school included. "The RJA believes putting up the Black Lives Matter flag is imperative for both demonstrating our school's fight for equitable education for our Black Students, and modeling a brave and appropriate challenge to the status quo impeding public institutions across the country," said the student representatives from the Montpelier Racial Justice Alliance.

In the end, persistence and hard work of Montpelier students, with support from their teachers and school leaders, was a simple reminder of our core mission. Our students helped us remember that our work in school needs to focus on helping the historically disadvantaged. Our students asked us to update our curriculum so that it allows them to address the problems facing society today—the ones that matter most to them. Our students brought us back to our school mission that says that *all* Montpelier students will become "able and motivated contributors to their local, national, and global communities."

In a word, in raising a Black Lives Matter flag, our students reminded us what school is for. They also reminded us that our democracy depends on it.

Next Steps

Challenging your own belief system and asking colleagues to do the same is difficult, and at the same time is both rewarding and necessary. Because when beliefs are challenged, they lead to action. As you begin or continue your journey, consider the following next steps.

- Share your definition of social justice with a colleague, preferably someone who shares the same group of students as you, and ask them to draft one as well.

- Calibrate your definitions. What was similar? What was different? What can you agree on? What can you agree to disagree on?

- Discuss what these definitions look like in action. How will you ensure that you and your colleagues will be held accountable to these "look-fors." What does it look like to be held accountable? What can students hold you accountable to and how?

- Tell other colleagues and school leaders about what you're doing, explicitly focusing on the commitments that you are making.

Reflection Questions

- What stage is your community in, in regard to social justice and equity work?

- Have you taken the steps that we have recommended? If not, which steps do you believe will be the most challenging and which will be the most rewarding?

Once you have made a commitment to social justice and have named that commitment for your students, your professional development must continue to revolve around ways to learn, discuss, and reflect on this subject matter. Not for the sake of being a successful practitioner. That is secondary, but first and foremost for the sake of being a human being with the courage and confidence to embrace and not run from the messy space of being authentic about your humanity, imperfection, mistakes, assumptions, and your very imperfect journey. We can't depend upon external "experts" to help us navigate this space. Ultimately, we must assume responsibility for holding ourselves accountable to the standards of social justice.

In the next chapter, we will share the importance of the collective power of educators to lean into discomfort and take action to deconstruct our systems.

The truth and power of this book is that social justice in our world is literally in our hands as educators. We have the privilege to make changes that allow us to create classrooms and schools that are linguistically appropriate, culturally responsive, socially just, and universally designed. To do this, we have to create communities where we empower all students to embrace their identities, personalize their learning journey through Universal Design, and to create their own pathways to success. For us and our colleagues, we feel a calling to this work. We acknowledge the inequity and privilege in our world and we refuse to stand by and allow them to persist.

CHAPTER THREE

SOCIAL JUSTICE THROUGH COLLABORATION AND COMMUNITY

"If one feels like what they have to say is of value in a particular place, they are more apt to transform the place into a community and partake in activities that are valued within it."

—Christopher Emdin

SETTING THE STAGE

Universal Design for Learning (UDL) reminds educators that fostering collaboration and community is critical to provide multiple means of engagement. In order to implement UDL and create more equitable classrooms, educators need to commit to ongoing professional growth and continuously examine their own individual practices and beliefs. In this chapter we will share specific strategies for addressing opportunity gaps for all learners through the creation of collaborative communities that examine the academic, social, emotional, and behavioral needs of students through a social justice lens.

INTENTIONAL LEARNING COMMUNITIES

The great redwoods, the tallest trees in the world, dig strong roots before they reach nearly 300 feet into the sky. Just as these roots anchor a tree, creating Intentional Learning Communities allows educators to begin their journey to deconstruct the status quo in order to challenge assumptions and beliefs and take action to ensure that all students have equitable opportunities to succeed and reach higher as they grow.

As educators, we have to be intentional about identifying and eliminating barriers that prevent students from learning so we can meet the needs of all students and create equitable systems. One way to begin this critical work is to create Intentional Learning Communities with our colleagues that provide us with opportunities to examine the impact of our practice and its effect on students.

> Intentional Learning Communities are professional learning communities that are rigorous, collaborative, focused on learning, and built upon shared norms and values. They are groups of educators who meet regularly with the goal of improving teaching and learning and are characterized by (1) skilled facilitation, and (2) the use of protocols to guide adult learning. In summary, they need to be intentional (School Reform Initiative, 2019).

We need to commit to these communities because we cannot hide behind the mask of "I got it," "I understand," or "I know." Universal Design for Learning (UDL) has a goal of expert learning. The book *UDL Theory and Practice*, written by the founders of UDL, defines what it means to be an expert learner (Meyer, Rose, & Gordon, 2014).

The word "expert" probably conjures up a person who has mastered a particular skill or domain of knowledge, a professional, or a highly skilled amateur who can perform at a high level. But if we think a moment, we realize that expertise is never static. Developing expertise in anything is always a process of continuous learning—practice, adjustment, and refinement. In the context of UDL, we focus on learning expertise: the lifelong process of becoming ever more motivated, knowledgeable, and skillful. (p. 15)

If we expect students to become expert learners, we need to commit to our own lifelong process of improving teaching and learning. Committing to an adult learning community affords us opportunities to embrace the fact that everyone has room to grow. Expert learners, when working cooperatively, acknowledge that there will be multiple entry points to grow, and that is okay. Success revolves not around the notion of perceived expertise, but rather around a willingness to authentically commit to the work. This is what it means to be an "expert teacher."

[Expert teachers] need to be able to model and mentor the process of learning, with all its hills and valleys, for their students. Exposing their own learning and making it explicit both in action and in personal reflection might be one of the most powerful parts of teaching. How do teachers develop expert teaching practices? And what strategies and insights help them? (Meyer, Rose, & Gordon, 2014, p. 22)

How do we, as educators, develop expert teaching practices? And what strategies and insights help us?

That is the core of this chapter. We develop expert teaching through a shared commitment to growing and changing to meet the needs of all our students, ongoing collaboration and community-building, reflecting on our practices and belief systems, as well as being strategic about our own improvement.

Oftentimes, when we participate in professional learning communities, we want to dive right into curriculum or lesson design. We want strategies we can use *tomorrow*. We get it. But if a well-designed lesson could eliminate inequities, we would all be implementing that lesson. The reality is that before we can truly design for all students, we have to examine our own beliefs, privilege, bias, and how they impact learning.

We have both worked with countless districts and we know that often, this is a critical step that gets skipped. First, it's incredibly uncomfortable, but we must, as educators, embrace that discomfort because only then will we be able to design for all. Many of our students see this feeling of discomfort as a weakness, but it is necessary for growth. We need to have the courage to model for them what it means to lean into discomfort to create brave spaces.

Later in the text, we will dive into designing lessons using the UDL framework. Before effectively tackling the design of curriculum and instruction, we must first create structures that allow us to reflect on our learning and ask difficult questions about who is being served and who is not. Such structures, which we call Intentional Learning Communities, openly acknowledge that UDL is intended to eliminate inequities—rather than to create lessons that are fun and engaging for select groups of students at the expense of others.

One person who is an expert at facilitating Intentional Learning Communities is Kari Thierer. Kari Thierer is the executive director of the School Reform Initiative (SRI), a nonprofit organization with a mission to create transformational learning communities fiercely committed to educational equity and excellence. She provided us with guidance on having difficult conversations, specifically around race, as a foundation for social justice work in a school. Thierer shares:

> *If we, as educators, are truly committed to educational equity then we have to learn how to engage in challenging conversations about race. These conversations cannot only be theoretical but must also dig deep into how race and bias impact our teaching and learning practices. It isn't enough to say, "We are committed to equity," and then go about business as usual without interrogating our practices and our systems.*

Being committed to social justice isn't enough. Commitment requires difficult conversations, taking action, and creating learning communities both in and out of the classroom with a focus on eliminating inequities. This work can be done with students, but also needs to become a part of the school fabric, where teachers work together to build a system that works for all learners. The "Implementation Spotlight" that follows provides guidance on the key considerations for creating Intentional Learning Communities in your school. As you read, consider if these are in place in your own schools. If they are, know that you are on the right track. If they are not, take some time to identify the barriers that prevent the work. Then, take action with colleagues to ensure that these roots are planted because truly deconstructing an inequitable system to build it back in an equitable way requires that we experience discomfort and embrace it.

IMPLEMENTATION SPOTLIGHT

BY KARI THIERER

Engaging in challenging conversations takes time, a culture of trust that allows for risk-taking, an intentional agenda, and skilled facilitation. These four elements combine to grow the capacity of educators to learn from and with one another, and develop an equity lens that pushes them to have a fierce commitment to serving each and every student. Only after creating these communities is the foundation laid for meaningful development of universally designed learning experiences.

Dedicating Time to Intentional Learning Communities

There is never enough time in the day for us to do all that we need to do, so peer collaboration time has to be beneficial both for individual growth as well as to inform instructional practice. Developing community and doing intentional work around educational equity takes time.

1. In most schools, the structures for such conversations are already in place—that is, the weekly team meetings that go by a variety of names, such as common planning time, data teams, or PLCs. With Intentional Learning Communities, we apply an equity lens to every endeavor. We need to use the time we have to probe matters of great urgency. Advocate to help facilitate the session so you and your colleagues can begin to have difficult conversations.

2. Once you have identified time for Intentional Learning Communities to meet, do not allow it to be interrupted by the menagerie of disruptions that affect schools. Protect time to think about your practice rather than talking about lunch duty or the upcoming field trips. Those other conversations are important too, but what often happens is that the immediate gets our attention, and we neglect the long-term conversations that lead to improved instruction and equity. The deeper conversations get pushed to the occasional professional development day or before/after the school year. Regular, ongoing collaboration time is essential for schools to take up issues of social justice and equity that will improve school success for all students.

Time often gets blamed as the excuse to avoid challenging conversations. If the school is committed to serving all students, then that commitment needs to be demonstrated through the way we use the time we already have. We make time for what is important.

Intentional Culture Building

In order to increase engagement in UDL, we have to minimize threats and distractions. For some practitioners, conversations about race, class, and educational equity can cause anxiety, fear, and guilt. Developing a culture of trust is imperative for us to feel safe enough to take risks and know that we will be supported. This does not mean creating a space where people do not feel discomfort; on the contrary, discomfort is an important part of this equity-based work.

Setting Agreements

Many of you are likely familiar with the concept of norms or agreements. However, in equity work, these agreements need to go deeper. Agreements are important for groups to define so they know how they will be working together. They help to create the conditions for risk-taking, building trust, and mutual accountability for the improvement of instructional practice and individual learning. Within social justice and equity work, these agreements need to be thoughtfully developed and analyzed.

Gorski (2019) writes, "Too often, ground rules that are put in place, whether by an educator/facilitator or by participants, privilege the already-privileged groups in a dialogical experience. For example, in a dialogue about race, white participants will often support ground rules meant to keep anger out of the discussion- ground rules focused keeping them comfortable. When we consider who is protected by ground rules like 'do not express anger,' it becomes apparent that, intentionally or not, they protect the participants representing privileged groups."

When developing agreements, it is important to be open and honest about what each person needs in order to make the space work for them and their learning. Agreements are also living and must be revisited regularly. As a group grows, what they need shifts, and the agreements should grow and shift with the individuals of the learning community. There are some great examples of agreements that have been developed by equity-based facilitators. (See the Additional Resources at the end of this Implementation Spotlight.)

Planning Your Work

Once your learning community has discussed how to work together—allocating time, shared understanding of why, and agreements to begin to build the culture—then it is time to plan the learning of the group. Intentional planning is necessary so that people are pushed into their risk zones, while avoiding places that are too comfortable or too dangerous. The work the learning community engages in must be thoughtfully scaffolded to keep people at their growing edge. It is helpful to think of this scaffold in terms of risk—starting with lower risk learning and moving the group into more challenging and risky spaces.

Protocols that structure conversations are instrumental to helping groups engage and stay in challenging conversations. As group members are beginning to work with one another, protocols serve as a system to hold the group, as participants begin to develop the skills, knowledge, and dispositions of surfacing and challenging assumptions and biases.

Opening Moves

Opening moves are activities and practices that include learning with and from one another and beginning to build a community. Opening moves are designed to help individuals and groups

(Continued)

(Continued)

learn more about themselves as individuals and as educators and start to uncover their own assumptions, biases, and beliefs. In this phase, protocols help provide the structure for engaging in honest conversations that allow reflection on individual practices and beliefs and help guide and focus such conversations through active listening and questioning skills. A few protocols (all freely available on the SRI website) that are helpful in this stage of community building include:

- Micro Labs. A protocol designed to build active listening skills within a group while also allowing group members to learn more about one another and their practice. It involves participants working in triads, with each participant answering a specific sequence of questions. There is no discussion, just listening. Questions can be related to a person's educational journey, experience with equity conversations, understanding of pedagogy, and so forth. The questions allow a group to grow together by deeply listening to one another.

- Paseo/Circles of Identity. This protocol helps groups to begin to examine issues of identity, diversity, beliefs and values. The protocol asks participants to think about the different elements of their own identity, allowing participants to reflect on their own, while also learning to listen and talk with others about identity.

Each of these protocols works to help participants know each other as individuals, not just in their role at the school/organization, but who they are and how they show up in the world. Identity is a key component of engaging in conversations about race and social justice. It is important for educators to explore their own racial identity, so they can think deeply about the implications of their identity on their teaching practice.

Going Deeper

As participants in your learning community begin to know each other, the group will be able to go deeper into issues of race and equity. In this phase of group development, protocols can help support the group to have conversations about race and equity in a variety of ways.

- Use text protocols to make meaning of articles or books the group reads together. Texts that focus on issues of race, white fragility, and implicit bias are all helpful to develop an equity lens and begin to support the group's conversations. As group members have built community, they will be able to have more meaningful conversations about the texts they read, focusing on the implications on teaching and learning for the students they serve.

- Look at data through an equity lens. As groups begin to develop skill at having conversations about race and equity, the next step is to analyze data through an equity lens. Who are the students who are not being served by our school? How do the policies and practices we enact privilege some students, while potentially oppressing others? How do the units of study we provide represent the cultural diversity of the students we serve and the world we live in? Data becomes more than the quantitative numbers that are gathered from standardized tests and broadens to include evidence about attendance and discipline, as well as looking deeply at student work.

Skilled Facilitation

Intentional Learning Communities do not just happen, they take time and care. Growing your capacity and the capacity of your colleagues to engage in these types of communities means helping to grow the facilitation skills of your team. Protocols alone cannot hold a group completely and help them go as deeply as they need to go. A facilitator with experience in protocols and an understanding of adult learning theory can help both support and grow groups to develop the capacity to engage and stay in conversations. Growing capacity is necessary for the long-term viability of an intentional learning community and for the larger organization.

As your learning community practices collaboration and reflective dialogue, with an emphasis on race and equity, you will grow your capacity to continue to go deeper. Ultimately, the goal is to help you and your colleagues know yourselves and each other well, begin to know your students, and to use this newly developed equity lens to create a teaching and learning environment that is designed to support the success of all students. These practices move beyond the traditional learning communities and into the Intentional Learning Communities that will ultimately shift practice.

Next Steps

- Examine your school calendar for the year. Determine how much time you have available to foster these Intentional Learning Communities. Leverage your existing blocks of time to service your equity focused goals. Could you facilitate Intentional Learning Communities during faculty meetings? Professional development sessions? Common planning time? Without time to have these difficult conversations, student outcomes will likely not shift significantly.

- Identify your agreements and norms for these conversations. We like using Singleton's "Four Agreements of Courageous Conversation": Stay engaged, speak your truth, plan to experience discomfort, and expect and accept non-closure.

- Review some of the protocols mentioned that are available on the SRI website: http://www.schoolreforminitiative.org/protocols/. Consider ones that you could use with your colleagues.

- Identify, train, and support a facilitator for these groups. Maybe it will be you! Step forward and ask for the professional development that you need (reading this book is a great first step!).

Reflection Questions

- Leaning into discomfort can be challenging but it is such an important part of growth and learning. How can examining and sharing your own beliefs and biases help to create a space for more equitable systems and policies?

- How can protocols such as Micro Labs and Circles of Identity help your Intentional Learning Community facilitate difficult conversations and growth? And why is it important to go beyond these protocols to have deeper, more meaningful conversations?

- Think about your school or district. Who do you think are the students who are not being served? Do you think there are certain policies and practices that privilege some students, while potentially oppressing others? Write down your answers and examine them after you analyze data to see where your inclinations may not be in line with the data.

(Continued)

(Continued)

- What makes fostering collaboration and community within an Intentional Learning Community a critical strategy to provide multiple means of engagement?

- How can minimizing threats and distractions lead to increased engagement when having difficult conversations with our colleagues about social justice?

- How is expert teaching linked to expert learning?

- After reviewing the key considerations for an Intentional Learning Community, do you believe that you have this type of professional learning community in your school? Why or why not? In your position, how could you help to build it?

Additional Resources

- School Reform Initiative is an organization made up of educators throughout the world that are fiercely committed to educational equity and excellence: www.schoolreforminitiative. org. They provide professional development for participants and facilitators, as well as tools and resources for educators to develop and implement strong Intentional Learning Communities.

- Check out this incredible resource to learn about how to run a better equity-focused meeting: *Color Brave Space Agreements* by Equity Matters, https://fakequity.com/2017/05/26/color-brave-space-how-to-run-a-better-equity-focused-meeting/

- Email Kari Thierer: kari@schoolreforminitaitive.org

EVIDENCE-BASED INTENTIONAL LEARNING

In addition to fostering difficult conversations, Intentional Learning Communities can meet, plan, and work together around four focus areas: team building, logistics, instruction and learning, and social, emotional, and behavioral learning through data. Every educator should have the opportunity to work with colleagues to ask, *"How do we grow, develop, and collaborate as a team?"*

In Chardin's school, teachers have these meetings as a part of their professional culture. During these meetings, teachers work together to cover all of the logistical issues that arise during our day-to-day work, as well as plan town halls and other matters related to school culture.

Instruction and Learning meetings are facilitated by the instructional coach. The framing question for these meetings follows: *As individuals and as a team, how do we design learning that values impact over intentions, is objective driven, reflects the learners, and is authentically relevant?*

Universal Design for Learning (UDL) is the key framework that supports the work during these meetings. To ensure the work is relevant and authentic, teachers collaborate to engage in cycles of analyzing student work (using protocols) AND looking at teacher work (video) where they reflect, ask questions, identify barriers, and provide one another with feedback for growth. If you don't have an instructional coach, take charge and offer to facilitate a meeting where you ask these difficult questions.

Social, emotional, and behavioral learning through data meetings are facilitated by members of the counseling team (guidance and adjustment counselors). The framing questions for these meetings follow:

- What does the data tell us about our impact, and how does that inform our actions?

- How can we best meet the needs of a diverse population of learners?

During these meetings, teachers examine a variety of data (assessments, warning notices, office referrals, etc.), work to identify root causes, and match support based on students' needs (Table 3.1). Note that there can be fluidity between categories. For example, team building can be cultivated by engaging in the other components and collaborative analysis of student work can be an examination of data.

GOING BEYOND ACCESS

Building Intentional Learning Communities is the first step to creating a more equitable system that will empower every student. Once educators are prepared for these difficult conversations, they can begin to participate in what Mirko refers to as the *Going Beyond Access* framework of valuing impact over intentions, ensuring learner visibility in the work, and ensuring authentic relevance.

UDL notes the importance of designing learning experiences that are relevant, authentic, and meaningful, but this is often determined by what we, as educators, deem to be worthy of study. When examining the UDL Progression Rubric (Novak & Rodriguez, 2018) (see Appendix B), it is clear that the power of design and learning shifts from teachers to learners as UDL implementation moves from emerging toward expert practice.

For example, when noting what emerging practice looks like, the rubric notes that teachers "offer choices in what students learn (e.g., 'choose a country to study' rather than 'study France'), how students learn (e.g., use books, videos, and/or teacher instruction to

Table 3.1   Meeting Structures That Support Going Beyond Access Framework

	Team Building	Logistics	Instruction and Learning	Social, Emotional, Behavioral Learning Through Data
What is it?	Time to collaborate and build your team	Time for announcements, planning, and organization	Time to grow our skills as teachers in planning, instruction, and reflection	Time to use data to identify instructional and social emotional strategies for student growth
Framing question(s):	How do we grow, develop, and collaborate as a team?	What do we need to be aware of? What do we need to plan for as a team?	As individuals and as a team, how do we design learning that values impact over intentions, is objective driven, reflects the learners, and is authentically relevant?	What does the data tell us about our impact, and how does that inform our actions? How can we best meet the needs of a diverse population of learners?
What do teachers do during this time?	Some of the ways that they use this time are co-planning with colleagues and special educators, and coordinating and brainstorming around portfolio and team-building activities.	Teachers work together to cover all of the logistical issues that arise during our day-to-day work, as well as plan town halls and other matters related to school culture.	Teachers collaborate to engage in cycles of looking at student work (protocols) AND looking at teacher work (video) where we reflect, ask questions, and provide one another with feedback for growth.	Teachers examine a variety of data (assessments, warning notices, office referrals, etc.), work to identify root causes, and match supports based on students' needs.

build understanding), and how they express what they know (e.g., 'you can create a poster or write a paragraph')." It's clear here that teachers still hold all the decision-making power when UDL practice is still emerging as the options are "allowed" by the teacher. Teacher-directed work often lacks relevance to all students since it is generally designed to be "one-size-fits-all" and is often framed by the dominant culture and curriculum.

When working toward expert practice, however, students are empowered to create authentic learning experiences. When observing this practice on the UDL Progression Rubric, educators "empower students to make choices or suggest alternatives for what they will learn, how they will learn, and how they will express what they know in *authentic ways.* Free them to self-monitor and reflect on their choices with teacher facilitation and feedback but not explicit direction."

This *Going Beyond Access* framework, coined by Chardin, ensures that students experience authentic relevance and are visible in the work by building on three principles:

- Good intentions are not good enough, and educators must regularly reflect upon and evaluate their impact in and on the lives of their students (Tatem, 2017).

- If students see themselves as valued and visible in classrooms and curriculum and feel like they are being welcomed, they can and will be successful.

- The current lived experiences of students need to drive all pedagogical practices in order to feel relevant and connected to students' lived reality (Emdin, 2016; Lawrence-Lightfoot, 2005).

COGEN DIALOGUES

Intentional Learning Communities promote reflection and help to facilitate a shift to more socially just practices and learning opportunities. Another practice that supports this shift are Cogen Dialogues. Educators can honor Chardin's *Going Beyond Access* framework and add a depth to Intentional Learning Communities by instituting what Dr. Christopher Emdin (2016) has coined as "cogenerative (cogen) dialogues." According to Dr. Emdin:

> *Cogens are simple conversations between the teacher and their students with a goal of co-creating/generating plans of action for improving the classroom. . . . They allow teachers to more effectively deliver complex subject matter to students*

*to bridge their cultural divides before addressing content. . . .
Instances where the youth and the teacher are from different cultural
backgrounds . . . effectively introducing and implementing the
cogen . . . has proven to be effective in motivating students to engage
in dialogues with teachers in ways that allow them to share with their
teachers their suggestions for improving the classroom. (p. 66)*

Cogens should be seen as structured dialogues about the inner workings of the social field people cohabit. A social field is any location where humans interact under rules and/or hierarchies; for our purposes, we are referring to classrooms and schools. Cogens welcome self-expression and value the voice of the student as well as students' critiques of the classroom with the aim to create more authentic, socially just learning opportunities for students, which in turn motivates them to be more socially conscious and engaged in social justice work. This happens because they are being given the opportunity to have a powerful personal experience with sharing their voices, thoughts and opinions, while being able to both see and experience firsthand the results of such.

As we learned in Chapter 1, there is a tie between Universal Design for Learning (UDL) and social justice education as the connection requires us to examine our own implicit bias and how it may affect the design of learning experiences that work for all students. Cogen dialogues, or advisory groups of students in schools or classrooms may help to uncover some of the barriers that may be in educators' blind spots due to implicit bias, by elevating student voice, specifically to provide critical feedback on their experiences as learners within specific classrooms.

Eight Tips for Creating a Cogen

1. Identify possible participants based on differences in social, ethnic, or academic groups. For example, the group should consist of high-achieving and low-achieving students as well as highly engaged and disengaged students.

2. The group should accurately reflect the diversity of the classroom. It is the differences revealed in the cogen that lead to rich dialogue, which also leads to more opportunities for teachers to understand the different realities of students in the classroom; therefore, the cogen should not be homogeneous.

3. Invite students to participate. Students should not feel pressured to participate, and they should have the opportunity to opt out.

4. Introduce cogens to students in a way that does not make students see them as an additional classroom responsibility

or assignment. They should be framed as a privilege, not a punishment. Tailor invitations to each individual student; allow students' input in terms of when the dialogues will take place.

5. Plan the initial dialogue over a meal or snack. This helps to communicate that this is an informal and safe structure that will revolve around sharing together.

6. Establish rules/norms during the first dialogue. For example: No voice is privileged over another; one person speaks at a time by usage of a talking piece (individuals can only speak if they are holding the talking piece). The cogen results in a plan of action to improve the classroom.

7. Start with a small issue that has an obvious easy answer, which the group can solve together in order to ensure a positive experience for participants.

8. Provide the opportunity to involve new voices. The initial group should meet three to four times max; then students should be asked to invite one to two new students to join and an existing member to opt out. This keeps the group small and provides opportunities to involve new voices.

Mirko and his colleagues at the Putnam Avenue Upper School incorporate cogen groups in their practice. At times, they facilitate cogens specifically to inform and direct their teaching practices or connect with certain cohorts of students. Please consider the following example of such as recounted by Mrs. Pamela Chu-Sheriff, the school's founding assistant principal.

IMPLEMENTATION SPOTLIGHT

BY PAMELA CHU-SHERIFF

As I walked past the copy machine on the way to my office, the French teacher called out a hello to me, and I could immediately tell that something was on her mind.

"Hey, do you have a second?"

"Sure, come on in," I said.

We stepped into my office, and she proceeded to tell me that she was concerned about her eighth grade French class. This was her third year with this particular cohort, and things weren't going well.

"It's become pretty toxic in there," she said.

(Continued)

(Continued)

When I pushed her to explain why she thought things were the way they were, she was able to name that she had this class since they were in sixth grade when she was a first-year teacher. She acknowledged that as many first-year teachers do, she had struggled with classroom management and student engagement, and over time, a negative climate had developed with that class. Things seemed to be getting worse. And fast.

"We're already through the first quarter, and I think I just need to wait it out until they graduate and then go off to high school. I think it's just this particular class," she said.

It was early November, and she noted how she wasn't having any difficulties with her other classes of sixth and seventh graders, who had had the benefit of starting with her after she already had some teaching experience under her belt.

"I have an idea," I said.

Although she hadn't articulated it that way, I wasn't about to let her give up on herself or the students. I suggested that we initiate a short-term cogen, which I ran as a restorative circle, to give the students a space to discuss what had been happening and to share their input on how to make things better. Giving the students a voice, I reasoned, would help them take ownership over their actions and be instrumental in ensuring that things could turn around. However, was she ready to hear some hard feedback?

Two weeks later, I walked into the French classroom, and the teacher had already set up 15 chairs in the alcove section of her classroom. Since that first impromptu conversation that started by the copy machine, the teacher and I had met again to plan the discussion rounds, and I had also met individually with a few of the power brokers in the class—who were, importantly, also the leaders of the majority of the troubling behavior in the class—to hear from them what they thought was going on and to encourage them to share some of the honest feedback they had shared with me in private when the class convened as a group.

Over the course of the next 45 minutes, the talking piece went around and around as we discussed the following:

1. When you think about French class, what does it look like? Sound like? Feel like?

2. How have you, your classmates, and the teacher contributed to making the class this way? What do you think has motivated your actions and/or behaviors?

3. When you think about French class moving forward, what would you like it to look like? Sound like? Feel like?

4. What can you, your classmates, and the teacher do to make the class look, feel, and sound like the class you want it to be?

5. What needs to happen in order for you to feel seen and heard in French class?

We couldn't have asked for a more honest, powerful conversation. The students shared their raw emotions ("When I come into this class, I feel depressed and bored." "I'm in a bad mood whenever I come in here." "The teacher is always in a bad mood."). They took ownership over their own role in the class's downward trajectory and discussed what they needed to do moving forward (e.g., ignore distractions, don't retaliate when a classmate bothers you, hold each other accountable). They gave concrete suggestions for what the teacher could do to make the class more interesting and manageable; they suggested separating certain students who tended to feed off each other, mentioned really enjoying a station's activity that the teacher had done once and requested doing more station work, asked whether they could choose their own groups from time to time, said they would love to play more academic games, and stated how incorporating more video clips could help them stay more engaged.

One student sagely advised the teacher, "Do it; don't just say it." And most importantly, throughout the period, the teacher listened, acknowledged her own role in contributing to the negative atmosphere, and committed to implementing the changes the students suggested.

After the students left, the teacher and I debriefed, and I informed her that her next few classes were extremely high stakes. The students needed to see some clear signs from the teacher that their voices had been heard; otherwise, I warned her, if the students had made themselves vulnerable and been made to feel some kind of hope that things could improve and if this was not followed through on, the students would most likely turn, and things would probably be worse than before.

The teacher and I decided that the very next class, to symbolically demonstrate that things were going to be different, she would change the seats, play music as students were entering, and focus the next class on community building activities. I even suggested having a snack potluck, and the teacher eagerly agreed and spread the word to the students.

A few days later, I saw one of the "power brokers" who I had pre-gamed with before the circle/cogen session. I asked him how class had gone since the circle had been held.

"Awesome," he said, and smiled.

I later heard that he had brought a whole tub of cookies to share with the class for the snack potluck. This was a far cry from the picture of the combative, checked-out student that had been painted of him before the circle.

As is my usual practice, I scheduled a follow-up circle to conclude the cogen, for after the winter break to check in on how things had gone since our initial meeting. I could sense a change the moment the students walked in. Instead of coming into the classroom and dejectedly sitting in their seats with scowls on their faces as I had witnessed a couple months prior, the students bounded into the room and were happy to report that not only had the students stepped up in their attitudes and behavior, but the teacher had also implemented many of the suggestions that they had given her.

While they acknowledged that there were still some slight improvements that could be made, the class and the teacher expressed how much more enjoyable the class was and how they felt that they were learning even more academic content than before.

Next Steps

- Respond to the following quote from Dr. Christopher Emdin: "Equity is hearing somebody's voice about what they need and providing them with that."

_____

_____

(Continued)

Reflection Question

- How can cogen groups help us benefit our practice?

Additional Resource

- To further explore the concept of gogenerative dialogues/cogen groups, watch the following video of Dr. Christopher Emdin sharing about five strategies that can transform urban education: https://youtu.be/2Y9tVf_8fqo

OPTIMIZING STUDENT VOICE

Another way to empower student voice is to consider whether or not you have an authentic sense of how students perceive what their experience in your classroom is. If you think students are engaged, how do you know? If you think they are bored, how do you know? You can optimize student voice by employing cogen groups or by surveying your students. We strongly recommend that if you choose the latter, that you start by drafting a set of questions or prompts that you will also respond to, along with your students. You can then compare their responses to your own to get a sense of calibration on how close or distant you are in your understanding of their experience.

For example, in Chardin's school, the administrators distributed a climate survey to students and staff, which asked the exact same questions. After the surveys were completed, the team triangulated the data and focused on unpacking questions that showed the greatest disconnect in thinking between the two groups. The most significant example of such was a question that asked teachers: "Do you believe that students feel well known and cared for?"

There was an overwhelming response from 80 percent of the adult participants that, yes, they believed this. While on the student survey, when they were asked if they felt well known and cared for in school, there was similarly an overwhelming response from 80 percent of the student participants, that, **no, they did not feel well known or cared for.**

This survey and questions were instrumental in pushing the staff forward in their understanding—that their perception of the student experience of their school was very different from the actual lived experience.

The state of Massachusetts created Model Feedback surveys that are designed for educators to use with students. The tools offer some great prompts that would be great for educators to reflect on their own professional learning if there are discrepancies between student and staff perception. See sample statements below.

Model Feedback Survey Sample Prompts

- In discussing my work, my teacher uses a positive tone even if my work needs improvement.
- In my class, my teacher is interested in my well-being beyond just my class work.
- My textbooks or class materials include people and examples that reflect my race, cultural background, and/or identity.
- To help me understand, my teacher uses my interests to explain difficult ideas to me.
- My teacher helps me identify my strengths and shows me how to use my strengths to learn.
- My teacher encourages us to accept different points of view when they are expressed in class.
- My teacher uses a variety of ways to help all students learn (e.g., draw pictures, talk out loud, use slides, write on board, or play games).
- In this class, I can decide how to show my knowledge (e.g., write a paper, prepare a presentation, or make a video).
- My teacher gives students a chance to explain when they do something wrong

Source: Massachusetts Department of Elementary and Secondary Education, (2020)

Next Steps

- Ask your students: Do you feel cared for? What do you expect their answer would be? Try administering a student survey to students and staff and then reflect on the results.

In this chapter, we introduced three approaches for creating learning communities and collaborations that value all learners and create a foundation to have courageous conversations about the outcomes for our students: creating Intentional Learning Communities, aligning work to the *Going Beyond Access* framework, and fostering student voice through cogen groups and feedback mechanisms. Using these three practices ensures that all educators have opportunities to reflect on their practices and examine the critical connection between design and outcomes.

(Continued)

(Continued)

Additionally, by fostering cogen groups and examining student feedback during data meetings, students have opportunities to have their voices heard. Providing opportunities to foster collaboration and community in schools is critical to foster expert learning among students and teachers. Only when structures exist for educators to have difficult conversations and truly listen to students will they be ready to identify and eliminate barriers that affect student outcomes, especially those students from culturally and linguistically diverse backgrounds.

Additional Resources

- Visit the Tripod Project website to explore videos, articles, and research on why collecting student feedback improves teacher instruction. https://tripoded.com/

- Read "3 Ways of Getting Student Feedback to Improve Your Teaching," which identifies three ways you can get feedback from students. Although the article is about collecting feedback at the end of the year, the strategies could be used any time. https://www.edutopia.org/blog/student-feedback-improves-your-teaching-vicki-davis

Reflection Questions

- How do the creation of cogen groups and the implementation of cogen groups communicate high expectations through hidden curriculum?

- Implementation of the *Going Beyond Access* framework requires that all educators collaborate to reflect on the academic, social-emotional, and behavior needs of all students. Does your school/district have common planning time to have these critical conversations? If not, what is the impact on students?

CHAPTER FOUR

PERSONALIZED LEARNING FOR EQUITY

A powerful voice at the level of a whisper will be deemed inaudible and unimportant.
A powerful voice that is silenced and stomped out will be hindered but not altered.
A powerful voice masked by rage and anger will lose the message and make others guess the motive.
A powerful voice must be stewarded, prepared, preserved and educated.
A powerful voice deserves to be heard.
Empowerment of those deemed powerless is the most powerful voice.

—Tesha Fritzgerald

SETTING THE STAGE

This chapter is focused on the design process and how it can be leveraged to create flexible, meaningful learning opportunities for all students. When educators are committed to intentional learning communities and social justice education, they design curriculum and teaching that eliminates barriers that prevent all students from learning at high levels. The foundation for this work is Universal Design for Learning (UDL).

THE DESIGN PROCESS

Opportunity, or lack thereof, often comes to students in the classrooms where they are served. As we have shared, we have the authority and privilege to design learning environments that empower students to become motivated, purposeful, resourceful, and strategic or expert learners, the goal of Universal Design for Learning (UDL). As educators, you hold a great deal of autonomy and power in your learning environment, and knowing how to universally design it with all students in mind is a step toward eliminating inequity.

We have discussed the importance of creating procedures that create communities committed to eliminating inequalities and addressing barriers, but ultimately, these practices have to change teaching and learning as we know it. Our expectations are not high enough, our curriculum is not relevant enough, and student voices are not elevated and celebrated enough. This is where UDL provides a foundation for designing instruction that challenges and supports all students with authentic, meaningful, powerful instruction that is culturally sustaining and linguistically appropriate.

At its core, UDL was created to eliminate inequities. The framework recognizes that effective systems begin with identifying barriers that prevent equal access and engagement. One hard truth that we continue to press in this text is that our systems do not equally support students because they were not *built* to support all students. They were built to support privileged or mythical "average" students who face little or no barriers culturally, economically, academically, behaviorally, socially, or emotionally—while oppressing others, particularly those who have been traditionally marginalized. We can—and should—ensure that all students have a voice and visibility in our classrooms by recognizing how to design and deliver instruction that is universally designed.

To begin, it's important to consider what we know about design thinking in general before we dive more deeply into how to apply Universal Design for Learning to lesson design. Angie UyHam, the founder of the Cambridge Design Lab (d.Lab), helped us to better embrace design thinking and its relationship to social justice. She showed us how design thinking begins with an awareness of people, power, and equity. She shares, "We each experience our world with a unique perspective. If we can tap into how to communicate and learn about the experiences of others, we have the gift to look beyond what we originally see. It is in that space that new connections, ideas and potential solutions live. Design Thinking, if done with an awareness lens, can bring us closer to innovating in spaces that have embraced the status quo. It's a framework that encourages us to listen, look and trust in the power of collective insight and creativity."

Khari Milner, a colleague of Uyham's and co-director of the Cambridge Agenda for Children Out-of-School Time, adds, "The process of learning and teaching is inextricably linked, continuous and infinite, even more so, it's an experiential and unpredictable journey that educators must humbly embrace, particularly those who understand the essence of their role and calling to be the dismantling of racial, economical and societal injustice."

Design thinking, with its roots in both awareness, empowerment, and experiment, provides a solid foundation for learning environments that are learner-centered. We want to share Uyham and Milner's design process as a cycle that supports UDL. The implementation spotlight below can be used for the design of products, policies, procedures, and processes. In the section that follows, we will align with the UDL Design Process.

IMPLEMENTATION SPOTLIGHT

BY ANGIE UYHAM AND KHARI MILLER

Step 1: Decide on Design Challenge

Start with generating a list. What keeps you or your students "up at night" or "gets you or them out of bed in the morning"? What are the things that you are collectively concerned or inspired about? Consider the barriers that prevent all students from succeeding. From there, turn your concern or inspiration into a challenge.

For example, the catalyst for creating the Cambridge Educators Design Lab was the overwhelming number of district mandates and the need for educators to be shared decision-makers. Obligation was prioritized over inspiration, and educators, as well as students, felt a loss of power. Given that situation, we reframed our goal into a collective challenge: *How might we capitalize on experiences, expertise, and passion of educators by changing the way in which problems are identified and addressed as a district?*

Step 2: Be Aware

Before embarking on the Design Process, individuals or design teams "dig deep" to learn more. They reflect on their own identity and biases as well as mapping out all the stakeholders involved in their design challenge. By doing so, they can be more aware about their intended and unintended influence on a design process. Understanding the various stakeholders in a process helps us to see how power and context greatly impact a situation and potential solution.

Step 3: Learn

In Design Thinking, you will often hear the term "empathize." In our lab, we like to use the terms "learn" or "discover." We recognize that there are certain experiences that we can relate to and others that we cannot. So by using the term "learn," it opens up the lines of communication between different stakeholders in a design process. The Learning Phase is just that—it's all about learning as much as we can about the experiences of others given our own personal identity and context. We ask questions through thoughtful interviews, and we engage in observations when welcomed. Interview questions are mostly open-ended—for example, "Tell me about an experience when you felt powerful. Tell me about an experience when you did not, but wish you did." Observations may happen in multiple spaces—in the classroom, cafeteria, or a local gathering spot. These observations let us see people in different contexts, which help inform a greater picture.

(Continued)

(Continued)
Step 4: Interpret

After gathering information through observations and interviews, we begin to make sense of it. We lay it out, noting it for what it is. What exactly did we observe? What are some direct quotes we heard and documented? From that we look for motivations, frustrations, emerging themes, or patterns. Then we identify essentials that we need to include in our design process or outcome. These essentials or "North Stars" can range from agreements in the process like we must have "diverse student representation" to something more concrete like "this needs to happen during the school day."

Step 5: Brainstorm

The spaces created during our design sessions are grounded and propelled by a mindset to be open-minded, to seek and see the possibilities, and to think creatively. The attributes of these mentalities are shared by effective designers, educators, and change agents across the globe. In addition to supporting each other to ideate and think outside of the box toward new ideas to launch, we also encourage the generation of concepts and experiments that can lead to shifts in practice, disruptions to norms, and the elimination of barriers.

Step 6: Prototype

Design thinkers must learn to plan and implement their ideas and experiments with an ultimate focus on collecting and valuing all types of feedback. As we embark upon the important task of documenting how a new idea is going, we consider *who* we will learn the most from as well as what kinds of feedback we will need to know in order to determine how the idea is progressing and whether there are additional ways to test it. Prototyping takes time, but as importantly it takes a game plan.

Step 7: Improve

Experiment, get feedback, improve . . . repeat! These are constant themes as educators of all types progress through their design journeys. In order to confront the inequities we seek to dismantle, it needs to get messy—so we need to learn to be comfortable with that—and the messiness must be accompanied by increased efficacy and the broadening of our collective perspectives. Only then will continuous improvement (and progress) be a possibility.

Ongoing: Reflect

If the Cambridge Educators Design Lab was an oceanic ecosystem, then reflection would be its salinity. Reflection of multiple variations: periodic, continuous, personal, and communal are all staples throughout the d.Lab process. It is especially critical for our model to be steeped in reflection because we bring together educators and community members who arrive with a wide range of experiences with respect to learning and education, and we want each of those varied perspectives to be shared, understood, and leveraged.

Reflection Questions

- Why is it important to reevaluate our lesson design process with an equity lens to ensure all students have a voice and visibility in our classrooms?

- How can thoughtful interviews and observations help us inform a greater picture of our design challenges? Why is it important to go through this "learning phase" of the design process intentionally?

- How is Design Thinking a continuous process, and why is it so important to reflect, improve, and reflect again when addressing challenges?

Additional Resources

- The National Equity Project in collaboration with the K–12 Lab at Stanford's d.school developed an equity-centered approach to design called Liberatory Design. http://nationalequityproject.org/services/liberatory-design

- The Teacher's Guild Design Thinking for Educators Toolkit is a way to understand Design Thinking in schools. It helps educators by providing tangible steps for individuals or teams. https://www.teachersguild.org/approach

- Equity-Centered Community Design, created by Creative Reaction Lab, is a creative problem-solving process based on equity, humility-building, integrating history, and healing practices. http://www.creativereactionlab.com/

- Learn more about the Cambridge Educators Design Lab by visiting https://www.cpsd.us/office_of_curriculum_and_instruction/innovation_design_lab, where you can view videos and visit more links

UNIVERSAL DESIGN AS DESIGN THINKING

Design thinking requires amplifying the voices of all stakeholders, especially highly diverse student voices, and also a willingness to become an expert learner who is continually improving. When you are committed to consistent reflection, improvement, and change, you begin to recognize that one-size-fits-all fits no one. You begin to understand, at your core, that a scripted curriculum, no-tolerance discipline policies, and top-down mandates often result in disproportionality particularly for traditionally marginalized groups—no matter if they are marginalized because of gender, race, income, religion, sexual identity, disability, or something else—and that you can do better.

This is where UDL comes in as a framework to support your design thinking process. This is where, as an educator, you provide equitable access to high quality teaching and learning for *all* students.

As educators, we have to recognize our privilege. Of course, all of us have different levels of privilege based upon our race, gender, language, sexual identity, religion, and disability. But positionality requires us to take a hard look at the fact that we are educated, we have succeeded because of or in spite of the systems that were created, and we are here to do better for our students. Even if we may not have the authority to create schedules, allocate resources, or create policies (yet!), we have complete control over our mindset and the design of the learning experiences we provide to students. Through the social justice lens, all educators have the responsibility to design curriculum, instruction, and learning experiences to meet the needs of all students using design thinking.

In UDL, a curriculum is defined as the combination of goals, methods, materials, and assessments. In many classrooms, some of which are not inclusive to begin with, a teacher chooses the goals, methods, materials, and assessments for students, but those may not be accessible or engaging. For example, in a traditional English Language Arts (ELA) classroom, many teachers choose a single text to assign to students. All students read that text, often grasping a worn paperback novel written by a white male, and then they all write an essay on the same thing—theme for example. Clearly, if you're reading this book, you know that simply doesn't work for everyone, nor is it culturally responsive.

UDL, however, focuses on heightening the salience of goals and objectives and helping educators to see that there are many paths that can lead students to the same destination while honoring students for who they are as individuals. In the following section, we share some quick and dirty tips for thinking about designing a UDL curriculum so it meets the needs of all students. This four-step process is in no way a substitute for learning more about UDL, but it's a start so you can see how critical student voice and choice are in the framework.

Step 1: Identify the Goal

Since the first step in a UDL curriculum is to identify goals, this is the best place to start. Seriously, take out the dusty old copy of the state frameworks or navigate to them online and actually read them. You will note that "Read a paperback of *Of Mice and Men* or *The Great Gatsby*" isn't on there. Instead, standards identify specific destinations, which provide teachers with an incredible amount of autonomy and creativity when they design and deliver curriculum. For example, one reading anchor standard in the Common Core is "Cite specific textual evidence when writing or speaking to support conclusions drawn from the text." Well, that certainly opens up a lot more doors and provides an instant opportunity to allow students to make choices about how they will learn and how they will share what they know. Even when pairing that standard with "Determine central ideas or themes of a text and analyze their development," there are endless options and choices.

To align this step with the previous definition of design thinking, consider your standards as your design challenge. Ask yourself, *"How can I design learning experiences so that all students can cite textual evidence to support conclusions drawn from text?"*

Step 2: Involve Students

To make yourself more aware and to learn about potential barriers, as well as what would support and challenge students as partners in the design process, the next step is to share the goal(s) with students and then ask a lot of questions to optimize their voices. For example:

- What do you think you need to know or do to be able to meet this goal?

- How would you best like to learn it?

- What materials can I provide you that will help you to meet this goal?

- How will you share with me that you met it?

When we, as educators, have high expectations for all students, we believe that their voices and perspectives matter. If we teach them to be reflective and self-aware and we are inspired by their ideas, we welcome them into the learning community by asking them these critical questions. Also, when we have inclusive classrooms with diverse partners, we allow students to appreciate variability and see all the many journeys that learners can take to arrive at the same destination as they answer these questions.

If we imagine the goal as being a treasure on the top of the mountain, we have to consider how to become trail guides—to mark all the possible paths and scaffold the journey as much as possible. We also must understand that sometimes students will take their own paths, and sometimes we have to step out of the way. Failure is seen as an opportunity for reflection and choice becomes the responsibility and the privilege of the students.

Step 3: Plan Your Curriculum Buffet Style

At this point, you can interpret and analyze what you have learned from students and you create a curriculum "prototype." Since curriculum is a combination of goals, methods, materials, and assessments, educators can collaborate with students to create a buffet of methods, materials, and assessments to meet the intended goal. For example, if we expect all students to cite textual evidence as they write about a book's theme, we first have to identify all the possible ways for students to learn about theme and provide them with examples of how to cite textual evidence. For example, students can choose to read articles and sections from textbooks, watch educational videos, sit with teachers in small groups for mini-lessons, learn online in a virtual space, or create collaborative groups to jigsaw information under study.

Once students understand the concept of theme, they can choose the materials they need to achieve the goal. They can choose texts that inspire them, graphic organizers that will help organize their thinking, exemplars to guide them, or collaborative groups to work with. When you create a buffet of options, students can self-reflect on their interests, their needs, their personal culture, and the logistics of making the best choices for them. In the same class, some students could be reading *Of Mice and Men* by John Steinbeck in paperback while others listen to an audio version of *Breaking Through* by Francisco Jiménez while still others jigsaw *At Swim, Two Boys* by Jamie O'Neill. As they read from the diverse offerings, they can share their perspectives, look for similar themes, and collaborate to build understanding. Finally, students have an opportunity to choose how they will express their understanding of theme and their ability to cite textual evidence. Note that nowhere in the reading standards are students required to write. Some students may choose to write a traditional response using Google Read&Write while others create a podcast and publish it on their online portfolio. Some students may choose to design a lecture on the theme of their text to present to the grade below them while other students ask to produce a rap video to share on their YouTube channel. All students are reading grade level text, citing textual evidence, and examining the concept of theme, but they are personalizing their journeys and honoring themselves as learners. All products can be graded on the same rubric, but in this scenario, students have been exposed to multiple ways of thinking, multiple expressions of ideas, and an environment that embraces differences, creativity, and innovation.

Step 4: Reflect/Repeat

After implementing a UDL lesson or unit, it's time to dive into outcomes, set goals for improvement, and reflect on how to better design learning in the next unit. What worked well during this lesson or unit? What didn't? What can you do differently next time to improve outcomes? Ask yourself and your students these questions as part of the reflection process. At this time, assessment data can be used to help to define the goal for next steps and students can be a part of a reflection on how their choices allowed them to build meaningful, personalized learning experiences while also meeting the same goals. Continuing to ask students to reflect and reflecting on your own learning provides them with a model of what it truly means to be inclusive, accept diversity, and embrace your own identity.

***

To look at the importance of UDL another way, imagine going to a restaurant, opening the menu, and finding only a single entrée with the faded words on the bottom that read "no substitutions." Similarly, imagine you're preparing for a big event and you walk in your favorite clothing store and see there's only a single outfit in one size. Obviously, both of these examples are ridiculous, and yet in a world that embraces customization and personalization in all things, students are often required to sit throughout the school day with little or no choice about how they learn, what they learn, or how they share what they know.

So often people want to know, what does UDL look like? The answer is that it looks different for every district, every school, every classroom, every teacher, and every student. And so when people ask how it would look with urban students, special education students, a large class, or a remediation course, the answer is, "it depends," but in all cases students will be seen, loved, valued, and challenged. You'll be able to see that students have choices for how to meet their goals, how they choose to learn, what materials they use for their learning experience, and how they express their knowledge in a personalized, authentic assessment. And so, if you're wondering what UDL looks like, you have to think about the individual learners and how they should get to decide what learning looks like for them.

One resource that can help you to visualize if your practice is universally designed is the UDL Flow Chart (Figure 4.1) (Novak, 2019). As we have outlined in the UDL design process, offering choice is just skimming the surface of UDL implementation. When UDL is done well, its efforts result in expert learners: students who are purposeful and motivated, resourceful and knowledgeable, strategic and goal directed. When you examine this—the end goal of UDL—it's clear that you will need to go far beyond offering choice in order to fully implement UDL in your classroom.

At its heart, UDL is a goal-based framework with high expectations for all students. This means if your students don't meet a standard—whether that standard is a content standard (something students should know) or methods standard (something students should do)—then you haven't done enough to remove barriers to learning in your lesson design and you need to revisit the design process with your students.

UDL isn't a framework you can implement overnight. It takes time, patience, and continued practice to eliminate academic, behavioral, and social emotional barriers that prevent all students from learning at high levels. Even the most experienced teachers can sometimes struggle with universally designing learning experiences, but that's okay. Struggle isn't a bad thing. It means you're sustaining effort and persistence as you work toward a goal that matters. Sometimes, like students, educators need the option to access scaffolds,

Figure 4.1

UDL Flowchart

Dr. Katie Novak, EdD

Is there a **clear goal, aligned to state standards**, for the lesson? Note: It must be clear to all stakeholders what students should know or be able to do as a result of the lesson.

No → You're not quite there yet! UDL is all about "firm goals, flexible means," and requires a clear goal to design options and choices.

Yes

Before the lesson begins, do students have **options to self-reflect** on the standard and their background knowledge; take a diagnostic assessment, or view exemplars, rubrics, etc... to help foster self-reflection and goal-setting?

No → You're not quite there yet! UDL requires students to self-reflect to foster strategic planning so you need to build an opportunity for students to reflect on goal/standard and consider what they already know and how they learn best, so they can make appropriate choices to personalize their learning as they work to meet/exceed the standard.

Yes

Do students have **options of the methods and materials** they will use to learn the content and/or skills? For example, through multiple means (books, digital tools, teacher instruction, collaboration, etc...), multiple scaffolds (exemplars, reference sheets, peer-review, rubrics), and tech materials (assistive tech).

No → You're not quite there yet! UDL curriculum is focused on providing multiple pathways in to meet firm goals through multiple methods. If all students are expected to learn the same material in the same way, without options for them to build background knowledge, access additional resources for support/challenge/etc... it would be considered "one-size-fits-all."

Yes

Are there numerous opportunities for students to **monitor their progress so they can self-reflect and make better choices, optimize challenge and/or receive additional support** as necessary?

No → You're not quite there yet! The goal of UDL is to help all students become expert learners, or purposeful, strategic, resourceful students. They need numerous opportunities to reflect on their progress, set goals for their improvement, and monitor the effectiveness of their choices on their ability to meet the standard.

Yes

Do students have **options and choices for how they will demonstrate that they met the standard**? (Note: ALL options have to demonstrate standards are met, so if the standard is that students will SOLVE quadratic equations, all options/choices/tools need to align to the standard.)

No → You're not quite there yet! UDL curriculum is focused on providing multiple pathways so students can demonstrate competency using multiple means of action and expression. Without options for scaffolds and supports and/or more rigorous challenges, not all students will be equally engaged.

Yes

Did all students **meet/exceed the standard** set forth at the beginning of the process?

No → It's time to look at data and determine which students may need intervention and/or enrichment and consider which barriers prevented them from meeting the standard. This will support you in incorporating additional options and choices on the next lesson. Don't worry – you're getting close!

Yes

Woohoo! It looks like you universally designed a lesson toward a specific standard. Next, maximize generalization and transfer to determine if students can apply the skill on a more standardized measure. If they know the content and can apply the skill, and they understand themselves as learners, they should be able to transfer that knowledge! If not, consider which barriers prevented the transfer and design a lesson with a goal to eliminate that barrier!

Novak
EDUCATIONAL
CONSULTING

rubrics, exemplars, and graphic organizers to help self-assess, monitor progress, and set goals for continuous improvement. That is what this UDL flowchart is here for. It's a visual that helps you to imagine what a lesson would look like if you eliminated all barriers to student learning. Now, of course you may be implementing aspects of the framework all the time. But if you're looking where to grow, consider this tool as your map to eliminating inequities.

When you design a learning experience and you want to determine if you have, in fact, considered all the barriers that prevent students from learning, take a moment to look over the UDL Flowchart.

- Have you addressed how you will provide options for motivation, ensured there are options for students to sustain persistence, and helped students cope when things get difficult?

- Have you provided a variety of materials and supports to assist students with comprehension?

- Have you allowed students to take ownership of their education and choose the way that they express to you what they have learned as they work toward a standard?

- And finally, have your students met or exceeded that standard or goal?

It's a lot to think about, no doubt, but don't get discouraged. If you commit to the design process with your students, you will eliminate the barriers that prevent them from succeeding while helping them to recognize their power.

Next Steps

- Start including your students in the design process. In the spirit of UDL, give them multiple formats to offer feedback and ideas—Google forms, paper, open discussion forums, and so forth.

- Start experimenting with offering options with materials, methods, or assessments. Expect some bumps in the road, and persist through hiccups. Change can be stressful, but consistency and flexibility will help you get closer to universally designing your lessons.

- Use the UDL Flowchart as you plan your lessons to help identify barriers. Check it again during and after each lesson to see where there is room for adjustment and growth.

(Continued)

(Continued)

Additional Resources

- CAST, a nonprofit in Wakefield, Massachusetts, is the founding organization of UDL. Their web site includes numerous resources that unpack the UDL Framework and provide information on the UDL principles and guidelines, which are the building blocks of a universally designed education. Learn more at http://www.cast.org/

- The UDL Progression Rubric helps educators understand how to provide choices to students as they personalize their education using the UDL Guidelines. Educators can explore the guidelines at udlguidelines.cast.org/ and explore how the classroom shifts from being teacher-directed to teacher-facilitated through the UDL model that is focused on student voice and choice (see Appendix B).

Reflection Questions

- Why is it important to include students in the lesson or unit design process? How can their feedback and perspective help you eliminate barriers to learning, particularly for those students who have historically been marginalized?

- How can the UDL Flowchart help you as a learner meet the goal of eliminating barriers to learning? Do you think this tool will be useful for you? Why or why not?

- Are you comfortable with providing learning options to your students "buffet-style"? What barriers do you expect as a teacher when beginning this process, and how do you think you may be able to overcome those? How do you think this technique will help you pique student interest and be more culturally relevant?

THE POWER OF STUDENT VOICE

UDL is focused on optimizing student voice and choice, because when we see and hear our students, we give them power. Providing students with curriculum and instructional strategies that elevate and celebrate their voices helps them to reach for the privileges they deserve as their voices become vehicles to identify barriers and help to eliminate them. One educator who is a brilliant implementer of UDL is Andratesha Fritzgerald, the author of the poem at the beginning of this chapter. Fritz, as we call her, is committed to excellence in urban education through the lens of UDL. She has worked in urban education for 17 years as a teacher, building leader, and currently serving as director of federal programs in East Cleveland. Here's her stance on education:

> *When learning becomes deeply personal, it becomes deeply rich. When the audience is no longer just the teacher or the students in the classroom, the effort of the student increases. When we help our students discover the truth—that their voices are powerful enough to speak to experts, to question the powers that be, and cause*

an earthquake strong enough to shake the status quo—then the floodgates of learning are not just opened to them, but controlled by them. When learning is personal, then it matters.

In the following implementation spotlight, Fritzgerald shares the power of student voice in honoring all learners to create rich, personalized learning experiences that matter.

IMPLEMENTATION SPOTLIGHT

BY ANDRATESHA FRITZGERALD

The local newspaper described the city as "three miles of misery." It was a small article about the possibilities of merging this small urban suburb with its much larger metropolitan counterpart. I overheard some of my students dialoguing about this depressing phrase used to describe their lives, their homes, and their schools. They discussed what was missing from their community and their world. What troubled me in particular was the overall tone of their conversation: "It is what it is." Instead of incensing them, they were accepting this misnomer as truth. They were silenced. It bothered me that a reporter was coloring their perception of their city from the outside in. Someone else was allowed to speak, with authority, for the entire city—their city.

Some time after this conversation, a veteran teacher from the Social Studies Department invited me, an English teacher, to participate in a professional development session. She had been to a training and felt a sense of commitment and vocation to the work of the organization. After the utilization of every propaganda technique she knew, she somehow convinced me to give up a full week of my summer, with no additional compensation, to attend a seminar titled "Holocaust and Human Behavior" offered by Facing History and Ourselves. I didn't readily see a connection with the curriculum I was prepared to implement or a connection with our 99 percent African American demographic, but I went. I didn't know anything about the organization and had never heard of it. It is difficult to describe the transformation that took place during that extraordinary training. At the end of that week I saw myself differently. I saw my world differently. I agonized over the silence of my students and the apathy of me, their teacher, who did not push them to speak at all.

Facing History and Ourselves is a unique nonprofit organization that integrates "the study of history, literature and human behavior with ethical decision making and innovative teaching strategies." This organization offers programming for secondary teachers "to promote students' historical understanding, critical thinking and social emotional learning." Students and teachers constantly confront their own beliefs in the mirror of their actions. The training explores the impact of individual choices on the history of our world and how human behavior can either help us or haunt us when confronted with ethical dilemmas of today.

This strategy helps students to explore history and literature while at the same time reflecting on modern-day dilemmas where they are faced with the life-altering choice of silence or

(Continued)

(Continued)

speaking out. Students learn to weigh the caustic divide of upstander or bystander and decide the worth of the risk or the impact of the silence. The students explored literature, videos, poetry, and primary documents to gain a better understanding of what has happened in history when bystanders are plenty and upstanders are few. Students worked through what Facing History refers to as the scope and sequence. This structure is simply the road map of the journey of discovery that both teachers and students take together. This structure promotes inquiry and personal discovery but most importantly is a clarion call to action.

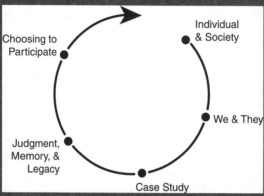

Source: Facing History and Ourselves. www.facinghistory.org. Used with permission.

To Facing History, pedagogy is not a set of teaching techniques that can be used to get across particular ideas or encourage effective practice of specified skills. It is an active process of engaging young people with challenging content through a process that builds the knowledge, skills, and dispositions of deep civic learning.

Facing History created the Pedagogical Triangle for Historical and Civic Understanding to serve as a touchstone for balanced program and lesson planning. "The arrows between intellectual rigor, emotional engagement, and ethical reflection are bidirectional, as these processes strengthen each other. At the center is the students' civic agency, their belief that they can play a positive role in their peer groups, schools, communities, and the larger world."

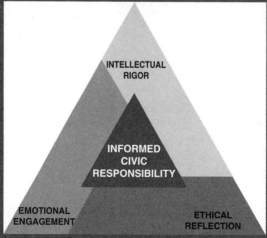

Source: Facing History and Ourselves. www.facinghistory.org. Used with permission.

After working through various ideas about culture, identity, and human behavior, students were given the option to choose an area of need in their school, city, state, country, or world to speak on. This alignment to Universal Design for Learning (UDL) ensured that they had the power to identify their own barrier. This was learner-centered and directed. They were given the opportunity to write a letter to a person who had power to make a difference on the issue they had chosen to speak on. The letter writing gave us an opportunity to explore nuances of language covered in the language arts standards but with the invigoration of a personal issue to fan the standards into a flame in action. Students wrote drafts, and because they had carefully chosen the eyes they wanted to read their words, they proofread. They recruited other teachers, classmates, and friends to read over their words, fostering collaboration and community to increase engagement. They solicited feedback to ensure the final product was perfect. I loved to hear students hold steady on their stances when challenged by others. I remember one girl telling her classmate, "That's what you would say in your letter, but this one is mine."

After careful preparation, a slew of letters went out to members of the school board, the mayor of the city, the cafeteria manager, local news anchors, national press correspondents, actors, actresses, football players, doctors, and even the president of the United States. They had spoken. They had used their voices to make a ripple in the waters of complacency. They had a voice because teachers allowed them to have a voice. The power is ours, and we need to transfer it to our students.

I was cautiously optimistic about sending the letters out because I knew that rocking the boat and challenging the status quo is not always welcomed—whether you are 13 years old or 73 years old. I prepared my students with the obligatory speech about speaking out being its own reward regardless of the responses. Then the most ridiculously beautiful thing started happening. Responses started coming in from local legislators, national activists, and even a form letter from the office of the president of the United States.

There was a shift in our classroom from, "No one wants to hear from us," to "Everyone needs to hear from us." From this point on the same teacher who invited me to the training continued to partner with me on cross-curricular lessons that empowered the students to "Choose to Participate," the true power of UDL. With the same students, she helped them build on their letter-writing campaign to increase their influence. The powerful outcomes of the scope and sequence led to students identifying bullying as an issue they desired to tackle. They crafted a program to present at elementary schools, and a video documenting their work was featured on the Not in Our Town website. They also continued working with elementary students as mentors.

After the video, our students continued to develop their own challenge-based personalized experiences because our district is committed, at its core, to the implementation of UDL. They even presented to pre-service teachers to help prepare them for success in urban school districts.

Social justice in education happens when students move from silence to empowerment. Increasing the reach of a student's voice from the fluorescent lights of the four walls of our classrooms to the echoes of the SHARE buttons on social media is truly freedom and empowerment.

Equity in education is best evidenced when the students are empowered to impact the world around them. Keeping their voices caged in for our own eyes and ears cheats them of the

(Continued)

(Continued)

opportunity to influence the world in real time. Building lessons around two questions will jump-start social justice in your learning environment:

1. What do you see in this world that bothers you?

2. What are you willing to do about it?

Authentic interactions with real-world movers and shakers empower the voiceless to speak up and be heard. Every student deserves the opportunity to be heard. Socially just, inclusive instruction is the mechanism that empowers a whisper with a megaphone. I believe in giving students the gift of developing, hearing, and sharing their own voice with you, their classmates, and the world. Social justice is not teaching and learning for the sake of any assessment but rather striving for teaching and learning that improves the quality of life for all by providing them with options and choices to meet rigorous standards while participating in authentic, powerful learning.

Additional Resources

- To connect with Andratesha Fritzgerald, visit her blog at https://teacherteshablog.wordpress.com/

- Facing History and Ourselves is a nonprofit organization committed to engaging students of diverse backgrounds in an examination of racism, prejudice, and anti-Semitism in order to promote the development of a more humane and informed citizenry. https://www.facinghistory.org/

- The video created by students for the Not in Our Town project, referenced in the section above as a response to challenge-based personalized instruction https://www.niot.org/nios-video/students-teach-students-stand-bullying

- Teaching tips on how to use the Not in Our town website. https://www.niot.org/nios/how-do-i-use-site

SUPPORTING EXECUTIVE FUNCTION THROUGH UDL

UDL is all about voice and choice, and we've seen the power of student voice through Fritz's story, but how do we support our students to make authentic choices and use that powerful voice wisely? That requires our learners to build executive functioning skills.

Scaffolding executive functioning skills in students is critical, as executive functions (including attentional or cognitive flexibility, working memory and inhibitory control) are strong predictors of academic achievement (McClelland et al., 2014). When examining the UDL principles of "Provide options for action and

Executive functions are a set of mental processes that allow individuals to engage in goal-directed behavior. The term commonly includes skills such as planning, organization, impulse control, emotional regulation, working memory, task initiation, flexible thinking, and self-monitoring.

expression," we are reminded to "provide options for executive function" to support learners as they plan, organize, and problem solve throughout the learning experience. The UDL Guidelines (CAST, 2018) help to further define executive function:

> At the highest level of the human capacity to act skillfully are the so-called "executive functions." Associated with networks that include the prefrontal cortex, these capabilities allow humans to overcome impulsive, short-term reactions to their environment and instead to set long-term goals, plan effective strategies for reaching those goals, monitor their progress, and modify strategies as needed. In short, they allow learners to take advantage of their environment.

If we provide students with options and choices to personalize their learning, we have to also ensure they have the skill to set personalized goals, create strategies, and organize the resources they need as they monitor their progress. In some ways, having strong executive function allows for an internal "trial and error" process. When choosing learning methods, materials, and assessments, students must consistently reflect on their progress and be flexible enough to choose more appropriate strategies in an attempt to successfully complete the task (Rosen, Boyle, Cariss, & Forchelli, 2014).

Because of the critical role of executive function, universal design is not only about providing students with the resources they need to personalize their education in meaningful ways but also about supplying the tools to support that learning journey. One of our colleagues, Amanda Hughes, shares with us the power of executive functioning—our ability to plan, organize our thoughts and actions, make choices, delay gratification, and complete tasks—when supporting personalized education that builds a foundation for social justice.

Amanda Hughes is an English Department chair in Baltimore County Public Schools. She has taught middle and high school English and holds a master's degree in educational leadership from Loyola University Maryland. She also completed a fellowship at Kennedy Krieger Institute's Center for Innovation and Leadership in special education during which she studied neuroscientific research and its implications for education. Amanda is passionate about designing curriculum in a way that reduces systemic barriers to success, and she uses the Universal Design for Learning (UDL) framework to guide her instruction.

Hughes argues, "All students can be successful when given the appropriate support, and there is plenty of research that tells us what strategies we should be using in the classroom to support students."

IMPLEMENTATION SPOTLIGHT

BY AMANDA HUGHES

Executive functions are often referred to as the air traffic control system of the brain; executive dysfunction is when students struggle to use these skills to reach a goal. While executive functions may not initially seem connected to social justice, they actually have a critical role in reducing (or augmenting) barriers to equitable educational opportunities. Research has suggested that executive functioning is more important for school readiness than IQ and also predicts later academic success and other later life outcomes, including career success and health status (Diamond & Lee, 2011). Students' proficiency with these skills is due to a combination of genetic potential and experiences, and some disabilities, such as ADHD, interfere with executive functioning. It is important that all children have experiences that allow them to develop executive functions over time, yet students living in poverty often have fewer opportunities to develop these skills than their counterparts with more socioeconomic privilege (Blair & Raver, 2015).

The toxic stress associated with living in poverty negatively impacts students' executive functioning, and children living in poverty lag behind other children in terms of executive function development at an early age (Hackman & Farah, 2008). This limits their educational experiences, as students with poor executive functioning receive less instructional time and have fewer opportunities to engage with their teachers and peers than students who are proficient with these skills (Williford, Vick Whittaker, Vitiello, & Downer, 2013). Teachers, often due to implicit, unconscious biases, tend to label students with executive dysfunction as lazy, unmotivated, or disinterested in the class. Students with executive dysfunction have often experienced repeated failures in school and may see little point in continuing to put forth effort; they internalize the idea that they are not capable of success, which becomes a self-fulfilling prophecy. For educators who are interested in striving for social justice through education, executive functions are a necessary part of the puzzle.

Since teachers cannot control their students' genetics or the environments in which they live, it is easy to be discouraged after learning about the causes and impacts of executive dysfunction. Fortunately, teachers have the power to intervene by designing experiences that help students develop their executive functions; research suggests that well-designed, supportive instruction can improve students' executive functioning (Jacobson & Mahone, 2012). While the most effective way to address executive dysfunction is to intervene early, secondary educators are still faced with students who need executive functioning support. Since executive functions continue to develop well into adolescence (Best, Miller, & Naglieri, 2011), secondary students without executive dysfunction also benefit from these supports. All teachers should strive to design environments that minimize unnecessary drains on executive functions to reduce the mismatch between students' executive functioning and environmental demands. In order to empower students to be successful, educators must implement strategies to support their executive functioning. The following strategies provide a starting point for administrators and educators to implement executive function support.

Strategy 1: Explicit Education

The first step is to explicitly educate students and teachers about executive functions. This is essential to change belief systems and enable teachers to empower students. When teachers understand what executive functions are, why some students struggle with them, and how to provide support, they are less likely to label students as lazy or incapable of success. When students understand executive functions and learn strategies to help, they no longer view themselves as bad at school. Teachers can start the school year by teaching their students about executive functions and strategies they can use to improve their executive functioning. This is a great time to explain the strategies listed below and the supports that will be available at all times in the classroom.

Strategy 2: The Pomodoro Technique

Classes in secondary schools tend to be long, and it is unreasonable to expect students to maintain their attention on instruction for an entire class period. The Pomodoro Technique, developed by Francesco Cirillo, is a strategy that helps with this. When using this technique, students work uninterrupted for a set period of time (traditionally 25 minutes), track their progress, and then take a short break. After four work sessions, or pomodoros, students take a longer break. Many online versions of a pomodoro timer exist that allow teachers to customize the work and break times based on their students' needs, working to increase the time between breaks as the year progresses. The timer helps with sustained attention as students can more easily attend to instruction and resist the impulse to engage in off-task behavior when they know they will soon get a break to check their phones and talk about their weekend plans. In addition, the timer also helps with task initiation; starting a task that will last for over an hour can be daunting, but tackling a shorter work period seems much more manageable to students. The Pomodoro Technique is also a useful tool for teaching self-monitoring as students check their progress at the end of each working period. Teachers can encourage students to set their own pomodoro timers when working independently and to use time intervals that work best for them.

Strategy 3: Checklists

It is easy for teachers who have fully developed executive functioning to forget how many steps go into successfully completing even seemingly simple assignments. For students with executive dysfunction, these various steps can be overwhelming and can prevent students who have mastered the content from showing what they know. Using checklists is a simple strategy that makes a huge difference. For all assignments, it is helpful to provide students with a checklist of all the tasks that need to be completed in order to be successful on the assignment. Checklists aid students with planning their approach to the assignment and keeping the various steps organized. They also help students who struggle with working memory to keep track of the different things they need to do as they progress through the assignment. In addition, students are more likely to be successful with task initiation once they view the project broken down into manageable steps, and they can use the checklist to help with monitoring their own progress toward the end goal. As the year progresses, it is important to teach students how to create their own checklists for

(Continued)

(Continued)

various assignments, and they should be working toward independently creating checklists by the end of the year. They will then be able to use this strategy in their other classes and daily lives.

While these strategies are effective, they only scratch the surface of the myriad of ways that teachers can provide executive function supports. Whatever strategy is used, the goal is to minimize barriers to success caused by executive dysfunction. In addition, it is important to teach students how to use these strategies outside of the classroom so that they are empowered to be successful in life. This is especially true for students living in poverty as they often start school with underdeveloped executive functions. Helping students develop their executive functioning is an essential aspect of striving for social justice through education.

Next Steps

- Explore one to two of the following resources to learn more about executive functioning.
- Try out the Pomodoro Technique when lesson planning or completing some other task and monitor how it affects your productivity.
- Make a checklist (see, they work!) or plan for how you will begin to teach your students about executive functioning and how you can regularly incorporate strategies into your lesson and unit planning.

Reflection Questions

- Before reading this chapter, did you imagine that executive functioning and social justice could be connected? How has that changed?
- In your learning environment, do you currently employ any strategies to teach your students about and support executive functions? Discuss creative ways to do this that will engage your students.
- Think of a time you were experiencing executive dysfunction due to stress or distraction. How did you get back on task, and what techniques and strategies do you find most helpful for supporting your own executive functioning?

Additional Resources

- Harvard University's Center on the Developing Child has numerous resources for various topics related to child development. Their website includes an activity guide on strategies to practice executive functioning with children of all ages. The activity guide is available at https://developingchild.harvard.edu/resources/activities-guide-enhancing-and-practicing-executive-function-skills-with-children-from-infancy-to-adolescence/
- The National Center for Learning Disabilities has published an e-book that provides information on what executive functions are and how to support them in the classroom and at home. Executive Function 101 is available at https://www.understood.org/~/media/040bfb 1894284d019bf78ac01a5f1513.pdf
- For more information on the Pomodoro Technique, visit https://francescocirillo.com/pomodoro-technique. Many different pomodoro timers are available online; one example can be found at https://tomato-timer.com

CHAPTER FIVE

IDENTITY, MIRRORS, AND FUNDS OF KNOWLEDGE

"School needs to be a place where individual students can feel their whole self is welcome and valued—meaning their culture, language, gender, sexual orientation, race and ethnicity. And we need teachers and leaders who know how to embrace those wonderfully varied individuals."

—Linda F. Nathan

SETTING THE STAGE

This chapter is focused on curriculum and techniques that honor student identity and culture and increase tolerance of diversity in schools. We will explore windows and mirrors as a way of assessing our own identities, recognizing privilege, and embracing differences in others. We will then discuss how we can use the UDL framework and funds of knowledge to shape and change curriculum to ensure that students are valued and represented for who they are.

The Southern Poverty Law Center (2020) is focused on fighting hate in the United States and teaching tolerance. Their Teaching Tolerance project provides resources for educators to combat prejudice and promote equity and justice in their classrooms.

One resource published by Teaching Tolerance (2013), "Social Justice Standards: A Framework for Anti-Bias Education," unpacks social justice as four constructs: identity, diversity, justice, and action. If we are to create a world that is socially just, we must first embrace our own identity and recognize privilege and how it has contributed to the world in which we live. To do this, we need to look in windows and mirrors (Style, 1988); that is, we must take action as we look in the mirror to deconstruct the pyramid of privilege and hate that stands around us. Looking in the mirror at our own identity is not enough. We must look outside ourselves, through windows, to embrace the lived experiences of others so we can analyze the harmful impact of bias and injustice. All of our students need to do the same.

When classrooms serve as both windows and mirrors, they become inclusive across identity domains (Style, 1988). This allows students with diverse experiences and identities to feel both validated by being included and to have the opportunity to humanize others whose background may differ from them, which enhances school climate by allowing all learners to feel seen and represented (Cohen & Freiberg, 2013). Classrooms that reflect students' identities as they are engaged in content are also associated with higher levels of student engagement and academic achievement across multiple indicators, including but not limited to high-stakes standardized assessments (Cabrera, Milem, Jaquette, & Marx, 2014).

Our hope is that if we are courageous enough to explore and honor the identities of our students, systems of social justice will extend beyond our classroom walls and inspire policy changes that embrace diversity and inclusion.

One of our colleagues who knows this well is Arthur Lipkin, EdD, former chair of the Massachusetts Commission on Gay Lesbian Bisexual and Transgender Youth and the author of *Understanding Homosexuality, Changing Schools* and *Beyond Diversity Day: A Q & A on Gay and Lesbian Issues in Schools*. His work on social justice and equity is focused on transforming curriculum to represent the vast experiences of the students who we teach. Lipkin contributed an implementation spotlight that provides us with a framework for how we can fight to change curriculum to better meet the needs of all students, so everyone has an opportunity to explore mirrors and windows. We are excited by how his contribution highlights changes to curriculum on a state level to ensure that students are valued and represented for who they are, not merely through shallow recognition of identity but by means of a deep focus on culturally sustaining practices at a state level.

This Implementation Spotlight is lengthier than previous pieces, but it is rich and heavy, emphasizing how deep inequity and injustice can affect the selection of curriculum. After this spotlight, take time to answer the reflection questions that ask you to consider how curriculum reflects the lived experiences of not only our LGBTQ learners but also all our marginalized learners.

IMPLEMENTATION SPOTLIGHT

BY ARTHUR LIPKIN, EdD

LGBTQ Curricula: The Next Step Toward Equity and Inclusion

"Over 25 years ago in Massachusetts, the Governor's Commission on Gay and Lesbian Youth (sic) issued recommendations to the governor to meet the needs of LGBTQ students in schools. Governor Weld wanted nothing to do with either library books or curriculum, perhaps because controversy in New York City schools over a teachers' resource book about a nontraditional family (*Heather Has Two Mommies*) seemed to doom their education commissioner. Moreover, some conservatives at the time saw LGBTQ-related library books or curriculum as instruction manuals for 'aberrant lifestyles.'"

As a result, the MA Board of Education unanimously passed recommendations that schools should develop policies protecting gay and lesbian students, offer training to school personnel in violence and suicide prevention, offer school-based support groups for LGBTQ students, and provide school-based counseling for family members of those students.

The MA Department of Education established the Safe Schools Program, eventually renamed the Safe Schools Program for LGBTQ Students, and provided assistance and training to help schools and staff meet these goals.

More recently, the state enacted an LGBTQ-inclusive anti-bullying law and added gender identity to its civil rights law. In 2015, State Commissioner Mitchell Chester presented the Board of Education a memorandum updating the above 1993 recommendations.

Among them were a variety of proposals, from demands for policies that ensured compliance with the law to mandatory suicide prevention content, designated staff familiar with LGBTQ identities and sexual orientation, curricula that encourages respect for the human and civil rights of LGBTQ individuals, and the review of academic and non-academic policies and procedures, including all available data, to identify patterns that build barriers to a safe and successful learning experiences for LGBTQ students.

"As in 1993, these recommendations passed unanimously. Thus, after a long delay, library offerings and curricula were part of the vision. Moreover, staff expertise and role models were added. Although only advisory, these official acts and recommendations serve as a touchstone for a clear-eyed discussion of where Massachusetts schools—or any schools—stand today vis-à-vis LGBTQ-inclusive curriculum and instruction."

Teachers and Administrators

Most teachers and administrators are limited in their exposure to LGBTQ-related matters. Both pre-service and in-service educators need to unlearn biases and examine why they resist creating affirmative spaces for LGBTQ students. This examination should include intersections of oppression based on gender, race, physical ability, and so forth.

"In 2002, I reported on the limited success of a Massachusetts program to integrate LGBTQ topics into teacher education courses in the 60-odd college and university-based programs that had a formal relationship with DESE's teacher certification division (Lipkin, 2002). Nearly all

(Continued)

(Continued)

teacher educators, in my experience, prefer to have a one-day visiting 'LGBTQ expert' in their classroom than to equip themselves to integrate LGBTQ topics across their curriculum.

Others more recently have noted the marginalization of LGBTQ issues in teacher education (Dykes & Delport, 2017; Sherwin & Jennings, 2006).

"LGBTQ topics are rarely touched upon in school principal preparation programs either – even those labeled 'social justice programs.' When the topic is raised, it is a one-off, not an integrated part of the syllabus (O'Malley & Capper, 2014).

"The importance of educating school administrators in these matters is magnified when one learns that school leaders who push back on LGBTQ-related professional development cite the irrelevance of the topic to their schools, teachers' lack of interest, and community and school board backlash (Payne & Smith, 2018). These findings explain why in a recent national survey only 36.8 percent of students reported that their school administration was supportive of LGBTQ students and more than a quarter of students (28.5 percent) said their administration was very or somewhat unsupportive (Kosciw, Greytak, Giga, Villenas, & Danischewski, 2016).

"Courses and textbooks in multiculturalism in schools may pay scant or passing attention to LGBTQ student needs and the needs of children from LGBTQ families (Gorski, Davis, & Reiter, 2013). The same study found that multicultural educators' approach to LGBTQ issues tended to be conservative, focusing on identity rather than on both identity and oppression. The latter approach was limited to race/ethnicity. The danger of the conservative lens is that it locates the 'problem' of homophobia among its targets rather than challenging the heteronormativity of the school and society at its source."

In contrast, the National Association for Multicultural Education (NAME) sets an inclusive and intersectional goal: *Students develop language, as well as historical and cultural knowledge, that affirms and accurately describes their membership in multiple identity groups (such as identities related to race, ethnicity, gender, sexuality, nationality, language, ability, religion, socioeconomic status, age, and geography).* They recognize how peoples' multiple identities interact to create unique and complex individuals.

"According to one comprehensive Canadian study, in-service teachers evince a seemingly contradictory mindset about LGBTQ student support and affirmation (Taylor et al., 2016). On the one hand, they characterize their schools as 'safe' for LGBTQ students; on the other, they report that many LGBTQ students would not feel safe in the same schools. Although over two thirds of educators expressed comfort with LGBTQ-inclusive education in their classrooms, only half reported that they used inclusive language or challenged homophobia, and far fewer extended that practice to transphobia (18 percent). Only 16 percent critiqued heterosexual privilege and a mere 9 percent had invited a speaker on these issues to class."

Recent studies show that teachers take active roles in supporting LGBTQ students at a far lower rate than they express the importance of doing so. Educators cite discomfort, lack of intervention skills, and lack of knowledge or training as major obstacles. Similar disconnections between a sense of duty and actual intervention in LGBTQ harassment have led school leaders to call for better training and direct contact with LGBTQ individuals. (Swanson & Gettinger, 2016; Greytak & Kosciw, 2014; Nappa, Palladino, Menesini, & Baiocco, 2018). But whatever attention has been given to the preparation of educators in the support of LGBTQ students, transgender, and gender nonconforming youth have only recent entered the discourse (Brant, 2016a; Kean, 2017).

"When the introduction to their needs comes in the context of bathrooms, schools may be left in a reactive mode. Mainstream and social media are accelerating public awareness of transgender lives and concerns; teacher education programs and schools are racing to catch up. A school's experience and progress with LGB students could ease the addition of T students, but that may be wishful thinking. Despite the salience of gender norm violations in understanding homophobia, gender identity and expression should not be conflated with sexual orientation."

Reaching the Goal: Libraries and Curriculum

"Transmission of knowledge, skills (both vocational and social), and values is at the core of the educational mission. The inclusion of LGBTQ topics in library resources and the school curriculum should increase students' understanding of sexual and gender diversity and lessen anti-LGBTQ bigotry. There is some evidence that LGBTQ-inclusive curricula are associated with higher LGBTQ student reports of safety at the individual and school levels, and lower levels of bullying (Snapp, McGuire, Sinclair, Gabrion, & Russell, 2015). But heterosexual and cisgender students' intellectual, ethical, and psychosexual development can also be enhanced. Inclusive curricula should foster the healthy development of *all* youth. Because the world is not 'straight' (i.e., monolithic sexually or in gender identity), learning about these kinds of diversity and how they intersect with other aspects of identity should be encouraged.

"Moreover, the belief that multicultural education is merely a form of reparation to overlooked minorities is a failure of vision. Granted, *Brown v. Board of Education* rightly addressed the consequences of discrimination for black students. In addition to decrying the impact of segregation on funding for black schools, Chief Justice Earl Warren added that black children's segregation 'generates a feeling of inferiority as to their status in the community that may affect their hearts and minds in a way unlikely ever to be undone.' Yet separation hurt white children, too. It crippled their understanding of the human experience by limiting social and intellectual discourse with their black neighbors.

"Lessening bigotry helps not only its targets but also the bigots themselves. All multicultural education should be undertaken both to protect the oppressed and to free all students from what multicultural educator J. A. Banks calls 'their own cultural boundaries.' In the case of LGBTQ curricula, students can also transcend psychic and emotional boundaries, as well as broaden their understanding of the human experience."

Toxic masculinity is just one of the penalties of the normalization of restrictive sexuality and gender norms. Many cisgender, heterosexual boys are taught to banish emotion, pain, and empathy to fulfill the requirements of manhood (Way, 2011). Their sexuality is suspect if they don't measure up to the classic image of the strong, often virulent male. Many become obsessed with ridding themselves of ostensibly feminine qualities, like emotion (Pascoe, 2011), which are a source of shame that has been called "the primary or ultimate cause of all violence, whether toward others or toward the self" (Gilligan, 1997, p. 110).

"Heterosexual girls, commonly given more leeway in emotional expression and in same-gender relations, may yet face pressure to stifle their voices, self-confidence, and physical prowess. Although many educators understand the importance of stopping self-destructive behavior, few see how an inclusive curriculum can help. Studying the range of human sexual feeling and gender expression can help relieve straight-identified students from the pressures of narrow,

(Continued)

(Continued)

inflexible sexuality, and gender norms. Some might also come to see the arbitrariness of sexuality and gender labels themselves.

"LGBTQ topics should be included in the curriculum for the same reasons any sexuality or gender topics are there. Sexual and gender identities and roles are important parts of adolescent development (i.e., social and emotional learning). When curricula are scientifically informed and destigmatized, they balance pervasive media exploitation of sex/sexuality for commercial purposes."

A frequent far-Right dog whistle is the claim that LGBTQ curriculum is equivalent to "sex lessons." But sexuality is more than erotic preference. It is a matter of health, self-discovery, romance, pain, growth, and enlightenment. Sexuality and gender are indispensable to literature and constitute a major portion of the history of all civilization.

"Clearly, heterosexuality has ruled in mainstream curricula from the beginning of schooling and universal heterosexuality has been assumed, unless, at least recently, one is informed otherwise. The absence of LGBTQ experiences in our curricula reflects the fact that most schooling has been devised to transmit dominant cultural content and values, including sexual and gender norms—not, alas, to stimulate critical thinking and imagination. Some who would bar LGBTQ curricula might claim that schools are sexuality-free zones. That is not true. Most schools are deliberately or unconsciously heteronormative, heterosexist, and trans-averse. LGBTQ students are hyper-aware of this curricular invisibility (Castro & Sujak, 2014)."

Media portrayals of LGBTQ issues and stories, fictional or otherwise, cannot be a substitute for inclusive school curricula. Such portrayals must lead to *more* teaching, adding context and substance where they are absent, and providing counter narratives to sensationalism and stereotyping across all nations, races, classes, abilities, and faiths.

"An LGBTQ-inclusive curriculum should enable a student to

- analyze how the homo/bi/queer/gender identity of an historical figure, author, artist, and so forth influenced or might have influenced his/her/their life and work;

- come to a fuller understanding of the overt and hidden themes in literature;

- know something about the history of the LGBTQ community in the West and current issues in LGBTQ life;

- appreciate the diversity and different experiences of same-gender-loving and gender-expansive people in cultures around the world.

- understand the nature of sexual identity, gender identity, same-gender attraction, and how they have been expressed in various times and cultures;

- understand the significance of past and current research and theories about the 'causes' of homosexuality and gender nonconformity.

"Even in a progressive state like Massachusetts, systemic hurdles are rife. High-stakes standardized testing provides little to no incentive for inclusion—multiculturalism may be regarded as an 'add-on' frill. Textbooks may be outdated, omit or give short shrift to LGBTQ topics. For the most part curriculum-setting authority lies with local districts, where fear of community resistance may restrict such innovation. And parents must be notified of and are allowed to opt their children out of 'any curriculum that primarily involves human sexual education or human sexuality issues' (MA Parental Notification Law, § 32A, April 7, 1997)."

As of 2018, seven states ban curriculum that "promotes homosexuality," which includes the mere act of mentioning it: Alabama, Arizona, Louisiana, Mississippi, Oklahoma, South Carolina, and Texas.

Opponents of LGBTQ-inclusive curricula insist that both sides (pro-LGBTQ curricula advocates vs. anti-curricula advocates) of the issue should be presented. An honest portrayal of any group, minority or otherwise, ought not to be an idealized, blemish-free vision. Instructive imperfections, like those of Roy Cohn or Ernst Rohm, may be broached, encouraging healthy skepticism, especially of cultural hagiography.

"Being honest and historically accurate, however, does not mean being neutral about intolerance of LGBTQ people. Public schools are obligated to adhere to their own codes of non-discrimination and multiculturalism. They are not bound to any religious doctrine, yet should be respectful of students' and their families' religious beliefs. If students or parents say, 'It's in the Bible that homosexuality is sinful,' getting into Biblical or Koranic interpretation is inadvisable. A possible response is, 'Our school affirms all people. Some faiths accept LGBTQ people without exception; some do not. Since this is a public school, we won't debate the Bible or other religious text. You can talk with your family or with your religious advisor instead.'"

There are numerous professional supports for curricular inclusion, including those from national teachers' unions like the National Education Association and American Federation of Teachers:

- *Eliminate discrimination and stereotyping in curricula, textbooks, resource, and instructional materials, activities, and so forth (NEA).*
- *Integrate an accurate portrayal of the roles and contributions of all groups throughout history across curricula, particularly groups that have been underrepresented historically (NEA).*
- *Identify how prejudice, stereotyping, and discrimination have limited the roles and contributions of individuals and groups, and how these limitations have challenged and continue to challenge our society (NEA).*
- *Eliminate discrimination and stereotyping in curriculum, textbooks, resource and instructional materials, activities, and so forth (AFT).*
- *Integrate an accurate portrayal of the roles and contributions of all groups throughout history across the curriculum (AFT).*
- *Identify how prejudice, stereotyping, and discrimination have limited the roles and contributions of individuals and groups (AFT).*

Preparing Teachers and Administrators for LGBTQ-inclusive Curriculum

Even prospective teachers who indicate familiarity with LGBTQ-related terms and some confidence in being able to work with LGBTQ students show less confidence about being able to identify curricular bias and teach LGBTQ content (Brant, 2016a).

"Progressive administrators, from whom one might expect stronger support and leadership, may disappoint. One recent study had difficulty even finding respondents (Steck & Perry, 2017). Six self-selected principals and one vice principal in the Northeast who had dealt with LGBTQ
(Continued)

(Continued)

curricular inclusion in their schools were interviewed. They were not a representative sample. Only one had more than three years in the role and six were white (31 state district superintendents had been asked unsuccessfully to suggest names), but even among this non-representative group who recognized the importance of inclusion, passivity prevailed. Unless the state or other higher authority mandated such content, they abrogated their roles as curricular leaders.

"Putting the onus on individual teachers to include this content, these administrators implied permission would be given, but not without qualms. They were sensitive to the fact that LGBTQ teachers, likely introducers of such topics, took some risk in so doing. Moreover, not all teachers might be equipped to handle student reactions to having their heteronormative worldview disrupted. Overall '[F]ear of negative reprisals, professional and community ostracism, and loss of financial security for challenging current educational practices served as strong deterrents . . .' (Steck & Perry, 2017, pp. 342–43).

"Lastly, none of these administrators offered a solution to insufficient pre-service or in-service teacher training regarding content or pedagogy for LGBTQ curricular inclusion and merely regretted the hit-or-miss nature of whatever was being done. Thus, although they wrung their hands over not being effective change agents, they continued to wait for instructions from above – an unlikely source of leverage, except in a few states. Thus, even forward-looking administrators fall back on informal curricular and pedagogical means for change" (Steck & Perry, 2017, pp. 344–45).

Administrators depend on faculty to implement inclusive curricula, but many reject the proposition. In a study of K–12 teachers enrolled in an online multicultural literature master's course at a major research university, 75% at both elementary and secondary school levels responded negatively to LGBTQ curricular inclusion, while still claiming to have neutral or positive attitudes toward LGBTQ people (Thein, 2013). Some felt "sex" did not belong in a literature class; others anticipated negative student, parent, or administrative responses, expressed concerns about legality, feared reprisals against LGBTQ students, and expressed concerns about discrimination *against anti-LGBTQ views* (Brant & Tyson, 2016). Many felt unequipped to detect heteronormative biases in existing curricula.

"The English Language Arts class is a rich arena to explore human relationships in all their permutations. When it comes to same-sex relationships in fiction, biography, or memoir, students can inquire how they resemble or differ from 'opposite' sex relationships, romantic or otherwise. They can bring the same critical gender lens to Twelfth Night as they bring to Romeo and Juliet. In most English literature before the 1960s, LGBTQ romantic relationships were not overt and the challenge is to find the clues in, for example, Melville's *Billy Budd*, Willa Cather's 'My Antonia' or Langston Hughes's 'The Weary Blues.' The authors are many and the relationships even more numerous.

"Writers whose sexualities are open to debate may also be already included in existing courses. The crucial point in studying them from an LGBTQ perspective is not to prove them homosexual, but to gain insight through hypothesis. If it can be shown that certain authors experienced same-gender attraction, the facts that modern gay labels did not exist 110 years ago or that no evidence can be found of their erotic practice and group affiliation ought not frustrate the enterprise. The valuable academic questions in each case are: did these feelings have any significance for the author and was there a possible influence on the work?

"For example, analysis of Thoreau's poem 'Sympathy' ('Lately, alas, I knew a gentle boy') is enriched by considering its homoromanticism. Further, examining Thoreau's sexuality creates an interesting new criterion for probing the mindset of *Walden* (Abelove, 1993). This exercise would be intellectually satisfying, even if one could not find reference to gay self-awareness either in *Walden* or in the journals.

"Langston Hughes's poem 'Café: 3 a.m.' is about undercover police officers arresting 'fairies' around 1950. In eleven lines it sketches the cruelty of homophobia, the causes of homosexuality, and, archly, not being able to differentiate a lesbian from a policewoman. Besides the provocative issue of Hughes's sexuality, students can think about how being black and writing in Harlem might have shaped his empathetic view of homosexuals. The poem can also serve as an introduction to other Harlem Renaissance figures who were openly gay and lesbian, like Bessie Smith, Gladys Bentley, Ma Rainey, Countee Cullen and Wallace Thurman.

"Some teachers have actually taught Willa Cather's 'Paul's Case' without reference to the sexuality of either the title character or the author. Though it may not be critical to know details about Cather's women companions, 'Paul's Case' comes alive with an LGBTQ lens. Discovery of Cather's early condemnation of Oscar Wilde and her own masquerade as a man lends even greater nuance to this short story.

"A similar argument can be made for studying *Billy Budd* as a tale of repressed homoerotic desire. Alternative readings of *Moby Dick* and 'Bartleby the Scrivener' might come from learning about Melville's views of sexuality in the South Seas islands and the passionate relationship between him and Hawthorne.

"Language arts teachers should also consider LGBTQ topics for student writing, such as opinion pieces about civil rights questions, research on historical figures, fiction with LGBTQ characters, and first-person exercises in the voice of an LGBTQ person.

"For LGBTQ students, personal writing is an outlet for self-expression that is at once tantalizing, daunting, and crucial: 'Narrative writing, telling our own stories and telling the truth about our own experience, is essential to the attainment of literacy (Hart, 1989).' Ambivalent and closeted students might not risk the disclosure that genuine, even passionate, writing demands. Teachers could break down this reticence by communicating receptivity, creating respectful and discrete writing groups, or guaranteeing that they will be the only readers of designated pieces."

Teachers should not slight the importance of sexuality in the fine and performing arts, including painting, sculpture, photography, music, dance, and film, all of which are capable of communicating sexual imagination and desire. Renaissance art is ripe with homoeroticism in, for example, Michelangelo and Caravaggio. More modern figures include Beardsley, Kahlo, Romaine Brooks, Johns, Rauschenberg, Warhol, Hockney, Bacon, and Lucian Freud.

Yet, if one is to reach those most in need of information, an integrated approach is more effective. LGBTQ-phobes and adolescents struggling with their identities are unlikely to enroll in separate courses. Helmer's (2015) crucial research on a "Gay and Lesbian Literature Course" observed how "students moved from discomfort to confidence and ignorance to knowledge which in turn enabled them to become more supportive allies and advocates related to LGBTQ issues. . . . However, they also acknowledged that the class targets a specific student population which means that students who exhibit a more homophobic stance often are not represented in the class because they choose not to take this elective" (pp. 288–289).

(Continued)

(Continued)

"Teaching about LGBTQ topics is more than informing students about a particular kind of person. It can also challenge them to think about how same-gender attraction became a marker of a type of person in the first place. They can investigate other characteristics that 'constitute' identity labels and analyze how these tags influence their own understanding of the past and the present. Discussions of culturally imposed categories of sexual identity can lead to conversations among groups of diverse high school students, asking 'Who does this culture say I am and you are? On what basis does it make those assessments, and why should we believe it?'

"In short, teachers and students can employ new concepts of identity to link sexuality to a variety of equity issues grounded in socially constructed identities. Integrating LGBTQ content can be more than a multicultural add-on where the dominant paradigms and values are not challenged. LGBTQ identities can destabilize the verities, invert the viewpoints, undermine the models, and test the values. It can be quite appealing to young people for whom society's dictates are a locus both of self-reference and potential rebellion. It is important to make visible the experiences of and give voice to lesbian, gay, bisexual, transgender, and queer people."

Reflection Questions

- As an educator, why is it important to go beyond acceptance of diversity and move into action?

- Lipkin discusses common concerns among teachers and administrators regarding the incorporation of LGBTQ content in curriculum. Do you feel comfortable approaching LGBTQ content or other diversity content in your curriculum? Why or why not? If not, what would you need to feel supported?

- Through Lipkin's excerpt, we see how diverse curriculum can increase acceptance of differences of those traditionally marginalized but also for those who may be considered part of a privileged group. For example, Lipkin notes LGTBQ curricula can help heterosexual transgender boys by building more acceptance of more "feminine" traits into society. How could similar curriculum that explores issues of race, ethnicity, religion, or nationalism similarly broaden our perspectives beyond acceptance?

EMBRACING FUNDS OF KNOWLEDGE

Hopefully, you will have a more critical lens when examining curriculum and whether it truly represents the identity of our students, while asking them to look deeply into mirrors and also simultaneously embracing their own identity. Empowering students to co-design ensures they make their learning relevant, authentic, and meaningful, but sometimes they too are blinded by their own identity. It is up to us, as teachers, to provide all students with opportunities to peek into windows to create a more empathetic, socially just world.

In addition to ensuring all students see themselves in the curriculum, we have to embrace their identities as we are teaching. One way to embrace student identities is to learn more about student funds of knowledge to ensure authentic relevance. Tapping into students' funds of knowledge provides an opportunity for the current lived experiences of students to drive and influence all pedagogical practices, which supports greater relevance and connection to students' lived reality. This following section on Funds of Knowledge was contributed by our colleague, Joni Degner, who is committed to embracing students' identity in all learning environments. Degner is a member of the CAST Professional Learning Cadre, a rock star presenter on culturally responsive teaching and Universal Design for Learning (UDL) and a full time UDL facilitator for Bartholomew Consolidated School Corporation (BCSC) in Columbus, Indiana.

"Funds of Knowledge" grew out of an extensive study led by Luis Moll in the late 1980s and early 1990s. Studying a group of drastically underserved Latinx students, Moll noticed a drastic gap between their outcomes and the outcomes for white students. In studying and researching the Latinx's home lives, including their familial practices, languages, and values, they discovered that Latinx students were underserved because their cultural heritage and familial proficiencies were ignored in their learning environments. Moll's formal definition for funds of knowledge is the historically accumulated and culturally developed bodies of knowledge and skills essential for household or individual functioning and well-being (Moll Amanti, Neff, & Gonzalez, 1992).

FUNDS OF KNOWLEDGE ACTIVITIES

IMPLEMENTATION SPOTLIGHT

BY JONI DEGNER

At its heart, Moll's study was about building connections between home life and school life that so many of our students feel are profoundly separated. When a student comes into a learning environment, he either knows something about area and perimeter or he doesn't. A student either knows something about simple machines or she doesn't. That prior knowledge resides solely within the student, and to a degree, it is somewhat static until the student starts making new learning connections. Think of prior knowledge as WHAT students know. Funds of knowledge, on the other hand, is HOW and WHY students have to come to know what they know. Funds of knowledge are not fixed or static but rather dynamic and ever-changing. Funds of knowledge does not reside solely within the student; it comes from families, neighborhoods, and community groups.

(Continued)

(Continued)

Our students are like rivers teeming with an array of life experiences, values, beliefs, perspectives, stories, and resources, and funds of knowledge is the headwaters that feed those rivers. Every part of the river is composed in some measure by the water from the headwaters. All learning must flow through these headwaters in order to reach the river.

"How does prior knowledge differ from funds of knowledge?

Prior Knowledge	Funds of Knowledge
• Cognitive approach • Based in knowledge • Resides within the student • WHAT a student knows	• Anthropological approach • Based in culture • Resides outside of the student (family and community) • HOW and WHY a student has come to know what he/she knows

As we work through the design process with our students when implementing UDL, we must build in opportunities for students to access their funds of knowledge. We can implement these activities as stand-alone exercises or content driven opportunities as you co-design or reflect on learning experiences. The rest of this section outlines 10 strategies that help students to embrace their identities and to access their funds of knowledge in classrooms where UDL is a foundation for equity.

Highs/Lows

Highs/Lows is a connection protocol that gets learners drawing on their funds of knowledge as they share their accomplishments, personal bests, and meaningful interactions as well as their worries, setbacks, and anguish in a safe environment. The goal of using the High-Low protocol is to foster collaboration and community and to create an environment that reduces threats and distractions so that learners feel connected to their peers and the learning environment.

Teachers can implement High-Low as a way to begin or end a week. It's also a great way to begin or end each class session if your schedule allows. Responses can include but should not be limited to academics. This protocol is a powerful storytelling tool, especially when it is implemented regularly.

The teacher begins High-Low very deliberately by saying, "Let's take a few minutes to share highs and lows." Be prepared to scaffold student understanding by modeling what you want.

The Rules:

- Not everyone has to talk.

- Just because you share a high doesn't mean you have to share a low.

- High-Low is not a time to gossip.

- No one is under pressure to have the right response to anyone's high or low. The right response is active listening, respect, kindness, and empathy.

- The class response to someone's high should be one of celebration.

Example: I made the travel hockey team!

Appropriate responses:

- ○ That's awesome!
- ○ Congratulations!
- ○ It's so cool that you challenge yourself!
- ○ You must have worked really hard.

- The class response to someone's low should be one of empathy, and although it may include some element of problem solving (see example below), we will not solve everyone's problems in this protocol. That's not the goal.

  Example: My grandfather is in the hospital, and it's all I can think about.
  Appropriate responses:

  - ○ I can see that you are worried.
  - ○ It sounds like you have a lot on your mind. That can make concentrating on other things difficult.
  - ○ It might be a good idea to share that with your other teachers today so that they know why you might seem distracted.

  Closing: Closing is also very deliberate. If you've specified a time frame, stick to it. Use a timer to provide options for self-regulation. Let students know it is coming to a close. "Let's take two more, and then we'll close Highs/ Lows."

Photo That Represents Your Idea of _____

Ask students to bring a photo that represents their idea of whatever theme they are studying. The beauty of marrying an exercise like this with the UDL framework is that we can build in all kinds of flexibility. For instance, instead of asking our students to bring in a picture of their family, teachers can think more flexibly and ask them to bring in a picture that represents their idea of family. When phrased in this way, you may get images of dinner tables, family vacations, sporting events, extended family, neighbors, and friends. I also had a student ask me if he could bring in a picture of a TV family and tell me how that family was similar to his. Brilliant! Yes! The goal of the exercise was to show me the idea of family as you see it, not as I see it. Don't forget to provide options for perception to eliminate barriers to student understanding. Doing a practice round in class with another concept and images students find either from Internet image searches or from their own digital library of images will help provide alternatives to auditory and visual information and increase understanding across languages.

Artifact That Represents Your Story

Artifacts are powerful. They represent something far greater than themselves. I have young children, and they love when a teacher asks them to bring in something from home. They meticulously look for that just-right thing. At the secondary level, asking my students to bring in an artifact was novel. It recruited their interest by allowing them to connect items that were valuable and relevant to them to our work together. My kids almost always responded to this sort of assignment. Even the ones who didn't would bring me a piece of clip art printed off to show me or they would ask, "Can I just describe it?" Absolutely! Although the artifact is powerful, it is not the goal.

(Continued)

(Continued)

Accessing their funds of knowledge, connecting their lives to school life, sharing with their peers, and giving me some great data to collect for future lesson design are the true goals of this activity. These goals allow teachers to build options for expression and communication and to allow students to construct their responses to this assignment using multiple media and tools.

I remember asking my freshmen at the beginning of the year to bring in an artifact that represented their own literacy. I was amazed at the variety of artifacts my students brought in. Some of the examples my students brought in were hunting and fishing magazines, children's books, a notebook of poems, and comic books.

All of these gave me a glimpse into how and why my students knew what they knew. It also helped me understand what helped shape their literacy. It gave me lots of great data to implement in my lessons so that I was able to provide better options for recruiting interest and more meaningful options for language support. Some students no longer had the artifact they wanted to share, so I asked them what they would like to do. Some did sketches, narration, oration, and collages. We worked together to remove the barriers.

An Invitation to Co-Design

At the beginning of the year, share with your students the standards and units of study you will be covering. Let them see an outline of your units of study and sign up for one that they'd like to help design. Not only does this get students accessing their funds of knowledge, but it also helps optimize relevance, value and authenticity. They can help you connect to community partners they may know, connect parts of your lesson to youth culture (trends, music, TV shows, and social media), select resources that they find to be current and relevant, and help integrate tech tools that your students will love using for expression and communication.

In addition to this being an amazing partnership with your students and lightening your load in planning, it also communicates a clear message to your students: "You are an integral part of this learning environment. Without you, this would fundamentally be a different experience."

Skills, Hobbies, and Talents

Ask your students and their families about what skills, talents, and hobbies they have. How did they come to have them? What is the family history of their development? Use the responses to create a flow chart that shows how the skills, talents, and hobbies they have relate to your learning environment.

We must remember that when we are digging into student funds of knowledge and using them to make our design more responsive, the connections that we build in don't always have to center on content. When I think about, for instance, the partner card games that I grew up playing, I realize that I brought a sense of collaboration and cooperative work with me to my learning environment. The storytelling and oration that my grandparents passed down to me served me well in my language arts classes. As we design this activity and we gather this information and involve our students in making a web or flowchart to connect what they know, we are honoring them and their families. We are bringing two worlds together that for many students feel emphatically separated. In honoring them through this work, we are also staying true to the mission of Universal Design for Learning which is to create opportunities for students to be expert learners. If we want students to be knowledgeable and resourceful, we must begin by letting them know that we acknowledge and honor the resources they bring to our learning environment.

What Kind of Teacher Would You Like to Have?

I've seen this activity represented many different ways on Pinterest and other lesson and activity collectives. Ask teachers what kind of question they want. If it's open house night, design a chalk talk so that families can use words, sentences, and images to answer the question 'What kind of teacher would you like your child to have?' You don't have to choose. You can do the exercise first with students and then with families. It's interesting to see the different kinds of responses you get and to guide students in the work of finding similarities and differences to highlight patterns, big ideas, and relationships. The products that result from this activity will serve as a reminder on your toughest days of teaching that your students and their families need a teacher that is loving, tough, silly, kind, funny, cool, and so forth.

What's Your Story? Where Does It Come From?

Empowering students to tell their own stories eliminates the threat of someone else's incorrect assumptions telling that learner's story. Unfortunately, sometimes learners develop narrow and limiting academic esteem. They actually perpetuate their own academic stereotypes, and this becomes the story that they (likely with some help from others) create and retell themselves each time they walk into a learning environment. The problem with these academic esteems is that they create threats and distractions in the learning environment, promote a fixed mindset, and actually work against the hopes and dreams students have for themselves.

We've all heard it before. "I'm not a math person. My mom and dad were both bad at math." OR "I'm just not a reader." We can address these academic esteems and chip away the threats and distractions they present by asking students, "What is your math story? Where does it come from?" Fill in the word "math" with any subject, theme, or content area. Let students know up front that we are digging into their beliefs about themselves as learners and where those beliefs come from. That's the first part of the work. The second part of the work is empowering students to tell a different story about themselves by drawing on a growth mindset and getting them to think differently about themselves as learners. Be prepared to scaffold this exercise by modeling what you want or showing exemplars and building in options for expression and communication. This exercise in storytelling can help mitigate the single stories students create about themselves and their own abilities. In doing so, you get a major return on your investment: digging into funds of knowledge and developing a growth mindset.

As you build in these exercises for your learners throughout the year, keep in mind that initially some students might not feel like sharing much. They might play it very safe for a while, and that is to be expected. The more students have an opportunity to get to know themselves and one another, the more trust they build. That trust will have a profound impact on how they engage in these funds of knowledge exercises. Writer Anais Nin said, "We do not see things as they are. We see them as we are." This is exactly the way a student views a learning environment, not as it is, but as he or she is. Exercises like these can help us understand our students' funds of knowledge and, in turn, design more relevant and meaningful learning opportunities.

When we ask students to do this work, we are inviting and empowering them to connect the cultural resources they bring with them to our learning environments. We are honoring the fact that they do in fact see the learning environment not as it is, but as they are.

(Continued)

(Continued)

Reflection Questions

- Brainstorm some ideas for collecting students' funds of knowledge in your learning environment. How could you change your lessons, assignments, or prompts to be more flexible?

- Why is it important to make connections for students between their home and school lives? What can you do in your learning environment to support that?

- When we hear stories of selves, it is easy to label our learners. But embracing their funds of knowledge and encouraging a growth mindset, we can see how a student's story of self can transform. What can you do differently to better understand your students' stories and what activities would you like to begin incorporating in your learning environment to help students reshape their stories?

Additional Resources

- Watch a short video of Luis Moll talking about Funds of Knowledge, https://youtu.be/EnAmARNgKEw here

- Read *Funds of Knowledge for Teaching: Using a Qualitative Approach to Connecting Homes and Classrooms* from Moll, Amanti, Neff, and Gonzalez, https://www.academia.edu/15916623/Funds_of_Knowledge_for_Teaching_Using_a_Qualitative_Approach_to_Connect_Homes_and_Classrooms

- Review Brown University's information on Teaching Diverse Learners while considering funds of knowledge, https://www.brown.edu/academics/education-alliance/teaching-diverse-learners/families-0

FACILITATING CONVERSATIONS THAT PEEK INTO MIRRORS AND WINDOWS

Another way to embrace both the identity of students and the importance of diversity is through rich, collaborative discussions focused on current or historical events. Earlier in the text, you learned about the importance of collaborative communities using cogen groups. The same level of collaboration and problem solving can be incorporated into classroom discussions as well. Having these courageous conversations is one of the cornerstones of the work of the Anti-Defamation League. In order to embrace identity and diversity, we must facilitate conversations with students and allow them to explore through mirrors and windows and to see how we are all connected, how we all have equal worth, and that when we collaborate, we can deconstruct the pyramids of privilege and hate that we have created.

Tammie Reynolds is a high school social studies teacher in Massachusetts. She holds a graduate degree in history, focusing largely on genocide and human rights, and is an advanced scholar with the Anti-Defamation League (ADL), the Shoah Foundation, and Yad Vashem. Recently, Reynolds created and launched a graduate course, Learning From Injustice, in partnership with these institutions. An educator and a philanthropist, Reynolds wears both of these hats into the high school classroom. Reynolds argues, "Worn alone, neither hat has the presence, the potential or the power that they do when worn in tandem."

Reynolds reflects, "At one time, I was given a formal directive to not be personal when doing my job. I analyzed this instruction, first cognitively, and then deep in my heart, and then chuckled. How could I ignore my own identity and what I saw in the mirror? It is silly to think that one can separate the two. In fact, they complement each other," Reynolds insists. "We bring our own identities into the classroom, and we must embrace that while also helping all students see into their mirrors, and then open up windows so they can appreciate how they are a part of the bigger picture, that they are critical for change, and that together, we can make this world a better, more inclusive, and more just place.

"Any historian will argue that all writing is subjective. And just as the author brings their ideas to the page through a unique lens, so does the educator, and so does every student we have the privilege to teach. To deny this human truth, that we as educators have our own mirror, to feign some omnipotent, objective classroom persona, is a farewell to countless opportunities for pure, genuine, dynamic learning. Further, avoiding contentious issues and matters of social injustice in the classroom setting is fruitless."

Across the curriculum, students have immediate access to current events in their pocket. If one is ever in need of an up to the minute news briefing, today's classrooms are filled with reporters. Reynolds notes, "Our young people are immersed in a world that increasingly segregates them into dichotomous communities—'us vs. them.' Countless posts about school shootings, gun control, racism, bigotry, right vs. left, immigration policy, terrorism, and such incredible suffering are at their fingertips and on their minds in real time."

During the school day, these ongoing, weighty discussions flow from the hallways straight into the classroom with each new group of young adults who are inherently exploring their own principles and value systems and developing their sense of individuality as they look in the mirror. Our students are in a constant state of growing up and forming perspectives and opinions. Should educators stifle these imminent debates in a controlled academic space? Where could be a better place for such conversations to take place to help students explore both mirrors and windows?

Reynolds has developed the following five Es to support educators in guiding students safely in and out of meaningful, productive, and inspiring conversations on topics of gravity that help them explore their own identity while also navigating that identity and looking through windows. Ideally, we as teachers are also learners in this forum.

IMPLEMENTATION SPOTLIGHT

BY TAMMIE REYNOLDS

The Five Es

In my work, I cannot engage students if I am not being real and if I don't embrace my own identity. I can present historical truths, and I can require the memorization of facts and dates, but to truly engage my students I have to be personal. It's only fair really, as I am asking them to personally invest in me if I want them to personally invest in themselves. I have to make the curriculum relevant to their lives, inform them, and invite them to take responsibility in working toward solutions in a universally designed classroom. Their world is so much more confusing than the one I grew up in. Their leadership in the future is my hope. The least I can do is wear two hats and embrace the five Es:

- *Embrace the Opportunity*
- *Elicit Meaningful and Safe Discussion*
- *Explore Sources and Resources*
- *Evaluate the Issue*
- *Empower Leadership and Exit Safely Out*

Below is a brief explanation of each of the five Es. Consider how to foster difficult conversations in your own class whether they come up because of news, current events, or within your curriculum or discussion of funds of knowledge. We need our classrooms to be safe spaces for students to examine their own identity and peer safely into mirrors.

Embrace the Opportunity

News happens. When it does, there are times when being flexible with mandated curriculum is important. Teachers are always torn. We are all bound to rigorous, demanding curricular mandates that require planning and pace to meet. At the same time, we must allow for the unexpected student interest about a particular topic to be explored and developed if it is important to their authentic learning and their identity as a learner. On any given day, a world event, however local, can consume the hearts and minds of any of us. Since it cannot be avoided, embrace it. When possible, plan ways to use these topics within your curriculum, and create the opportunity for students to see where they fit in to this news. These are moments to evoke empathy and to cultivate altruism.

Elicit Meaningful and Safe Discussion

Encourage students to share their thoughts and reflect on the news and moderate carefully. Take the risk to let students share their thoughts, in writing or in discussion, whichever is most meaningful for them, and appreciate that they are willing to put their faith in your ability to keep them safe. Begin any evolving discussion by clearly setting guidelines for appropriate behavior and language in an academic environment and stay true to your usual classroom protocol for courageous conversations. Immediately, firmly, but always kindly, intervene in monologue or dialogue that veers from that compass. When it makes sense, offer alternate phrasing that captures the student's main idea by providing sentence stems and guide students in considering different ways that an idea might be phrased to achieve the same meaning. Point out the power of language as you help students to explore windows and mirrors.

These discussions are not debates. Political debates in the classroom often are a reflection of the "us vs. them" approach and this must be avoided. Be sure to keep your discussions firmly rooted in civics, in an examination of their rights, and in an analysis of their responsibilities as a citizen and future leader.

Inherently, discussions of gravity are almost always the ones that bear contention. The deliberate educator can manipulate "*us v. them*" thinking and language to invite an examination of "*them's*" perspective. This is an opportunity to allow all students to look into windows, while never forgetting what they see in the mirror.

For example, ask students to construct a one-minute argument that they believe someone with an opposing opinion would use to persuade them to change their thinking. Make the time, either in pairs, in a discussion, or in a reflection journal to explore the reversal of roles. Be sure to leave time for participants to restate or reflect on what they heard and to comment. This activity in itself will cause students to examine why they feel the way that they do. It will help them to affirm their own identity while also exploring the identities of others. Keep in mind that students may parrot ideas they have overheard in their personal lives from adults they trust at home. They may be questioning ideas in your class that they have never really owned personally, and when asked to develop their ideas further, they are stymied. That's okay.

Do not get mired down in debate without providing a model to ask questions. Asking questions equals actively looking toward the future for solutions. The opposite of asking questions is "us v. them" thinking. The worst that could happen is that a heated conversation gets ugly and hurtful, and that scenario is avoidable.

Be prepared at the first indication of communications gone awry to terminate the conversation swiftly, firmly, respectfully and *temporarily*. Invite the opponents to cool off, and to do some research. Plan to revisit these topics when the time feels right. There is value even in this scenario as the educator clearly demonstrates the outcome of crossing the lines of protocol defined initially. Further, as unpleasant as this scenario might be, the participants are demonstrating an emotional investment and passion about a topic that provides an opportunity to the educator. Even if the passion is expressed as anger at first, that can be channeled easily into a more positive position that helps them to learn more deeply.

(Continued)

Explore Sources and Resources

There are so many ways to access studies and statistics, expert opinions, and the persuasive arguments of others immediately with technology. Have it handy. Use this as a portal into a lesson about the kinds of sources that are reliable (or not), about how to recognize bias and still extrapolate valid information from a given source, and about the difference between primary and secondary sources. It is important to infuse solid research into these conversations as often as possible (DeAngeli, 2017).

Beyond leading student expeditions for information on the internet, do some preparatory work, and expose students to several relevant resources. Having predetermined resources at the ready gives the educator even more control to introduce a topic or to steer a discussion back on track. In fact, choosing resources and providing discussion questions are essential elements in keeping the environment safe for disagreement. Consider providing a variety of documents, literature, brief eyewitness video clips, art, music and/or artifacts to launch a universally designed learning experience that shares perspectives of professionals who look like the students as well as people who are different. The balance is critical.

Always bring a human face to the discussion. This is key for a student to have awareness, relevance, and to develop empathy. Never, ever go for the "shock factor" when using graphic media, but always, always bring the human reality, suffering, and plight to the forefront of your audience's mind. This is a balancing act. Teach students to be merciful. That being said, use prepared resources judiciously, and be brave enough to let a discussion unfold unexpectedly.

Evaluate the Issue

This is the time for reflection and reflective writing. To maximize student growth, carefully craft the beginning of the end here. This is the educator's opportunity to provide closure and analysis by facilitating a solution finding mindset, endowing students with a mission and motivation that is personal, and equipping them with the tools they need to set goals and achieve them. This is where the design thinking challenge can begin for students. Empower them to identify problems and explore how to address them. Support students to see through windows as they embrace who they see in the mirror. These reflections are critical for learners to learn about themselves and where they fit into the world and to consider the power they have in addressing inequities.

Empower Leadership and Exit Safely Out

Always leave a discussion with students in a *solution finding mindset*. In order to achieve this mindset, one must feel empowered to lead. Empowering leadership, then, is built upon a foundation of **hope**. Inspire **hope**. If students leave your classroom devoid of hope, the discussion is simply not over.

Now more than ever is a time to facilitate the expression of these developing opinions and values, to highlight the value of listening to the ideas of others or looking into windows in forming one's own conclusions, and to encourage students to consider what role, if any, they might play in shaping the future. An altruistic, civic-minded, philanthropic educator will manage this conversation carefully while allowing it to happen spontaneously as well. This educator will pose questions and point out reliable sources. This educator will be brave and will be enabling new leaders to emerge.

- When facilitating courageous conversations with students, which of the five Es would you struggle most to adhere to? Why would it be difficult?

Additional Resources

- <u>Note:</u> Echoes & Reflections offers a rich trove of eyewitness testimony, model lessons, and sound pedagogical lesson planning tied to National Core Curriculum Standards. One does not need to be a history teacher or study the Holocaust for this resource to provide relevant, easy-to-access material. Please take the time to look at their general website at https://echoesandreflections.org/

- Indiana University Bloomington's Center for Innovative Teaching and Learning has published a very helpful guide, including step-by-step instructions for managing difficult classroom discussions and is rich with references to similar work: Indiana University Bloomington Managing Difficult Classroom Discussions: Diversity and Inclusion, https://citl.indiana.edu/teaching-resources/diversity-inclusion/managing-difficult-classroom-discussions/index.html

EXPLORING IDENTITY AND DIVERSITY THROUGH WRITING

As educators, it is our job to design opportunities for students to become expert learners—those who are purposeful and motivated, resourceful and knowledgeable, strategic and goal directed. We must also guide students to effectively communicate what they have learned, how they feel, and their goals for the future. We can achieve this by celebrating the voices of our learners through written and spoken language and modeling and embracing what it means to be a communicator. We can also achieve this by clearly and explicitly communicating expectations for success with academic writing and supporting students in reaching those expectations.

Given the context of a diverse environment, some would or could consider this code-switching, which has two consequences—placing the onus on students and devaluing authentic student voices so that they are perceived as a deficit and must be modified. Instead of placing the burden on students to know when, where, and how to adjust their message, what needs to happen is a shift of the responsibility from students to the teacher. The teacher must make the expectations of academic writing explicit, build upon the skills that students have already developed from the necessity of code-switching, and navigate this process in a way that honors students' voices. It is through this shifting of responsibility that allows us to teach students to appreciate and utilize the power of language and to employ the technical aspects of good writing without erasing students' voices. This shifting of responsibility also results in other benefits: It gives students the opportunity to honor and embrace identity and diversity while also providing a platform for students to take action. Critical lessons about speaking and writing can be integrated into every learning environment, so our students are empowered and not silenced—they are elevated and not ignored.

A reluctant writer herself, Dr. Christina Farese's work has continually been connected to and driven by the importance of being able to write effectively. She has taught writing in various contexts since college—as a writing lab tutor, a teaching assistant, an editor for advertorials at a global consulting firm, a middle and high school English teacher for more than a decade, and as an adjunct professor. This work has been fueled by her strong belief that most writing instruction alienates at-risk and struggling students by

1. failing to make explicit the underlying structures of academic writing, which leaves students without an access point with which to enter the conversation, and

2. failing to utilize content that engages students to the point where they want to write, which leaves so many students without a voice.

She has spent a significant part of her teaching career working in schools with significant populations of students who are culturally and linguistically diverse. Additionally, Christina also teaches at Endicott College, which serves a diverse population of adult learners; courses she has taught include Introduction to College Writing, Seminar in Academic Inquiry, Transitions to Academic Writing I and II (ELL), and Applied Research Methods.

IMPLEMENTATION SPOTLIGHT

BY DR. CHRISTINA FARESE

Universally Designing a Writing Classroom for Social Justice

As an English teacher, I have seen over and over again the fear that the blank page strikes in students, particularly students who are disengaged, who struggle, and who have not typically been successful in school. What is often overlooked are all of the strengths and creativity that these students can bring to writing if and when they feel comfortable. Although the literature on teaching writing is vast and many teachers are inundated with curriculum and directives, two principles have underpinned how I purposefully designed my writing classroom: respecting the learners in front of me and providing a variety of organizational structures to support students with accessing the material regardless of entry point. These principles have allowed a diverse body of students to successfully enter into the world of academic writing and have informed my four-step approach.

Start With Why

As author Simon Sinek has shown us, the heart of engagement is providing purpose and understanding from the start. So often, we focus on the "what" and "how" and skip over the why. But starting with why helps us heighten the salience of goals and objectives, optimize relevance, value, and authenticity, and capture the attention of our audience. Creating a frame and a context is an essential element of designing a writing classroom. Students need to contemplate what writing is and why it is important before embarking on their own writing journey. When "why are we doing this" is answered for adolescents (and, really, people in general), then buy-in for a task that is arduous at best is significantly easier. This is not to suggest that simply telling students why writing is important is the answer. Instead, allowing students to wrestle with their own ideas about writing by posing questions, allowing reflection, and engaging in discussion is paramount. Essential questions such as "What is writing?" "Why write?" "What makes writing worth reading?" and "How do I change my writing to communicate for different purposes or audiences?" are open-ended and broad enough for all students to engage with. Entering into this discussion provides opportunities to validate all of the voices in the classroom and provides a context for the work you will be doing as a class. As a teacher, this is also an opportunity for you to lay the groundwork with the following principles:

- Language and words are power; being able to communicate effectively gives you that power.
- Writing is not just a final product. It is a tool for thinking, learning, and communicating—formally and informally.
- Writing is a process—and a journey—that we are all in together.

Be Flexible

Flexibility is important in two regards: timing and pacing. Writing is a nonlinear process, which requires that our instruction also be flexible enough to be nonlinear. Although it is convenient to try and move the entire class forward as a group, this is a disservice to students in front of you and, probably, contrary to the way you would write outside the confines of the classroom. Instead, the use of checklists, criteria for success, and menus of options (see exemplar that follows) respects individual students' processes and provides the flexibility that the writing process authentically demands.

Exemplar

Good morning! Today is a "Choose-Your-OWN-Adventure" Day!

You may visit any centers you wish (no more than five people at each center, though), for however long you wish (until the period ends).

Suggestions:

- Refer to your checklist to see what work you still need to complete.
- Think about where you are in your writing process and what you still need to do in order to be on track for the due date.
- Pick the teacher center if you'd like to check in with me or ask a question.

(Continued)

(Continued)

Expectations:

- You are making progress, giving your best effort, and treating your colleagues respectfully.
- At the end of the class period, be ready to reflect on what progress you made, what you learned, and questions you have.

Menu of Options:

- **Center #1: Vocabulary**—What vocabulary work do you need to practice? Use this space to work with others on using the vocabulary words in writing.
- **Center #2: Research**—Do you need more information for your essay? If so, use the computers and library databases to search and print relevant research. Then, read and highlight.
- **Center #3: Peer Review/Peer Support**—Work with other students brainstorming ideas, talking through a difficult aspect of your writing, or reviewing each other's writing.
- **Center #4: Teacher Center**—Check in with me or the special educator.
- **Center #5: Writing**—At this center, you may wear your headphones as you brainstorm, draft, edit, and/or revise. Please note, this should be a silent area for writing.

Emphasize Revision

Revision is essential to the writing classroom and is also the part of the process that is eliminated most often due to time constraints, rigid deadlines, and a misguided attempt to force a recursive process into being linear. In my classroom all work could be revised and re-submitted until my grades were due to administration—and, even then, if I could convince students to revise their work, I would go back and change "official" grades. Due dates and time constraints are real, but if we tell students that their learning is the most important thing, then how can we not offer multiple opportunities for them to demonstrate that learning? Completely rigid deadlines not only alienate students who may struggle but also contradicts the authentic process of writing. Moreover, by modeling a recursive writing process and offering multiple opportunities for success, we provide students with a sense of ownership, control, and responsibility over their own learning, which makes explicit our respect for them as learners and as writers.

Truly honoring the revision process means that feedback—from peers, from teachers, from themselves—is an essential element. What we say and how we say things to students matters, and it matters even more to our students of color (Cohen & Steele, 2002). Honest appraisals of student work against specific criteria for success and within a context of support are essential for students who face stereotype threat, microaggressions, and racism on a daily basis—particularly when that feedback is coming from a white teacher (Cohen & Steele, 2002). Additionally, it is through the process of revision and providing feedback that the most significant learning takes place and is customized to what the writer needs in that moment. And, if done with respect, it is also a significant way to establish and build relationships with students.

Select Engaging Content and Provide Organizational Support

Selecting engaging content is so often touted that it is trite; however, I feel compelled to address it for two reasons. First, even if teachers know it is important, they don't always do it and second, competing curriculum demands can work in opposition to best practices.

For most of my teaching career, I've had the privilege of designing courses around essential questions and themes that are engaging and developmentally appropriate for young adults—justice, identity, friendship. I have also designed courses including authors and books that students have expressed a desire to read and write about—Malcolm Gladwell, John Greene, and *The Pact*.

These courses were not only about topics that students felt connected to—from driving laws to planning for life post-high school to life sentences for minors—but also featured people who looked like them or had similar cultures. This is key. In order to want to join a community of writers or scholars, students must see themselves reflected both in the work and as the creator of the work. Additionally, it is necessary to include student voice when selecting materials or creating open-ended opportunities where they can select their own, individualized materials. When students are engaged with the content and see themselves reflected in the content, then you can accomplish the first hurdle of writing instruction—getting students to start writing.

Another important element is providing students with choices—not just choices about what to read but choices about what to write about. For example, in a writing course that I taught around the concept of justice, students were tasked with an essay for every unit. Each essay had multiple elements of choice. First and foremost, students could pick which question they wanted to answer:

- Is plagiarism ever acceptable?
- Is it important to be judged by a jury of your peers?
- Is it right to take the law into our own hands?
- Do you agree with utilitarianism?

Then, they could pick what texts (videos, readings, articles) they wanted to use to support their response. Lastly, they created their own work schedule to accomplish the task and had workshop days where they could select how they wanted to use their time.

Finally, once students start writing, we need to support them in organizing their ideas. Organizational support is essential because it provides both a checkpoint for the educator and for the student. Nothing kills a student's willingness to write more than a teacher telling them, after completing a whole draft, that they need to start over because they missed the whole point of the assignment. Thesis organizers and paper organizers provide a stopgap to prevent this from happening. They are also a way of making students pause to consider whether they have a strong claim or sufficient evidence. An element of choice is important here as well; my students could choose what organizer they wanted to use or create their own. I also had students who used organizers as a way to check their essays once they were written; and, for students who complained that they didn't need an organizer, we orally talked through their plan. Regardless of how it happened, attention to the organization of their writing and supporting students with that was necessary.

Ultimately, when students feel respected, are met with flexibility, receive criteria-based feedback, have ownership and choice, and are supported with structures and organization, then their willingness to share their voice and their writing with us grows.

Next Steps

- Think about how you can better support students with communicating their thoughts and ideas through writing and spoken language in your learning environment even if you aren't an ELA or writing teacher.

- Gather a variety of scaffolds and resources to support students with their writing and provide them as options. Solicit feedback and reflect on what works and what could use refinement.

- Remember to always start with why when encouraging students to speak, write, and express themselves. Remind them of the power they have through communication and language.

If we are to build a world that is socially just, we must create learning opportunities for students to explore who they are, why they think the way they think, and why others may perceive them in one way. There are many resources that educators can use to help students reflect on who they are, how they fit into the world, and how to appreciate the beautiful diversity in our world. This concept of embracing both student mirrors and windows forms the foundation from which we make curriculum decisions, choose resources, and facilitate collaborative discussions. We must facilitate an environment that allows students to explore the world around them, the inequality and hate that stems from a lack of understanding, and most importantly, the hope that with education and mercy, we can and will create a world where we appreciate all people for who they are. Through a socially just education, we can come together, despite our differences, and truly embrace identity and diversity.

Reflection Questions

- Why is it important to "start with why" when teaching writing to students?

- What barriers do you have in your learning environment that you feel could interfere with being flexible with your students when teaching writing and communications? Brainstorm ideas that could help you overcome those barriers.

- Providing organizational guidance and scaffolds to support students during the writing process is essential. What scaffolds and exemplars do you offer to students to assist them with organizing and planning for writing? Which ideas provided by Farese do you like best?

- What is the significance of learner visibility?

- How does the idea of "windows and mirror" ensure learner visibility?

- What structures and/or strategies are currently being utilized in your school community to provide students with windows and mirrors?

- How do you support high expectations for writing for all students? Which strategies from this chapter could you begin to implement immediately in your practice to optimize and elevate student academic voice?

Additional Resources

Writing

- Graff, G., & Birkenstein, C. (2018). *They say/I say: The moves that matter in academic writing.* New York/London: W.W. Norton & Company.

- Tatum, A. (2013). *Fearless voices: Engaging a new generation of African American adolescent male writers.* New York, NY: Scholastic Inc.

- Atwell, N. (2002). *Lessons that change writers.* Portsmouth, NH: Heinemann.

- Gallagher, K. (2011). *Write like this: Teaching real-world writing through modeling and mentor texts.* Portsmouth, NH: Stenhouse Publishers.

- Tough, P. (2016). Helping children succeed: What works and why. Mindsets, http://paultough.com/helping/web/

Feedback

- Cohen, G. L., Steele, C. M., & Ross, L. D. (1999). The mentor's dilemma: Providing critical feedback across the racial divide. *Personality and Social Psychology Bulletin, 25*(10), 1302–1318.

CHAPTER SIX

CULTURAL RESPONSIVENESS AND EQUITY

"Culturally responsive teaching (CRT) is one of our most powerful tools for helping students find their way out of the gap. A systematic approach to culturally responsive teaching is the perfect catalyst to stimulate the brain's neuroplasticity so that it grows new brain cells that help students think in more sophisticated ways."

—Zaretta Hammond

SETTING THE STAGE

This chapter focuses on integrating culturally responsive teaching techniques within the UDL framework. We will explore what culturally responsive teaching means and how it helps create a more equitable learning environment.

UDL AS A FRAMEWORK FOR CULTURALLY RESPONSIVE TEACHING AND LEARNING

It's critical for educators to optimize student voice and choice through UDL so that curriculum and instruction can be culturally responsive and linguistically appropriate. We cannot allow students from diverse backgrounds to feel like afterthoughts that we've been obliged or guilted into making space for. We need to proactively and intentionally remove barriers as well as any and all known or unknown bias by providing educational experiences that are culturally relevant, responsive, and sustaining. We have discussed the design process and how to universally design curriculum to meet the needs of all learners, but it's important to consider how to ensure that teaching and learning is culturally responsive for all students.

> **Culturally Responsive Teaching** is a pedagogy that acknowledges, responds to, and celebrates fundamental cultures to offer equitable access to education for students from all cultures. Culture is central to learning.
>
> *Source:* Ladson-Billings (1994)

A culturally responsive pedagogy and curriculum allows all learners to have access to, and ownership of, an education that is reflective of themselves, their communities, and their lived realities. Such pedagogy and curriculum are intentional in acknowledging the importance of a student's sense of self in their learning and growth. It necessitates critical analysis of our beliefs around history, culture, and language as a precursor to creating environments that are conducive to student learning. It also calls upon us to cultivate and humanize parental and community involvement and address community issues that affect students' and families' daily lives. Culturally responsive education brings together Universal Design for Learning (UDL), funds of knowledge, and the importance of student identity.

A culturally responsive education is one that is free from the presence of barriers, in particular those related to identity including but not limited to institutionally racist, classist, and/or sexist policies and practices. A culturally responsive education acknowledges that positive intent does not prevent policies, practices, and decisions that may harm (intentionally or unintentionally) students, particularly those who have been historically marginalized. Our impact, not our intent, must be central to our work Tatem, 2017. In addition, an authentic sense of impact can only be ascertained by hearing and learning from the experiences of our students. Culturally responsive educators do this by first acknowledging and owning their own identity and the privileges and/or lack there of. They then acknowledge and celebrate the funds of knowledge that students and families bring with them and incorporate such in their planning and decision-making while celebrating student identities and stories.

We would be remiss if we did not also acknowledge that culturally responsive teaching is evolving into a framework of culturally sustaining pedagogy. In their book, *Culturally Sustaining Pedagogies: Teaching and Learning for Justice in a Changing World*, Paris and Alim (2017) make a distinction between culturally responsive pedagogy and culturally sustaining pedagogy. They explain how the frameworks relate in an interview about their book in *Education Week: Teacher* (Ferlazzo, 2017).

> *Culturally sustaining pedagogy (CSP) seeks to perpetuate and foster—to sustain—linguistic, literate, and cultural pluralism as part of schooling for positive social transformation and revitalization. CSP positions dynamic cultural dexterity as a necessary good, and sees the outcome of learning as additive, rather than subtractive, as remaining whole rather than framed as broken, as critically enriching strengths*

rather than replacing deficits. Culturally sustaining pedagogy exists wherever education sustains the lifeways of communities who have been and continue to be damaged and erased through schooling. As such, CSP explicitly calls for schooling to be a site for sustaining— rather than eradicating—the cultural ways of being of communities of color.

In the past 25 years, this research has importantly included work on the funds of knowledge (Luis Moll, Norma Gonzalez and their collaborators), the third space (Kris Gutiérrez and her collaborators), cultural modeling (Carol Lee), and, to your question, Gloria Ladson-Billings's seminal conception of culturally relevant pedagogy. Indeed, Ladson-Billings (2014) wrote in her recent article in the Harvard Educational Review that "culturally sustaining pedagogy uses culturally relevant pedagogy as the place where the 'beat drops'"; it does "not imply that the original was deficient" but rather speaks "to the changing and evolving needs of dynamic systems" (p. 76). It is these changing and evolving demographic, cultural, and social needs coupled with the persistence and even increase of deficit-framed policies and practices that make a more explicit commitment to sustaining the valued practices and ways of being of students and communities of color so necessary in the current moment.

For us, then, it is not so much about distinctions between CSP and CRP, but rather about the ways CSP can contribute to the ongoing work of educational justice that CRP and other asset pedagogies have forwarded.

SUSTAINING CULTURE THROUGH RELATIONSHIPS

There are small steps that we, as educators, can take to be more culturally responsive and sustaining to our learners. Our colleague, Juan Gallardo, has provided us with strategies to embrace all students, being mindful that such strategies are critical when working with students who are culturally and linguistically diverse.

Juan immigrated to the United States from Spain. He recalls:

In early 2001, out of extreme randomness, I learned about an interchange program for teachers between Spain and the United States that seemed interesting. I applied, I interviewed in Madrid with a very nice HR lady that worked for several school districts. The one question I remember is "What do you think about punishing students?" and I answered something in the vicinity of "I didn't know teaching was some kind of a fight." She smiled and asked me some more questions. I talked about my experiences as an English teacher and she ended up saying "I would like to offer you a position as a high school teacher in Texas." I had never been in the states, not even as a tourist, and Texas seemed interesting, although I didn't know much more about it than what was portrayed in Marlboro TV commercials.

[When I arrived] The culture shock was immense; as a westerner, I assumed life in the United States wouldn't be very different from life in Europe. It was. Adapting to my new environment was tough. However, one of the things that helped me find my place here in Texas was precisely the number of ELL students I had in my classrooms. Due to the many nationalities of its incoming students, the motto of Sharpstown High School was and still is "Where the World comes to school"; I felt like I was part of that diverse, incoming world to this new, scary world; my journey of discovery of this country and its culture ran parallel to the journey of my ELL students."

As an experienced educator and administrator, Juan shares strategies that can support educators as they welcome students and their families who are linguistically and culturally diverse into their classrooms.

IMPLEMENTATION SPOTLIGHT

BY JUAN GALLARDO

Supporting Language Learners Through Relationships, Family, Understanding, and Empathy

It is proven that students learn better from teachers they care about, who, in turn, must care for them. A positive relationship cannot be created between teachers and students if they don't get to know each other. Share with your students as much of your life, likes, and dislikes as you feel comfortable sharing, so they get to know you. The best way for you to get to know them is incredibly simple: *You must listen to them.* In Sharpstown High School we recently started producing a series of videos. At first, we had teachers and administrators discussing a variety of topics connected to education; then, we decided to have students talk about their educational experience without a clue of what awaited us.

Put a microphone and a camera in front of a newly arrived Latino student, show him or her that you care about what they have to say, take a deep breath, and get ready to be overwhelmed with emotion. In our first interviews we have heard stories of hard travels, terrifying experiences, love for their families, and a sense of moving forward, primarily, to make their families proud. Most of us educators haven't gone through even half of the hardships many of our newly arrived immigrant children have had to endure: Besides their often dramatic journeys and struggles with acculturation, many of them face tremendous language barriers and economic struggles and may suffer bullying or witness plain discrimination and prejudice targeted toward their parents and/or themselves, accentuated by our current and convulsive political environment—all of this when they are still children.

For privacy reasons, we have edited some dramatic parts of those interviews out, but I still invite you to check out our **Sharpstown Stories Project** playlist on YouTube.

Involve Student Families

When working with English language learners and their families, especially in newly arrived families, it is critical to make connections between home and the classroom. As we know from UDL, "one-size-fits-all" fits very few people so outreach must be varied, flexible, and culturally responsive. For example, it is possible that in some families taking part in school activities may feel to them as something disrespectful to the school and the teachers. Don't feel frustrated if parental participation is hard to gain at first. A special effort must be made to incentivize such families to attend school activities, meetings, open houses, and so forth. Many studies show the correlation between family participation and student's success (Roehlkepartain & Syvertsen, 2014). It is for that reason that every effort must be made to remove the barriers that may prevent some parents from taking a more active part in their children's education.

1. To minimize cultural barriers, teachers and administrators should be very clear to parents that they are not only welcome but also encouraged to participate in school activities and that doing so represents no disrespect.

2. To minimize language barriers, all information regarding such events must be distributed in English and in all first language, and the events must be also offered bilingually.

3. To reduce barriers to participation, provide childcare support for families with little kids. Additionally, if needed, buses or any other form of transportation must be provided to pick up families from their houses on the dates of events.

If your families aren't participating in school events, consider moving the event to their neighborhoods, be it in churches or other places those families congregate. Lastly, consider an additional, more subtle barrier: Parents may have never had the opportunity to earn a college education or a high school diploma. It is possible that their self-perceived lack of academic preparation may make them feel insecure in a school setting. That's why the expectations for those meetings and activities must be clearly communicated to them in advance in ways that are linguistically appropriate and culturally responsive.

Promote Understanding Through UDL

Imagine walking into a classroom with a culture and a language you do not yet understand. If you are to be successful, the educator in that room needs to provide culturally responsive and

(Continued)

(Continued)

universally designed learning. It is critical to implement both culturally responsive teaching and UDL with your English learners. It is clear that the UDL framework has a very special place for ELL students because at its center, it reminds all educators to provide options for language and symbols. Your ELL students don't necessarily have any sensory deficiency, so please, do not talk loud to your students the way you may need to talk to your 90-year-old grandma! Rather, from the moment you welcome students to your class, support them by exploring the UDL checkpoints in the **provide options for language and symbols** guideline:

Clarify vocabulary and symbols

Be sure to offer language support that can be addressed with anchor charts around the room, subtitles in videos, glossaries of key words, rich visuals, and realia.

Clarify syntax and structure

Contrary to the classical "immersion" approach that dictated that the original language of the student should be avoided at all costs, new research indicates that the student's knowledge of grammar and syntax in his mother language is beneficial when acquiring an additional language and should be embraced (Cohen, 2015). The research goes on to say that "translanguaging," a form of flexible bilingualism, should be encouraged. Hence, in my work, I often highlight similarities between Spanish and English and encourage students to embrace their first language.

Support decoding of text, mathematical notation, and symbols

Promote good, understandable pronunciation using text-to-speech and/or voice recognition software. It's right there on every smartphone, even in TV remote controls, and focus on "understandable" rather than perfect pronunciation. The main purpose of language is communication, so don't require your students to have a perfect pronunciation at first; focus on them being able to make themselves understood, and then you may focus on polishing their pronunciation. As I entered an English environment at age 27, I no longer have any hopes of losing my foreign accent, but I can communicate just fine!

Promote understanding across languages

UDL vocabulary is nowhere else as unequivocally connected to the ELL student as it is in this checkpoint. The UDL Guidelines (CAST, 2018) provide the following strategies when working with language learners:

- *Make all key information in the dominant language (e.g., English) also available in first languages (e.g., Spanish) for learners with limited-English proficiency and in ASL for learners who are deaf.*
- *Link key vocabulary words to definitions and pronunciations in both dominant and heritage languages.*
- *Define domain-specific vocabulary (e.g., "map key" in social studies) using both domain-specific and common terms.*
- *Provide electronic translation tools or links to multilingual glossaries on the web.*
- *Embed visual, non-linguistic supports for vocabulary clarification (pictures, videos, etc.).*

Illustrate through multiple media

This checkpoint points out a clear connection between visuals and text. You can provide visuals that are both universally designed and culturally responsive. For example, when working with predominantly Latino and Hispanic students, I would share the word "flag" next to Latino countries' flags, "president" next to a president of a Latino country, "monument," "food," and "city" all next to images of distinctly Latino images. This is more powerful than you may think: I remember becoming teary-eyed during my first week in Houston when I saw a map of Spain displayed in a classroom.

Key Word: Patience

When students are learning English, give them time to answer your questions in English. Do bear in mind that they are doing double work: answering the question itself and putting it into English words rather than in their first language. And let me emphasize this point: **they need to talk**, and as I mentioned before, their pronunciation doesn't have to be perfect. Their grammar will be less than exquisite, but they need to lose the fear to speak, and for that you will need to engage them, make them feel safe, and never be judgmental.

Videos in English with subtitles in students' first language will be very beneficial in the initial stages of English learning, but don't take too long before you start showing English spoken videos with English subtitles as the scaffolds benefit spelling and a deeper immersion in the new language with the images as contextual support.

Key Word: Empathy

Let's admit it: We have all been there as teachers. It's March or April, even May, and you have been working with your students very hard for the best part of a whole school year to get them ready for the state standardized tests, for your finals, and you get a brand-new child with no knowledge of your subject. To make matters more complicated, she doesn't speak English.

Picture that moment when, in the middle of your lecturing, an administrator knocks on your door and introduces you to your new student. What's your first reaction? Are you paying attention to what you feel and how your body language displays those emotions? Your new student may not know English, but she can tell how you feel.

Now put yourself in the position of the child. She has arrived at a new country with a new culture and a new language where everything she knew about life and functioning in it is completely different. She may have arrived at the country in an airplane, maybe? In a bus? Or maybe in ways that she wouldn't want to admit. Imagine how some, uncertain journeys may affect the psyche of a young person. Picture her the night before attending her first American school for the first time when all she could think about was to enter, without the protection of a parent or any close relative, a school setting, and how she would be surrounded by a microcosm of her new reality.

You must welcome every student the second they enter your world. I cannot emphasize enough how important that first week is, the first day, the importance of those first 10 seconds. Were you smiling?

My favorite part about working as a dean of students in Sharpstown has been, without a doubt, welcoming new students. Most of them are Latino English learners. As their dean, I am one of the very first people they get to meet in our school, even before they meet their

(Continued)

(Continued)

teachers. I am the one who has the privilege to sit with them, explain the basics of the Texas high school graduation requirements, how many credits they will need, which ones are mandatory, which ones are not, and which of the classes they passed in their countries will serve to get them credits here towards their graduation. The biggest honor I get is being the first person in my campus to ask them about their lives, about their country, community, and family members they left behind, about their journey, about their family situation, about their fears, and about their hopes. I get to walk the hallways with them for their very first time and introduce them to their new teacher.

Knock, knock.

Don't forget to smile.

Reflection Questions

- How do you currently empower families of all students, including English language learners, to participate in the school community?
- How can UDL provide a framework for elevating and celebrating the voices of English learners and their families?

SUSTAINING CULTURE THROUGH COMMUNITY

Supporting students and their families in culturally responsive ways also requires us to recognize how much families can support your goals and solve the problems that may create barriers in the community. As former state teacher of the year in Arizona, Kristie Jackson is committed to optimizing the outcomes of all students by making meaningful connections with the families and the communities in which they live. Her journey began working with student families and their community support systems as a teacher, but she soon realized that schools, districts, and state education systems can be transformed when educators are willing to embed themselves in the communities they serve—partnering with families to share decision-making about the district. She shared three anecdotes with us, which are both inspiring and possible to duplicate in our own communities if we are willing to recognize that solutions to barriers and problems within our schools cannot only be resolved within district office and school walls.

The power of fostering collaboration with the community cannot be overstated in the UDL model. Kristie Jackson shared concrete examples of how building meaningful connections can help address outcomes of all learners and the communities who serve them.

IMPLEMENTATION SPOTLIGHT

BY KRISTIE JACKSON

Oftentimes, although very well intentioned, we in schools hear the first part of a problem and jump to "This is what I'm going to do to fix it," as though our communities cannot contribute to a solution that cuts to the heart of the problem. Our responsibility, as educators, is to collaborate to clarify a problem and continue to collaborate to co-create solutions. If we don't commit to this partnership, it's possible that we will provide solutions that would work perfectly in our walk of life but the solution may not be culturally responsive for the communities we serve. We have to believe that solutions exist in these communities already and we have to empower families and the communities to share them with us.

Without taking the time to ask questions, listen, and discuss solutions, we are undermining a community's ability to deal with problems for themselves. We have to create space, time, and the opportunity to elevate the voices of our families and communities and only then can we design systems that are inclusive, equitable, and culturally sustaining.

At the School Level

I started teaching in a K–8 school with 1,000 students in a somewhat rural district outside of the Phoenix area. It was a proud, migrant farming community. All the students lived within a one-mile distance from the school. They had never had buses, and the mamas in this community walked their kiddos to school and picked them up every day.

In this community, as in many others, things started to change. An urban sprawl enveloped the migrant farming community, and given that the district was already overpopulated, a new school was built. As the bird flies, the new school was a mile away from the community, but there were railroad tracks that were fenced off, and these families did not have access to vehicles. Walking to the nearest overpass could extend the journey to over an hour. Parents were very upset because they could no longer walk their children to school, pick them up if they were sick, or have easy access to them. There was a clear problem, and the district, making assumptions about the heart of the problem, "solved" it by providing transportation to and from school. They even sent out buses for parents to take a ride to the school so they wouldn't be nervous about the transportation. The issue was that the parents weren't nervous about the bus ride. It was something else.

As a teacher, I met with the moms of my students to ask them to identify their concerns, and they were in tears. I learned that to a mama's heart, the new school and the transportation meant "If my little one is sick, it will take me an hour to get there and then I have to make her walk all the way back." This allowed us to understand the problem a little more, but again, the district swooped in saying, "But we have solved their transportation needs and if students have to, they can stay in the nurse's office until the end of the day." This was not a solution.

In meeting with a small group of moms again, I learned that they simply wanted quick access to their children. I listened, and then I asked them, "What do you do for transportation when you have to leave the neighborhood?" They explained there were a few active churches in the

(Continued)

(Continued)

community and the pastor would help them coordinate with someone who could arrange transportation. These mamas were problem-solvers and had solutions already.

I reached out to the pastors and additional community organizations and asked if there was a way to coordinate a ride share to support parents if they needed to pick up their kids. We facilitated community meetings, asking questions such as "How will people sign up?" "Who will coordinate the rides?" They were solving problems in their community that we didn't even know existed. It was an amazing opportunity to learn about the amazing work that was happening.

Experiencing the power of this collaboration was beautiful and interesting because the district was so focused on investing in bus runs and school tours that they missed the real problem and opportunities for a real solution.

At the District Level

The school district where I served was the fastest growing district in the nation. In 1 year, we built three new schools. One of the building projects was a school built in the heart of a retiree community. Land in those communities had never been used for schools until enrollment spiked and a new school needed to be built. The retirement community did not welcome this change. They were fearful that the migrant community would bring not only traffic and noise but also crime. They didn't want little kids in the neighborhood, and one citizen stood up in meetings and said, "Not only do we not little kids but we don't want little brown kids in our community." It was heartbreaking for educators in the system and created further animosity with the community. It seemed like it was "us" against "them," as the community didn't want the school, and we, as educators, were pushing back as advocates for kids.

In one instance, the school was in the final stages of construction, but students were not yet enrolled. One gentleman came in and said, "I can't even rest because all the kids are making so much noise on the playground." We had to explain that students had not yet stepped foot on campus.

Day after day, community members came in to complain, which was so disheartening. One day, however, a woman came in from a small church group to ask if there was any way that the church could support the schools. Finally! I asked if I could attend the church group, and she welcomed me. At our first meeting, I sat down and shared, "I love that you want to help the school, and I'd also love to know what some of the concerns are in the community because we want to support you too."

No one had ever come from the school district to come and talk to them. But once the door was open, everyone wanted to talk. I attended pinochle games, bridge club, pickleball tournaments, and Elks Club meetings. As an advocate for kids, I went where people were gathered. Every time I started with "I understand there are concerns and I'd love to know what they are and how we can work together to solve them."

One big issue, for example, was a fear of traffic. Many of these community members didn't drive often. They were fearful of not knowing the schedule so they didn't know how to avoid the lines of pickups if they were going to the doctor. I addressed their concerns by sharing bus schedules and school schedules. The most powerful part of these meetings was sharing my own concerns as an educator and asking them for help. At the time, I was a K–3 reading specialist, and I couldn't meet the needs of all the kids who needed my support. They needed extra practice reading—someone who could listen to them practice reading aloud. And so I asked these retirees if they would be willing to come in and read. They felt that they weren't qualified, so I eliminated that barrier by going into their community and teaching them active listening skills and reading games. At these training sessions, they built confidence, got a badge, and then they would come in as a crew of volunteers. As they read, they built relationships with these sweet children. They became nanas and papas to many of these kids. There were so many volunteers sometimes that you couldn't get a parking spot on campus.

Other community organizations wanted to partner too. We asked them, "What needs do you have?" Some of them wanted older students to come and read to retirees who were losing their sight. They wanted students to come in and clean up yards if they couldn't do it themselves. There were a number of people who needed help moving heavy items out on the bulk trash days.

The football team would go to work on bulk trash weeks! There was a symbiotic relationship. Instead of seeing us as scary or a challenge, they began to see our school, and our students, as a resource that could be tapped into. They could give as much as the community was willing to give back to them. We not only changed the perception but also saw a positive change in the voting practices in the areas. They were one of the strongest communities to support the school. We were able to change the minds of our retirees, but it was a learning experience for us as educators because we didn't see them as adversarial anymore. We never gave them a space to share what their concerns were or to help us address it. It was really about the change that the community was going through.

At the State Level

As an educator, you have an incredible opportunity to lead outside of your classroom if you partner with community organizations. After I became state teacher of the year, I had many opportunities to work with administrators and educators in different districts. One district was dealing with significant racial tension and had a complaint filed with the NAACP. The complaint was about a white teacher who wanted students to understand the horror of historical events and racism. She asked two black students to walk into her classroom while white students berated them and called them the N word. This carried over onto the playground. She stated she was simply reenacting the experience of the Little Rock Nine.

A part of the solution was going to be training on equity and racism, but I didn't want to be a part of a Band-Aid solution. A one-off training wasn't going to address the deep inequities and racism in the district. Instead, I wanted to be a part of a long-term solution, and this would mean partnering with the community, not just the teachers in the district. I connected with the NAACP leader Roy Tatem, president of the NAACP East Valley Branch, to discuss how to get the community together to support the schools. I recognized my privilege in this work. In a predominantly white school, having a white educator colead the work created pathways that weren't available previously. Once I got involved, I invited Roy Tatem to collaborate. He was more than willing to help but had never been invited.

He helped me connect to black and brown families to understand what was actually happening. Together, we listened to understand areas where parents were feeling challenged, but they weren't heard in the school. I then reached out to the superintendents and school districts and

(Continued)

(Continued)

tried to address those issues and created an open meeting with the NAACP and a mother forum and additional community organizations to begin to examine structural racism and how we could partner to address it. We worked together and realized we needed to learn and work from each other.

Because of the success of this model, Roy and I were invited to Harvard University to discuss race, equity, and leadership in schools. We attended that together—as education and community partners. This work is always in progress. Together, we continue to partner districts with the NAACP and other educational nonprofits to better serve our students. We are trying to educate across each other—allowing families to be heard and educated while educators listen, learn, and collaborate.

In writing this book, we had the pleasure of connecting with Angel Tucker and Samantha Feinberg from Race Project KC, which provides an incredible example of what can be accomplished when multiple community organizations come together to support learners.

Race Project KC serves communities in both Kansas and Missouri. Race Project KC is an annual immersive social justice initiative focused on the role of racism in the history of the United States and, more specifically, the Kansas City area. The project, which is a partnership between local schools, the Johnson County Library, and other community organizations, builds on the text *Some of My Best Friends Are Black: The Strange Story of Integration in America* by author Tanner Colby. Through a series of experiences, students learn about the impact of structural racism, collaborate with experts, learn vocabulary for talking about racism, build relationships with diverse peers, and learn the power of their own stories.

The Race Project KC grew organically because Angel Tucker, a librarian at the Johnson County Library, recognized the need for a partnership and made space for it in the community. Johnston County Library has 14 different locations within the system. Angel Tucker is the youth services manager who oversees programming and outreach to children beginning at birth until they reach 18, parents, caregivers, and educators. Her counterpart is an adult services manager who oversees in a similar capacity. In 2014 they decided to bring Tanner Colby, the author of the aforementioned text, to Johnston County. What resulted from this one book provides an example of what is possible when we are committed to this work.

Angel shared with us the following: "We wanted this opportunity to be about the community and considered one of two approaches. We could've simply brought in Tanner Colby and had a local person interview and/or facilitate a dialogue with him, have him share opinions and views, sign books and then head out the door, or we could've made it more of a community effort and that's the track we took." In this following implementation spotlight, Angel shares how she partnered with local educators and other community organizations to create an immersive experience that would make a lasting impact.

IMPLEMENTATION SPOTLIGHT

BY ANGEL TUCKER

To make Race Project KC a reality, we started off by partnering with a local high school. We took Tanner Colby to the school where students had read his book. He was in conversation with two local educators to make this happen. We also partnered with Johnston County Community College, the local community college, and pulled him into their campus where there were two professors who were in dialogue with him.

We also held an evening event that was open to the public. In the audience that evening were a handful of educators who did not realize the impact of racially restrictive covenants, red-lining and blockbusting in Kansas City, or how what was happening in Kansas City was imported to other major cities across the nation. Across the nation, people of color and Jewish people could not buy homes in entire neighborhoods, and to this day, that impacts the makeup of our schools and communities.

As an example, one of the high schools that sits in one of our neighborhoods is 0.8% black, which means you can go through all 4 years as a black student and never have class with another black student, and this contradicts the notion of why all the black kids sit together at the lunch table. At Shawnee East there aren't enough black kids to do that, so they don't interact. It was a fascinating look at why our neighborhoods look the way they do. After the event, high school teachers reached out to us, and we held a summit the following summer. It was both interesting and empowering to hear from teachers who wanted to talk about race but didn't have the tools to do it, but they knew it was important.

We chose *Some of My Best Friends Are Black: The Strange Story of Integration in America* because a quarter of it examines our city. Kansas City is featured in the text and so the redlining, blockbusting, and the racial covenant conversations in the text basically tell the story of our city. Choosing the text was an easy thing to do because it revealed the collective truth about our community. We never envisioned that it would go anywhere beyond that. We just wanted to say, "Here's this information, public; please read this book," and there was such a powerful response from educators that we realized we needed to continue to talk about this. We know that the library must continue to play a role. In other words, we gave educators this powerful information, and they expected us to commit to do something about it.

With their overwhelming reaction, we found that teachers wanted to talk about race in the classroom but didn't have the time or the tools to figure out how to do it collectively or even at all. As a public library, we recognized the opportunity to be a liaison and a connector. I had contacts

(Continued)

(Continued)

at the Kansas City Kansas School, and I had contacts at Shawnee Mission, which is a Johnston County School, and I worked to partner these teachers. That's how it all started.

We identified two teachers, one on the Kansas City, Kansas, side and one in Johnston County, who wanted to bring their students together. One of those teachers was Samantha Feinburg, who offers her perspective on this program in the implementation spotlight that follows this one. With these educators, we created a bus tour that took students around our city, looked at pertinent landmarks as they related to integration and segregation, and brought them together on a college campus where they had discussions about what they saw. It started that simply.

From there it's become a three-cohort, twelve-school initiative that brings high school students together around identity, representation, museums, and implicit bias. Now, we end our school year with a symposium that brings all students involved in the program together to attend workshops and interact with our author, Tanner Colby, and other nationally recognized authors like Ta-Nehisi Coates.

Libraries are all about access. We put the right book in someone's hands. That's what we've done with this program. And then we connected the right educators who work together to create and support these opportunities for their students.

The library continues to support the educators called to this work by partnership with other community organizations such as the Nelson Atkins Museum, which has educators on staff that create workshops for us. We have also partnered with the University of Missouri Kansas City and Rutgers University. We work with college students who have been trained on implicit bias to come in and facilitate dialogue with our students. My role is to continue to push collaboration as we all work collectively.

Through our continued work on this project, we are unearthing the fact that our county was not inclusive in nature and there is work that needs to be done. The Tanner Colby text revealed a truth: *You cannot deny history.* We needed this text to push this work forward. I'm proud that we have been able to use the history of our city to step into a powerful and much-needed conversation.

As educators, please tell others who are interested in this project to reach out to us. We want this work to be implemented elsewhere; we want to share what we have learned, what has gone well, and what has been challenging. If you use history to start the conversation, you have the ability to shed all the noise that comes with debate around whether or not race matters. It does. It matters because our history clearly shows us that it does. If we want to have a more socially just society, we have to confront these truths about ourselves.

Samantha Feinberg, an English teacher deeply involved with the Race Project, shares the impact of the project on her practice. Now that you know more about the project, the following is a peek into the power of creating such an opportunity in your own community.

IMPLEMENTATION SPOTLIGHT

BY SAMANTHA FEINBERG

"We all have numerous resources in our community that can support our work to create more equitable systems. The communities in which we live are rich with opportunity. There are relationships and connections waiting out there to exist and we have to find them."

I always had some deeply entrenched beliefs about what it meant to be an anti-racist educator. That work, however, was strengthened and deepened as a result of the collaboration and the work in the Race Project. Every member of our team viewed him-or herself as an activist, but connecting and forming relationships with them, reading, and planning—that to me has not only been really fulfilling and enjoyable but also stoked the fires that already existed. Growing and learning from one another has been a powerful piece of this journey. We all have to find someone to join the fight with. It's really powerful.

There are so many teachers who are already doing this work because they are professionals who are responding to what the kids in their schools need. I have come in contact with a lot of educators who are in the classroom, mostly white educators, who find themselves with a group of students who are beautifully diverse, and they think to themselves, "Gosh, I've got to up my game," and these educators learn how to do this anti-racist work as a professional and then bring it in their classroom. I am so impressed by all the colleagues who are working so hard. One universal truth of teachers is that we all want to do right by our students. When we are lucky enough to have the time and space to connect with each other, think about these things, and make changes to our classroom practice and teaching practices, it is so important. The Race Project has given me a place to do that.

For me, the Race Project has been fulfilling because I have watched students claim their power. After students are immersed in the Race Project, they seize opportunities to speak out and to be heard. No one has to give them the opportunity—the kids are taking the opportunity. We talk a lot about access, self-identification, history, belonging, and non-belonging. Some of our kids, even those who have been described as quiet—after they come back, they don't wait to be granted the opportunity to speak but they grasp it. They begin to identify monocultural perspectives, and they recognize that they have an opportunity to offer a diverse perspective.

A couple of years ago, I was in a workshop that changed my perspective about my role in the classroom. I have always talked about empowering students. Someone checked me and said, "Don't you think that's a little paternalistic?" After a conversation, I recognized that, it's not my place to grant students power. It's my job to help them tap into power they already have, help them seize power for themselves, and aid them in facilitating their path. I can provide them with meaningful opportunities for learning and growth, and that allows them to claim their own empowerment.

We, as educators, need to help all students see that they don't need to look toward someone in a position of power for their empowerment. If power grants power, we will never alter the status quo. We will maintain a hierarchy if a teacher is the only one who can give permission for students to speak their truth. Instead, we have to work with other anti-racist educators to teach students how to recognize and take advantage of the opportunities that are theirs.

CULTURALLY RESPONSIVE CURRICULUM DESIGN

As you have learned in the previous implementation spotlights, it's critical to embrace students who are culturally and linguistically diverse as they work toward rigorous goals and standards in our classrooms. Universal Design for Learning (UDL) reminds us to provide options and choices to support students in their language development and to welcome them into the school community. Culturally responsive teaching, however, goes beyond the pedagogy we use in the classroom. It also impacts the curriculum we design for students who we serve. All students should see themselves reflected in the methods, materials, and assessments we use to challenge and support them. It's critical to consistently reflect on our instructor materials to ensure we are optimizing choice and voice in ways that do not only reflect dominant culture. We partnered with one of our colleagues to provide an implementation spotlight to help you to support this work.

Meet Lissette (Castillo) Agyeman, an educator who is committed to culturally responsive education. Agyeman emigrated to the United States at the age of 12 from Santo Domingo, Dominican Republic with limited English language skills. Six years later, she graduated from Boston English High School and is a first-generation college graduate. She has over 14 years of experience working with youth of color, building community, and developing curricula while teaching the Spanish for Native Speakers program. Agyeman shares the following: "I believe all students should have access to culturally responsive education to learn about their ancestors and histories with dignity and respect. For them to see themselves reflected in the curriculum (in ink)." For this text, she contributes a beautiful description of the purpose of culturally responsive teaching.

IMPLEMENTATION SPOTLIGHT

BY LISSETTE CASTILLO AGYEMAN

During my first teaching year, my principal, Peggy Kemp, asked me if I could lead the Spanish for Native Speakers program. After reviewing the limited curriculum previously used, I noticed that the classes were originally and exclusively designed to focus on language acquisition and grammar. The resources and literature were Eurocentric in the sense of only displaying Spanish/Hispanic colonial themes without considering the competing discourses of identity and race in Latin America and the many intricacies inherent in the demographics of students in the classroom.

My professional practice, focusing on mindfulness and intentionality, clearly demanded a change in the program's pedagogy. I believed that culturally responsive, decolonizing strategies would improve the aspirations of my students, their sense of self as well as their civic engagement in the school community and beyond. Indeed, they gained ownership of their learning, saw themselves reflected in the histories (for healing and empowerment), and became both analytical and appreciative of their ancestries, culture, language/accents, their families' migration stories, and of the social justice struggles they shared with other oppressed groups. It became clear to me that there was a connection between a more culturally responsive curriculum that is deeply intertwined with students' identities, socio-emotional needs, families, ancestry, and learning outcomes.

Culturally responsive pedagogy has evolved over the years from culturally based education and has also been referred to as culturally responsible, culture compatible, culturally appropriate, culturally congruent, culturally relevant, and multicultural education (Irvine & Armento, 2001; Gay, 2010). This approach to teaching addresses the immediate needs of students learning by providing them with an inclusive learning space validating their presence and realities in the classroom and in society.

Over the years, I developed a curriculum for the students in the Spanish for Native Speakers Program, honoring them as heritage language speakers while tracing the foundations of my and their ancestry through Mesoamerican cultures prior to European colonization. This challenged students to understand theoretical and practical forms of influence in culture, identity, language, and the production of racial and ethnic classifications, the establishment and purpose of castas after colonialism and the Atlantic Slave Trade, while deeply reflecting on the current impact of their identity development now and in their understanding of their world today.

In 2016, while consulting at Sociedad Latina, I expanded the Spanish for Native Speakers curriculum to highlight additional dimensions of students' struggles as first-generation college attendees and the oppressive higher education obstacle of affordability that disproportionately affects communities of color. Through the *¿Quién Soy Yo?* (*Who Am I?*), students continue to develop a strong sense of self and identity while also addressing college and career readiness, affordability, and the many challenges ahead (literacy readiness, cultural shifts, adaptability, discrimination, and isolation) on campuses across the nation.

The social impact of the disproportionate racial and ethnic makeup of teachers and administrators, together with Eurocentric curriculum content, plays a crucial role in creating an unhealthy learning environment for students of color and the communities from which they come. Considering the contested politics of education and the miseducation of students of color (as reflected in the "Opportunity Gap," as distinct from the "Achievement Gap"), it is time to eradicate consistent and oppressive structures in education.

To develop a comprehensive model of teaching with dignity, culturally appropriate and responsive education demands a focus on both recognition, reconciliation, and inclusion.

(Continued)

(Continued)

Creating a learning environment where students and teachers feel connected demands a coproduced curriculum, which I pioneered through my Spanish for Native Speakers program. A culturally responsive, coproduced curriculum creates an understanding that students are both a) learning something that is relevant to their lives, struggles, and community, and b) feeding back their thoughts and experiences into the curriculum. This teaching style demands that educators see students' perspectives and experiences as a central pillar of the overall learning experience. There is growing evidence that intentional engagement in diverse classrooms demands a holistic approach.

As Paulo Freire (1972) states, "The teacher is of course an artist, but being an artist does not mean that he or she can make the profile, can shape the students. What the educator does in teaching is to make it possible for the students to become themselves."

Reflection Questions

- What is culturally responsive teaching, and how does it relate to Universal Design for Learning (UDL)?
- What is the significance of incorporating culturally responsive practices?
- What culturally responsive practices are currently being utilized in/at your school community?

HOW TO NAVIGATE HOLIDAYS IN AN EQUITABLE WAY

The way we approach holidays during the school year can be either a barrier or an opening to honoring our students' identities. To create a learning environment that is culturally responsive, it's critical for educators to universally design the celebration of holidays. Despite increasing focus on multicultural and inclusive educational practices across the country, it is often easy to gauge the time of year by scanning the artwork and symbols on school bulletin boards, newsletters, and worksheets. Across diverse geographic regions, there are persistent depictions of apples and pumpkins for Halloween, predictably followed by turkeys for Thanksgiving, snow and winter-related representations during winter holidays, Dr. Martin Luther King, hearts for Valentine's Day, shamrocks for St. Patrick's Day, and other calendar-related images.

We are sure many educators have fond memories of holiday celebrations in school and anticipate the same for our learners. The reality is that the world is changing, and in public schools, we cannot celebrate holidays the same way we did when we were young.

Despite good intentions to infuse the learning environment with morale rooted in holiday-related themes, the sometimes uncritical ways in which traditional practices are carried out may lead to students feeling left out or marginalized. How might Columbus Day and Thanksgiving be experienced by First Nation students? Is it possible that a celebration of the survival of pilgrims could be perceived as a celebration of the massacre of indigenous people? Our educational focus on colonialism has the potential to alienate students when we don't include and honor the other parts of the history in our lessons. While most schools have become more mindful of celebrating religious holidays such as Christmas, Easter, or Hanukkah, we must also consider how celebrating seemingly innocuous holidays such as Halloween as usual could also leave students out for a variety of reasons.

For students from some religious groups, for example, Halloween-related costumes and exchanges of tricks and treats may violate religious teachings given the pagan origin of the celebration. For children with food allergies or other dietary restrictions (e.g., diabetes or obesity), the predominantly sugary nature of the treats may limit some children's partaking. For students and families with socioeconomic constraints, public observations of Halloween in school contexts create pressure to purchase nonessential food or candy products and costumes. Finally, for young children and children who may have been exposed to trauma, "fun" Halloween depictions of graveyards, haunting ghosts and ghouls, and scenes characterized by blood and gore may trigger a traumatic experience. While these experiences may exist in neighborhood and community spaces without our control, we must be mindful of these potential barriers as we decorate our classrooms, plan celebrations, or discuss holidays to ensure that the content is meaningful, culturally relevant, and accessible for all students.

We discussed implicit bias previously, but it deserves another look as we discuss the celebration of holidays. Let's unpack

Invisibility is when certain groups are underrepresented. For children and families from other groups—be they Jewish, Buddhist, Muslim, atheist, or anything else—Christmas can be a difficult time. According to Teaching Tolerance (2013), "The intensity of the Christmas curriculum in public schools isolates children of minority faiths, while contributing to the development of ethnocentrism in majority children."

Selectivity – Classroom celebrations often perpetuate bias by presenting only one holiday that aligns to the dominant group. This imbalanced account restricts the knowledge of students regarding the varied perspectives that may apply to a variety of holidays.

Unreality – Lessons sometimes present an unrealistic portrayal of our contemporary life experience. For example, many Christmas celebrations focus on the commercial aspects of Christmas and ask students, "What do you want for Christmas?" Currently more than one out of five American children live in poverty. Discussions about Santa and gifts may set up kids for an inevitable feeling of loss and disappointment when expectations are not met.

three forms of implicit bias and highlight why the celebration of Christmas in classrooms, for example, could be problematic. We will also offer strategies for more inclusive, yet equally engaging opportunities for students to learn more about the world around them, build empathy, and feel as though their identity is embraced as well.

As with any design challenge, our task is to ensure that learning experiences meet the needs of all students. Before you have a class celebration, or read or discuss a holiday tradition or upcoming holiday, like Christmas, and embrace identity and diversity. All solid curriculum design begins with a standard and an essential question and then moves on to provide all students with options and choices to learn more about themselves and others.

For example, imagine you are working on a speaking and listening or writing unit. First, select your standard and then increase engagement by drafting an essential question. For example, instead of asking students "How do you celebrate Christmas?" or "What do you want for Christmas?" consider beginning with "What traditions are important to you?" This allows all students to make meaning in culturally sustaining ways and also taps into students' funds of knowledge.

Additionally, the following questions are great ways to encourage students to think beyond their own experience, which often results in implicit bias. If your focus is speaking and listening, you could use discussion protocols for the questions, or you could encourage students to research the answers to questions and write responses, create commercials, multimedia sites or brochures.

- What holidays/traditions do we have throughout the year?

- How have traditions in your family changed over time?

- How do the traditions represented in our classroom vary from one family to the next?

- How can we learn more about different holidays/traditions and beliefs that are not present in our classroom?

- How can all of our ideas and beliefs coexist in the same classroom, community, and world?

- What questions do you have about holidays/traditions or systems of belief that we have not discussed here?

If you universally design units or celebrate learning about multiple perspectives, holidays, and traditions, you and your students will see beauty in diversity and experiences. This is just one example that shows how this approach honors students and their families and people from non-dominant cultures. Although this may result in some students talking about Christmas, it leaves the door open to explore both windows and mirrors. All people in this world have value, and it is our task to help students learn that through our curriculum and instruction and not focus only on their own experience and the experiences of the dominant group.

Mona M. Abo-Zena and Christina Brown also provide strategies for using the design process and UDL to navigate more equitable lessons around the holidays. Abo-Zena is an assistant professor at the University of Massachusetts Boston with a focus on identity, diversity, and equity in teacher education. Brown is an educational consultant with a focus on teacher development. Both Mona and Christina consult together on diversity-and equity-related work partnering with administrators, teachers and staff, caregivers, and students in schools and school districts. While they acknowledge that teaching and learning involve risk-taking and feeling vulnerable, they maintain that failing to include even one student (or one dimension of a student's identity) presents a risk and a lost opportunity for the entire learning community.

IMPLEMENTATION SPOTLIGHT

BY MONA M. ABO-ZENA AND CHRISTINA BROWN

Our school calendar is designed around holidays, and oftentimes, educators infuse these holidays into curriculum design. Before doing this, consider the steps below, as they relate to the UDL design process.

Step 1: What are my instructional or developmental goals in navigating the holiday or event?

As you learned in Chapter 4, UDL is all about "firm goals, flexible means" and embraces co-construction with students. In order to develop classroom practices that move beyond the reproductive nature of educational traditions and realize the transformative potential of diverse and inclusive learning communities (Freire, 1972), educators need to have explicit instructional or student developmental goals to provide a compelling reason for how they dedicate instructional time.

For example, some families may deliver cupcakes, cookies, pizza, or other treats in honor of their child's birthday. Certain families may even prefer their child celebrate with friends at school instead of a celebration at home or a community location in order to include all members of a class (i.e., so some students do not feel left out if they are not invited or cannot attend the birthday party). While there may be good intentions behind this choice, for religious, dietary and other reasons, some children still may not be able to participate fully in a birthday celebration

(Continued)

(Continued)

at school. Exiled to the library or media room perhaps with a "fun" find-a-word or other puzzle, some students may be separated from the party and their peers. Others may feel pressured to host a similar school-based party, even though their family may not have the means to provide treats or goody bags.

To the teachers, what are the instructional goals of allocating scarce instructional minutes to such a celebration? What are the alternatives? One teacher posed the scenario to their students as a problem to be solved. Students brainstormed solutions and eventually decided that if one student would feel left out of a school-based activity because of their beliefs, social position, or identity, then the class should not host this particular celebration.

Through this exercise, students experienced an authentic opportunity to develop socially and emotionally and build empathy with classmates. As a class, they suggested different ways they might build morale and celebrate learning and engagement that would include all learners and be sensitive to their social positions (e.g., hosting dress-up days related to characters in history or books where students were encouraged to make or trade their own costumes; hosting class parties that celebrated class-based accomplishments, like a publishing party with discussions on how to provide refreshments in an economically sensitive and inclusive manner). Through class exploration and discourse, students engage in critical thinking and problem solving and contribute to engaging with instructional content, as opposed to perpetuating unreflective traditions in public educational contexts. In addition, students learn to identify their own blind spots related to social justice and inclusion and engage in collective practice to reduce the biases in their own classroom context.

Step 2: What are the strategies I will use to help actualize my instructional and developmental goals?

As an individual educator within a learning community, how will I develop strategies to allow students to meet instructional goals? On a basic level, it is important for individual teachers to develop the strategy of praxis, or reflective practice, that includes identifying their own values, assumptions, and biases. Reflective practice necessarily includes engaging in self-work to consider how to establish socially just practice, particularly as it relates to a range of holiday related issues. How does one's personal identity and social position inform this work? If "elf on the shelf" decorations are customary in home contexts, is there a justification for them to be displayed in nondenominational school contexts? On a collective level to ensure that our current practices are in the best interest of all students, antibias work requires engaging in observation, reflections, documentation, and questioning with a community of colleagues and other stakeholders (Kuh, LeeKeenan, Given, & Beneke, 2016).

Sometimes, this process may create a sense of personal disequilibrium, particularly after an individual engages uncomfortably with their own privilege, bias, and the denial of it. For example, a teacher may reflect on their own whiteness, privilege, and biased racial assumptions after viewing a student's photograph from home depicting a black Santa Claus or Jesus. This process may also result in a communal disequilibrium as in the case of staff members who were divided over extensive, heated discussions about whether they would continue the daily tradition of pledging allegiance to the flag of the United States of America given a range of religious and political reasons articulated by an assorted group of students and families that had requested to be exempt from the practice.

Such reflective practice may help illuminate how the Pledge of Allegiance, like many other well-intentioned and common school-based practices, may veil a host of issues that jeopardize socially just practice. The way schools navigate issues related to holidays may marginalize youth, particularly religious minorities, who may feel pressured to keep their own faith traditions invisible in order to blend in with others or who may face marginalization for their sometimes conspicuous religious-based differences through religious dress, diet, and practice (Abo-Zena, 2011).

Schools navigate these issues in a range of ways, including holding nondenominational and inclusive holiday or seasonal parties as well as including a range of holidays on the school calendar. While these inclusive practices may be well-intentioned, their impact and execution may still have undesirable consequences.

Step 3: How I will I assess the effectiveness of my approach?

In the design process, it is always critical to analyze and reflect. Educators may evaluate the effectiveness of their approaches on two levels: the degree to which the intervention achieved the intended goal, as well as the degree to which its implementation avoided unintended outcomes. In considering unintended outcomes, educators should begin by considering who and what may be left out or disproportionately represented. For example, in the zeal to be inclusive of different faith traditions, we often may overlook nonreligious individuals and families or interfaith families. In addition, we may risk creating a generic way in which we represent faith traditions or groups, glossing over the rich variations in which individuals, families, and communities believe and practice. Finally, religious identities intersect with other dimensions of identities and lived experiences as illustrated through celebrations like Kwanzaa, Three Kings' Day, and New Year's marked by different calendars with varied starting points and reasons for the yearly cycle. Because not all practices in faith traditions have analogs and there is a high chance to miss important markers, it is of vital importance for educators to actively solicit information from families and not expect young students or their families to insert their identities or self-advocate.

While children and adults may share their anticipation of a "day off" from school or work, it is also important to highlight the deep personal, social, and structural meaning and history behind holidays such as Labor Day, Veteran's Day, and Memorial Day and acknowledge that what they represent may be experienced differently. Even days like Dr. Martin Luther King Jr. Day that focus on racial justice may miss attention to complex societal factors (i.e., some may interpret a focus on the content of character as a "raceless" or "colorblind" approach whereas Dr. King's teachings focused critically on the intersections between race, socioeconomic status, and sociohistorical circumstances). In reviewing the way in which educators navigate holidays, it is important that they survey and partner with families and other colleagues to ensure that the holidays represented both mirror the identities of families in the community as well as provide windows to better understand the identities and experiences of individuals who may not be in the classroom (Sims Bishop, 1990; Style, 1988).

Concluding Thoughts

How holidays are taken up in schools and other places of living, learning, and working is a central issue related to social justice in that they provide institutional celebrations of who and what

(Continued)

matters. In such acknowledgments and focus, there is often a centering of attention on more privileged or dominant identities or positions, which consequently limits the regard for other individuals and groups and their experiences. In other cases, the uncritical observation of a holiday empties it of the original or intended meaning of the holiday, which marginalizes individuals or groups that hold the holiday in high esteem.

To promote social justice in our navigation of holidays, events, and people, educators must clarify their own intentions in their approach to promote instructional and developmental goals, develop strategies individually and collectively to meet the goals, and assess the intended and unintended consequences of their interventions. If one student is left out of a school-based practice because of an aspect of their identity, then school may not feel safe for that student and for any other individual who perceives the unjust exclusion. When educators aspire to and develop explicit ideas about holidays in working with colleagues, families, students, and other stakeholders in all steps of this process, educators will have promoted social justice, inclusion, empathy, perspective, critical thinking, and problem solving in their learning communities.

Next Steps

- Think about your current teaching practices, lessons, and celebrations. Reevaluate how you may change those practices, lessons, and celebrations to be more universally designed, culturally relevant, and accessible for all students.

- Expand your view of holidays and celebration by researching how other groups and cultures celebrate. Ask your students about their traditions at home and what those traditions mean to them.

- Think about how social justice and culturally responsive teaching are related. Examine policies and practices in your school that may be perceived as exclusive or inauthentic, and discuss with your colleagues and stakeholders.

Reflection Questions

- How does your school currently handle holidays?

- How can the guidance in this chapter help you to make teaching and learning more culturally responsive during times where holidays may be marked on the calendar?

Additional Resources

- Although antibias educational practices have roots in early childhood education, the beliefs and practices can be adapted to working with children and families across grade levels. http://www.teachingforchange.org/teacher-resources/anti-bias-education

- Lee, E., Menkart, D., & Okazawa-Rey, M. (1997/2006). *Beyond heroes and holidays: A practical guide to K-12 anti-racist, multicultural education and staff development.* Network of Educators on the Americas, P.O. Box 73038, Washington, DC 20056-3038.

- The Pluralism Project, Harvard University, http://pluralism.org/selected-links/education/. This website provides religion-specific resources inclusive of a range of world traditions and nonreligious groups, as well as links to educational resources on how to navigate religious-based issues in school contexts.

If we endeavor to provide equal opportunities to learn, we have to examine our practices, pedagogies, procedures, and policies and how they may be biased toward dominant culture. Reflecting on our practice through this lens is not comfortable, but it's not supposed to be. Deep engagement requires us to sustain effort and persistence and self-regulate through feelings of discomfort when we experience cognitive dissonance. That feeling is a sign that our mindset is shifting, and it is a calling to continue our journey. Colleagues may assert that it's "just a holiday," but for the students we serve, our willingness to address bias shows that we believe that the system should be designed differently and that we are willing to fight for it.

CHAPTER SEVEN

RESTORATIVE JUSTICE AND RESTORATIVE PRACTICES

"What if being called racist is the beginning, not the end, of the conversation?"

—Elizabeth Denevi

SETTING THE STAGE

Oftentimes, students face behavioral barriers that prevent them from accessing and engaging academically. In a universally designed system, educators eliminate these barriers by creating learning environments that foster self-regulation and minimize threats and distractions. In schools today, this work can be fostered with a focus on restorative practices.

We have discussed the importance of implementing Universal Design for Learning (UDL) as a framework for equity so all students have access to high expectations and a challenging, authentic, culturally responsive curriculum that supports their growth, challenges them personally, and provides them with opportunities to see themselves in the work. When academic work is designed with students as co-partners, we are able to eliminate barriers that prevent access and engagement, but what happens when students react in unexpected ways or need more social, emotional, or behavioral support?

UDL can also be leveraged to meet the social, emotional, and behavioral needs of students by designing experiences grounded in restorative justice.

Like cogen groups, restorative practices are opportunities for students to have their voices heard, to eliminate barriers, and to enrich learning experiences. In the case of restorative practice, the outcomes are focused not on academics but on self-regulation, problem solving, community, collaboration, and empathy.

Restorative Justice is an alternative approach to school discipline that seeks to address misbehavior by bringing together those who were most closely affected by the incident and working toward an agreement about how to repair the harm (Mayworm et al., 2016).

In this chapter, we will discuss how to proactively consider the behavioral and social emotional needs of students through restorative practices. The Center for Restorative Justice at Suffolk University refers to restorative practices, including circles and restorative conferences, as combined ancient wisdom and cutting-edge research to improve school climate and educational outcomes. Teachers can implement restorative practices in their classrooms by first laying the important groundwork of having high expectations and caring for students and then building on those practices with tiered supports.

First and foremost, in a universally designed classroom that meets the needs of all learners, educators make a real and just philosophical or theoretical commitment to believing that all learners both can and will succeed in the classroom. Educators should also consistently communicate high expectations in their classrooms by being "warm demanders."

Kleinfeld (1975) coined the term "warm demander" when studying effective teachers of Indian and Eskimo students in Alaskan schools. Kleinfeld found that although a personal rapport with students was necessary to elicit a high level of performance, it was not a sufficient condition. The major characteristic that differentiated effective from ineffective teachers was their insistence on a high level of academic work.

Students, especially those who are at risk, respond to these teachers because they understand that beneath the strictness and high expectations, the teachers believe they will succeed. These warm demanders teach a rigorous curriculum and expect students to rise to the challenge and this increases student achievement, which in turn increases student self-esteem, but they do it with a gentle touch and care.

Creating an environment that fosters academic, behavioral, and social emotional learning starts with believing that all students can learn and have the ability to self-regulate, collaborate, and be a part of the classroom community. It also requires creating an equitable classroom management plan where students are clear about classroom norms and consistently are held to high expectations to meet them. In Chapter 2, we shared the importance of participating in an Equity Audit. One of the audits asked teachers to reflect on their behaviors toward students. Take a moment to ask yourself these questions about your students before we discuss expected and unexpected behaviors and how to address them (Mid-Atlantic Equity Consortium, 2020).

- Do you model cooperative and collaborative behavior by encouraging students' participation in classroom management decisions?

- Do you demonstrate flexibility and fairness in situations that evoke conflict and potential classroom disruption?

- Do you rotate classroom management responsibilities to give all students an opportunity to be leaders and problem solvers?

- Do you reward and praise students' work equitably and consistently?

We must commit ourselves to thinking that requires us to consider our goal, and how we can partner with stakeholders to design learning that allows all students to meet those goals. Consider these additional questions.

- When we create our classroom management expectations, do we really believe that all students will meet them?

- Do we treat all students the same when they experience conflict, and do we empower all students to be leaders?

- Whether intentionally or not, do we expect some of our students to be disruptive? Do we plan for them to be disengaged and struggle? Do we assume that their background and/or current situation and circumstances will determine who they are, how they will behave, or how they will achieve?

These are difficult questions we need to ask ourselves as we work alongside our students to embrace the restorative justice process. We need to embrace the fact that our perceptions of students directly influence our expectations of them, and our expectations of them are directly correlated to how they perform as well as how they behave. The Pygmalion effect teaches us that the way we act toward others influences their behaviors, which in turn further influences our attitudes and behaviors toward them. For example, if we believe that students do not possess the capacity and/or potential to self-regulate, collaborate, and be a part of the classroom community, we give ourselves permission to make decisions about the design of our learning environments which reinforce these beliefs, therefore becoming a form of self-fulfilling prophecy as students then act in manners that are consistent with those beliefs.

Again, the only way to disrupt this vicious cycle is to commit ourselves to thinking in manners that require us to consider our goal and how we can partner with stakeholders to design learning that allows all students to meet those goals.

RESTORATIVE PRACTICE TO UPHOLD HIGH EXPECTATIONS

In order for you to get a better idea of what restorative practices may look like in action, we'd like to introduce you to our colleagues and their work in a series of three implementation spotlights. Each spotlight will highlight different aspects of restorative justice. First, Talisa Sullivan helps to define restorative practices as a process. The second spotlight, penned by Adina Davidson and Annie Levitt, focuses on restorative circle and how to implement it in a classroom. It provides insight into what to expect when implementing restorative practices as an educator. Finally, Dr. Sarah Coupet shares some wisdom for schools interested in incorporating restorative practices within the school community.

RESTORATIVE PRACTICE CONTINUUM

Like Universal Design for Learning (UDL), restorative practice isn't "one-size-fits-all." There is a continuum of intensity that discusses practices that help to meet students where they are. One educator who utilizes restorative practices, in the form of restorative circles, is Dr. Talisa Sullivan. Dr. Talisa Sullivan has been an educator for more than 17 years serving students, teachers, staff, parents, and the community in the California counties of Los Angeles, Riverside, San Bernardino, and Orange.

She specializes in alternative education, restorative justice, and leadership capacity and has built a rapport as an instructional leader at comprehensive, alternative, community, and correctional schools and programs throughout the Greater Los Angeles Area. As the director of access and equity at the Riverside Department of Education in California, Sullivan leads restorative work to eliminate barriers that prevent all students from engaging in deep learning.

When we chatted with Dr. Sullivan, she shared that during her first years of teaching, she volunteered with extracurricular clubs and teams. She recalls leading her student government, cheerleaders, and dancers in what she called, "feeling circles." When there was a problem or "girl/guy drama," the team would sit in a circle and each member of the team would take the opportunity to express how they felt about the situation. Dr. Sullivan has since conducted research on restorative justice and conducts training in restorative practices. She now recognizes that the feeling circles she conducted earlier in her teaching career were actually restorative circles. Circles are just one example of restorative practices that create opportunities for restorative justice to promote social justice.

IMPLEMENTATION SPOTLIGHT

BY TALISA SULLIVAN

The Restorative Practices Continuum can be used by teachers in the classroom on a daily basis. The continuum represents five types of restorative practices ranging from informal on the left and more formal on the right. Although these are not performed in particular steps, educators can use the practices on the continuum based on the level of infraction. Upon interacting with students who have broken a class/school rule or who have been involved in an altercation, educators can start by taking an informal approach using the techniques on the left of the continuum. For infractions involving the breaking of the education code and causing harm where consequences beyond restoration are involved, educators may use techniques from both ends of the continuum, starting with the affective statements and questions and eventually ending in a conference. The type of conference may be determined by the seriousness of the offence. Below, we will examine each of the responsive practices in more detail.

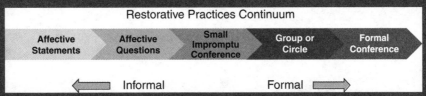

Source: Created by Talisa Sullivan using information from International Institute for Restorative Practices. www.iirp.edu

Affective Statements

Educators should begin with affective statements because it is the most informal practice on the continuum. Educators use affective statements to express how the offender's behavior made him/her or others feel. Affective statements should be expressive but should not add shame, judgment, or blame. Affective statements:

- Express feelings
  - pleasant and unpleasant (delivered privately)

- Acknowledge (specifically)
  - desirable behaviors
  - success
  - hard work

- Separate the deed from the doer

- Build relationships

Example: Instead of "Don't interrupt when I am speaking!" an affective statement would be "It's not polite to interrupt. It makes me feel like you are not listening."

Affective Questions

Next on the continuum is affective questions. Affective questions guide students in reflecting on their behavior and prompts answers that assist in reflections. Teachers can also use affective

(Continued)

statements or ask individuals who were affected by the wrongdoing. The purpose of affective questions is to do the following:

- Humanize individuals seen by students as an authority figure
- Allow students to reflect on their behavior
- Elicit what students think or feel about their behavior or the behavior of others
- Question those who have been affected by inappropriate behavior
- Question those who have committed wrongdoing to others

Below are examples of affective questions.

When challenging behavior, ask these questions (Costello, Wachtel, & Wachtel, 2009):

- What happened?
- What were you thinking of at the time?
- What have you thought about since?
- Who has been affected by what you have done? In what way have they been affected?
- What do you think you need to do to make things right?

To Help Those Affected

- What did you think when you realized what had happened?
- What impact has this incident had on you and others?
- What has been the hardest thing for you?
- What do you think needs to happen to make things right?

Small Impromptu Conference

Following affective questions on the continuum is a small impromptu conference. Educators can hold small impromptu conferences when students find themselves in verbal altercations or when students have a disagreement that may lead to a verbal altercation. Teachers can intervene with small impromptu conferences so the situation does not escalate and prior to involving the administration. The purpose of the small impromptu conference is to do the following:

- Ask affective questions when wrongdoing has taken place
- Address a problem and resolve it before it escalates
- Resolve conflict when multiple people are affected
- Actively engage all parties in expressing their feelings

Groups or Circles

Circles are the second to last practice on the continuum. Circles can be used to discuss wrongdoing or can be used to be proactive. Teachers can start the week or day with a circle to check in as well as end the day in a circle to have students check out. Circles have the following characteristics:

- A symbol of community
- Seating arranged in a circle
- Students take turns responding to prompts by the facilitator
- A talking piece is used so one person speaks at a time
- Can be used as a community response to wrongdoing
- Proactive processes for building social capital
- Means for check-ins/checkouts
- Classroom content can serve as a topic

Formal Conference

The final practice on the continuum is the formal conference. The formal conference can be conducted by any educator; however, it is during this conference that a formal response to wrongdoing takes place. It's likely that consequences beyond restoration will be issued during this conference. Below is information on restorative practices. Below are characteristics of formal conferences.

Two Types

1. Restorative Conferencing
   - All parties participate in the conference
   - Trained facilitator leads the conference to analyze the wrongdoing, who has been affected, and what needs to take place to right the wrong
   - Formal response to wrongdoing
   - Can include family and friends
   - Facilitator uses a script

2. Family Group Conferencing
   - Problem outlined by school or community
   - Family alone time—family and individual create a plan
   - Family explains the plan to the educational team

RESTORATIVE PRACTICE IN ACTION

Implementation of new strategies in schools is always complicated, and implementing restorative practices, which aim to shift the entire framework of how we see each other, is no exception. In a previous implementation spotlight, Talisa Sullivan shares restorative justice as a process. Next, let's examine a case study where one school started its journey into restorative practice by implementing circle practice.

In the 2014–2015 school year, the McCormack Middle School began "Year One" of its shift to using restorative practices. "The McCormack," one of the only large middle schools left in Boston, had many assets as a community and an incredible staff; yet few people who work there would disagree with the statement that it often felt like a hard place to be human. One of the middle schools with open enrollment in the district, the McCormack had about 600 students, many transferring in from other schools, with significant exposure to trauma, community violence, and ongoing loss and instability in their lives. There was a small group of staff members interested in implementing restorative practices who had been trained by Suffolk University Center for Restorative Practices in 2012, and the school started a whole school training process with the International Institute for Restorative Practices (IIRP) in 2014.

With a schoolwide commitment to trying to change practice, it was still up to school staff to make the leap into using restorative practices in their day-to-day work, with some use of restorative practices also happening in staff development time. The examples profiled here are some of the many examples from that first year led by Adina Davidson and Annie Leavitt, two of the many staff that led the effort, applying the philosophy and practices to the difficult situations that make up everyday life in a middle school.

Davidson, a lifelong social worker with experience in leading circles at the Curley Middle School, was in her second year as clinical coordinator at the McCormick when she began to facilitate restorative circles there. She shares her thoughts:

> *No matter how you slice and dice it, using Restorative Practices in real life, in the context of a living breathing school, is not going to be as simple as it appears in training. It requires a ton of adaptation, a willingness to leave many things unresolved, and the faith that trying things a different way is worth it, even if it's messy.*

Davidson and Leavitt wrote up many of their circles from that first year in an attempt to create an encouraging manual for others who were in the first year of trying to shift the paradigm. "It may be about a philosophy, but anyone who works in schools knows that it's entirely in the details; how much time did it take? What did you say to get the people in the room? What did you ask them to bring it to a vulnerable point? What works when you have only 10 minutes before the bell rings?"

The spotlight that follows is not presented as an example of completely unique work, as their work was influenced and supported by the IIRP, others in Boston working on Restorative Justice, and resources such as Carolyn Boyes Watson and Kay Pranis's epic manual *Circle Forward*. Rather, as Davidson puts it, "it's hopefully an inspiration for others who want to dive in, and move in the direction of becoming a restorative culture."

IMPLEMENTATION SPOTLIGHT

BY ADINA DAVIDSON AND ANNIE LEAVITT

Making It Right Circle: Between a Student and School Staff After a Hurtful Interaction

This circle is a great restorative conversation strategy to use after a few serious conflicts have arisen between students and adults (for example, a student pushes an adult or very hurtful insults are exchanged one or more times). These circles are voluntary, but students are encouraged to participate as a way to resolve conflict. In addition to taking advantage of a student's natural desire to be heard and to resolve and heal relationships, another incentive is the messaging to their parents after the fact—that he/she made a mistake, but handled the situation maturely. To be clear, circles are not intended to be the only consequence for what happened, and students knew there would be other consequences as well. Circles, when combined with other consequences, were by far more effective as a means of strengthening relationships that have a huge effect on a student's experience and learning in school.

Before-the-Circle Work:

As a guidance counselor, before conducting a circle between two or more parties, I would meet with the student to discuss the write-up of what happened and the teacher's description of what happened. During this time, we talked about the student's side of the story and I emphasized the need to make it right and have both parties talk about what happened. This usually wasn't a long meeting—10 or 15 minutes—depending on how much the student needed to voice their story to me. Generally students were receptive to the idea of doing a restorative conversation, as long as they knew they would have a chance to speak uninterrupted—and if they knew that being able to resolve the issue would make the phone call home much better (i.e., "John got into a bad argument but was mature enough to resolve it with the teacher today" versus "John got into a bad argument and refused to mediate it"). Once the student and I had come to an understanding at this pre-circle meeting, I'd tell the school staff involved that the student was ready to have a conversation. I made it clear that this wasn't just going to be an apology but a conversation that requires input from both sides and requires communication of feelings as a person (not just an enforcer of rules, etc.). If they were open (sometimes a cooling down period was necessary for adults too), I would set it up for the next free time the school staff member had in the day.

In situations where students or adults are still feeling ill will toward each other and don't believe that the other person is honestly ready to talk, I'd ask both parties to tell me the "one thing I wish I'd done differently." Then, I would share those sentiments at the start of our circle or have the parties involved start with those sentiments as a sign that there was regret on both sides. Expressing thoughtfulness can go a long way in these contexts to show goodwill and get buy-in into the process.

Guideline:

When conducting a circle, there are some standard Responsive Practices guidelines you can use, but I believe this one is the most essential: The number-one rule is that you must be listening and

(Continued)

(Continued)

not interrupting when the other person is talking. Even if you disagree or think that what they are saying is untrue, you will get your chance to speak after they are finished. And when it's your turn, you will also get to speak, uninterrupted.

Participants: Both parties from the interaction must be present for the circle to take place. If there was another person who was affected or tried to help (administrator, dean, another student, or teacher) during the conflict, it is also helpful to include them, if possible. However, I would avoid having too many people present, at least for the initial conversation between the two primary parties, as the added audience can sometimes make it more difficult for participants to be completely honest or vulnerable.

Set the scene: If it is necessary to get things moving, I would begin a session with having each party share what he or she wishes he/she had done differently during the conflict to show each other that they are willing to talk. Otherwise, we would just start with a more standard first round.

- Round 1: What happened? (Both share their perspective).
- Round 2: What were you thinking about at the time?
- Round 3: What have you thought about since this happened?
- Round 4: Who do you think was affected by this?
- Round 5: What can be done to make it right? (Ask for suggestions, whichever party wants to go first)
- Round 6: What can we do to prevent this from happening in the future?

After the circle, an administrator would hear about the plan made in the circle and decide if it should be combined with a standard consequence. Often it was reduced based on engagement shown in the circle process and commitment to the plan created together.

Lessons from implementation: Preparation is important (with each party individually), but it doesn't have to be extensive. Even when students started sessions believing they didn't think they could talk it through, they usually could—as long as there had been some prep and we had established some goodwill ahead of time. When teachers were involved, it was essential that they expressed their feelings rather than just followed their role as authority figures, and the process could be truly transformative (for both parties) if a teacher came to the table open to being changed by what they heard.

When using a similar protocol between students who needed meditation, we found that the pre-work was similarly important and the interruption rule became even more essential. If students started talking over each other, I'd cut it off and give them one more chance. If they did it again and things were getting unproductively escalated (not explaining emotions or thoughts, shooting each other down), it was best to cut it off.

Thereafter, I'd explore meeting again individually with each party but discontinue the joint session if the process was not being respected.

In conclusion, restorative circles are a great tool to use in restoring balance between students and teachers when the proper preparation and open-mindedness are in place and when the parties involved respect the rules of the process.

Now that you understand the process of restorative justice and have explored how it was implemented in a specific site, examine how you could help your school transition to a school-wide commitment to this work. Dr. Sarah Coupet is an educational consultant from the University of Miami. Coupet's research focuses on teacher development and building teacher capacity. "It is just as pertinent that students should be intentionally taught how to process conflict as they are taught academic skills in schools. I realized that I needed to create intentional spaces for students to process and develop language to express their emotions." Teaching these life skills transforms school culture and provides students alternatives to dealing with conflicts and other life traumas.

Expulsion, suspension, and other zero-tolerance punitive punishments do not improve poor behavior choices, nor have they curbed these problems. These punitive approaches or disciplinary processes cause students to miss instructional time, leading to academic skill gaps while not teaching students how to deal with or resolve conflicts. Furthermore, these outcomes perpetuate the high dropout rates and lead to the school-to-prison pipelines that plague urban public schools across the United States (Tyner, 2017).

Coupet explains, "Although, there is a disproportionate application of punitive measures in urban school districts; restorative practices is also appropriate in rural and suburban schools as they are continuously faced with violent school shootings and other hate crimes."

IMPLEMENTATION SPOTLIGHT

BY DR. SARAH COUPLET

In order for a school culture to shift, restorative practices must be implemented at every level of the school with all staff, including school leaders, teachers, paraprofessionals, lunch monitors, school counselors, bus drivers, and other personnel who come into contact with students. There are several approaches to implementing restorative practices. The following are some important considerations when considering restorative practices in your school.

Intentionally Teaching Expectations

We take for granted that students come to school and behave exactly how we expect them to. Likewise, if we get frustrated because we think our students have not met our expectations, then we have to ask ourselves, have we clearly articulated what those expectations were to them? Were those our authentic expectations of them? In addition, did we teach or model the expected behavior? And have we engaged with them to know what they are experiencing? Processing emotions, frustration, conflict, and other life challenges is a skill that has to be intentionally taught. Much like learning academic language, our students must also be taught social emotional language. Many times, we see students reacting to a personal life challenge or frustration.

(Continued)

(Continued)

As educators, we may interpret certain behavior or actions as being disrespectful, and then we revert to punitive measures. Punitive measures such as kicking the student out of class, sending them to the principal's office, or suspending them have one common outcome: The student misses crucial academic time, and this exacerbates the learning gap in their skills and content knowledge. However, applying restorative practices helps students articulate their frustrations, reflect, and make better decisions and help develop key life skills in the area of coping with and processing emotions.

Develop Awareness and the Language to Articulate Emotions

Many times, misbehaviors are a cry for help. Our students come to school with real-life stresses, anxiety, trauma, and other frustrations, and they do not always have the emotional awareness or language to articulate their frustrations. Their hurt, annoyance, or distress may reveal themselves in the form of disrespect and anger. Restorative practices allow for the opportunity to explore the root cause of the poor behavior and provide students with the tools to process, cope, and make better decisions. It is crucial to remind the students that they are not their behavior choices. They can choose poor behavior or positive behavior. However, they must also learn that their choices have consequences for themselves and others. By providing students with social emotional language and encouraging conversations, students will learn to resolve problems, reflect, and come to conclusions to help ameliorate their circumstances.

The Importance of Taking the Time to Listen

A teacher came to me to tell me about Hector, a student who is typically pleasant and engaged in class activity. She noticed a pattern with Hector, who had his head down on his desk every Monday. He would snap at his peers and always requested to go to the nurse's office. I came to the class to observe Hector the following Monday. He had his head down from the start of math class. The teacher and I pulled him aside after class and asked him what was going on. He explained that he and his siblings spent the weekend with their father. It was a loud neighborhood, and they did not get much rest. In addition, his father did not have time to feed them breakfast in the mornings, and he drops them off too late to get the school breakfast. This was a situation that was impacting Hector's emotional health, physical health, and grades. He expressed that he had a headache and stomachache, and the nurse gave him crackers.

Had I not taken the time to listen to this student's hardship, he would be getting into trouble with his peers and being referred to the disciplinary office on a weekly basis. Educators and administrators must spend the time to engage and develop relationships with their students and families. We reached out to his mother and shared this concern and the impact it was having on Hector. His mother decided that the kids would return to her house on Sunday night and allow them to start the week rested. She also dropped them off early to get school breakfast. During progress report conversations a few weeks later, we noticed an improvement in his grades.

Prevent Disruptive Behaviors That Deter Learning

Day-to-day disruptions in the classroom are the most common cause of lost learning time and a source of frustration for teachers. Teachers sometimes feel that they have to make the decision in the moment to remove a student whom they consider disruptive or sacrifice instruction for the entire class. The easy approach for most is telling the student(s) to go to the principal's office or a disciplinary space designated for students who've gotten into trouble. However, restorative practice offers teachers an opportunity for them to build a relationship and engage in conversation with students who are being perceived as disruptive.

Find out what is causing this behavior. What is happening in the student's life? What other approaches can the student utilize to get your attention and let you know what's going on? How can the student express their frustration without disrupting the learning of others? Discuss the student's strengths and discuss the importance of learning. This can be a space for teachers to share how certain behaviors can negatively impact class.

A teacher came to me to share that he had a group of boys in his class who he felt were purposefully disrupting his class. I observed the boys in other classes and noticed that they were respectful and focused in other spaces. They transitioned in the hallways with no disruptions. In the cafeteria, they got into the normal high-energy middle school mischief, but they pulled it together when they were redirected by the lunch monitors. The administrative team decided to have a conversation with the boys, the teacher, and a peer facilitator. The four boys admitted that they purposefully were being mean to the teacher because they did not like him. Each boy talked about a point earlier in the year when the teacher got them into trouble by calling home. They did not feel heard and felt that he unjustly targeted them. This conversation allowed the teacher the opportunity to hear the student perspectives, and he modeled humility by apologizing to them. This was a turning point for his teaching that year. The boys apologized too and promised to be respectful toward him moving forward. The remainder of the year the teacher intentionally had conversations with students prior to calling home. He engaged in conversations instead of jumping to conclusions and consequences.

Peer Mediation

Training student leaders for formal restorative circles is an important consideration for creating a climate of restorative practice. Training students to ask open-ended questions and listening to and engaging their peers in nonjudgmental conversations that lead to a peaceful resolution is a life skill. The students must learn to listen empathetically while also learning that conflict resolution is possible through listening and open, honest, authentic conversation.

Resolving Conflict

One year our faculty decided to start the school year by doing home visits for our advisory students. On a warm late August day, I went on a scheduled visit to meet twin advisees. They were pleasant and welcoming. Their mother had them serve me tea and shared some fun stories about her twin girls. I was excited to have them in my advisory. However, the first week of school came, and I realized a different set of twins showed up to my advisory. They were born leaders, very influential, and instrumental in unintentionally persuading their peers to be off task. During one of our peace circles, one of their classmates, Fiona, revealed that she was fed up and was tired of the twins' behavior. She fell apart, crying and sharing all of the nasty things that they had said to her. The twins were very popular and had a close circle of friends who would laugh and serve as bystanders, egging them on, when they were off task.

This was an opportunity for us to put our restorative practices to work. I invited Fiona, the twins, and the bystanders for a discussion. This conversation was led by a trained peer facilitator.

(Continued)

(Continued)

Fiona shared her frustrations with the twins. She felt they made fun of her because she covered her hair because of her religion. She said they called her ugly and all sorts of other names. Fiona said some of the bystanders were her friends too and she did not understand why they did not speak up. During the session, everyone got a chance to share their perspectives about what their roles were in this circumstance along with their feelings. Finally, one of the twins had a chance to speak. She was the most vocal of the two and had the tendency to take the lead. She revealed that the previous school year, they were victims of bullying. People made fun of them because they were from Nigeria and because they had accents. Her twin started crying. She said her peers told them they smelled and should go back to Africa. They decided that instead of being bullied, this year, they would be bullies as a means of trying to proactively protect themselves. The peer facilitator asked them how they felt when they were bullied the year before and how it felt now that they were considered bullies. One of the twins said they went home crying and it hurt all the time last year, but this year they were adamant it would not happen to them. After hearing Fiona's perspective and the reaction of their friends, the twins reflected and realized they were wrong. They had a choice to not be mean to others. They did not know that Fiona covered her hair for religious purposes. Both twins apologized and told their friends that they did not want friends who feared them; that's not real friendship. They want friends who like them.

This conversation ended with a resolution: that bullying was not ever okay. They developed the understanding that when these forms of violations happen, it is a violation of relationships. The twins knew how it felt. They took responsibility for their roles. The bystanders also took responsibility for laughing and not standing up for Fiona. I shared this conversation with the parents of the students involved. Full transparency in the process promotes accountability. Everyone does not have to be friends, but they all left knowing that they had to respect each other. The three girls took turns for the next few months leading our peace circles. Because of this experience and what they learned from it, they now choose to lead in positive ways.

Safety First

Restorative practice is preventative and creates a culture that fosters conversation to resolve conflicts. This approach provides students with the skills and the choice to communicate instead of reverting to violent language and physical altercations. Furthermore, it lends to a safe climate that deters the students who feel unsafe from feeling like they need to protect themselves. Even in situations when students revert to fighting and have to deal with punitive systems like suspension, restorative circles can support the reentry process to create a resolution to the initial conflict, create a safe space for the victim, and create an opportunity for the offender(s) to redeem themselves and take accountability for their actions.

I had a student who confidentially told me that he saw a knife in another student's bag. The other student, Mike, was a quiet student who kept to himself. He seldom volunteered to participate in class and mostly engaged with a small group of friends. Upon hearing that Mike might have a weapon, I called another administrator. We pulled Mike aside, and he was up front and told us he only brought the knife for protection. Mike was sent home, and he was asked to return with his parents the next day for a conference.

His parents were upset that he had a weapon in school, but they were more upset with the fact that he felt unsafe in school and he would feel the need to have a weapon to begin with.

They urged Mike to speak up and share why he felt so unsafe. Eventually, he explained that he was being bullied by another student who called him racial slurs and threatened to beat him up. After completing this initial meeting with Mike's family, we immediately called that student in to have a conversation with Mike. With the gravity and urgency of this situation, an administrator facilitated the conversation as opposed to a trained peer facilitator. Mike shared that he was afraid and was not going to allow this other student to hurt him. The other student, who at the moment realized how angry and hurt Mike was, apologized to Mike. He did not know that Mike had a weapon and that he took him so seriously. He stated that he was "just clowning around with his friends." His parent was called in, and the student took responsibility for making another student feel unsafe. Mike also learned that he needed to speak up when he was being threatened and he did not need to resort to bringing a weapon to school.

Implementing restorative practices in a school is not a quick fix, and it takes time and consistency across the board. This conversation ended in both students taking accountability, being reflective about their roles in making the school unsafe, and acknowledging and accepting the consequences that were the results of their respective choices. The process is continuous, and the conversations must perpetually occur to bring resolution to each and every conflict.

Outcomes

Even in the age of standardized testing, creating school cultures that embrace restorative practices is equally imperative to holding schools accountable through state standards. Overall, the successful implementation of restorative practices can create an environment and school culture that are focused and dedicated to learning and high academic achievement. Also, over time students develop the language and emotional maturity to discuss how they feel and resolve conflict and take accountability for their actions. Conflicts will always arise, but the goal is to teach students to talk through the misunderstandings, hurt feelings, anger, and frustrations. Schools should be safe learning communities that not only teach students academic skills but also focus on social and emotional competence and accountability for choices.

Next Steps

- Set high expectations for all your students, and become a warm demander when encouraging your students to meet those expectations.

- Take the time to get to know about your students' lives outside of school, and be open-minded to how their home and social lives may be influencing their behaviors and attitudes at school.

- Let your students know that you are there for them if they are faced with a challenging situation and that it is always important to speak up when they don't feel heard, supported, or safe.

- Engage in professional learning on restorative practices, and begin addressing disruptive behaviors with conversations in lieu of punishments. Use your team meetings as an opportunity to further unpack, apply, and analyze the impact of these new practices.

(Continued)

(Continued)

Reflection Questions

- Do you use restorative practices in your learning environment? How might using the techniques discussed in this chapter create a safer school environment?

- Think of a time where you had a student or group of students who regularly caused disruptions in your classroom. How did you handle that situation? What might you do differently now?

- How does using punitive measures such as sending students to the principal's office and/or suspending students have the potential to lead to unequal outcomes for students? How can restorative practices help us overcome these outcomes?

Additional Resources

- Trinity Foundation Boston: https://trinityinspires.org/
- *Circle Forward* by Carolyn Boyes-Watson and Kay Pranis: http://www.livingjusticepress.org/
- Information on Janet Connors, community leader, inspiration, and Circle Keeper at OurRJ: http://ourrj.org/janets-bio/
- Suffolk University Center for Restorative Justice: http://www.suffolk.edu/college/centers/14521.php

As you have learned, restorative practices are a range of approaches that aim to develop community and to manage conflict and tensions by repairing harm and restoring relationships. It is not a "one-size-fits-all" approach and requires educators to develop trust as well as welcoming and safe learning environments in order for the approach to be effective. Creating environments that foster academic, behavioral, and social emotional learning demonstrates the belief that all students can learn and have the ability to self-regulate, collaborate, and contribute powerfully to the classroom/school community.

We must consistently hold all students, particularly those who have historically struggled, to high expectations as they are in pursuit of behavioral, social emotional, and academic success. Antiquated exclusionary disciplinary practices do not support the development of behavioral and/or social emotional learning skill sets. Through the utilization of restorative practices, we provide our students, even at the most challenging moments, with the opportunity to reflect, grow, and develop both self-efficacy and self-advocacy skills. This is how we can ensure that all students become expert learners, the goal of a universally designed education.

Usage of restorative practices, through the UDL lens, also provides educators the opportunity to be socially just, even in the midst of addressing social emotional, behavioral, and/or disciplinary issues by relying on strategies that ensure that all that transpires within our classrooms, whether intentionally academic or not, can become authentic teachable moments. Restorative practice reinforces the notion that classrooms are places of partnership where learning occurs with and for students rather than to them by providing voice, choice, and the opportunity to reflect and process.

CHAPTER EIGHT

A STUDENT'S JOURNEY

"When you control a man's thinking you do not have to worry about his actions. You do not have to tell him not to stand here or go yonder. He will find his 'proper place' and will stay in it. You do not need to send him to the back door. He will go without ever being told. In fact, if there is no back door, he will cut one for his special benefit. His education makes it necessary."

—Carter Godwin Woodson

SETTING THE STAGE

In this chapter we will share why we believe in the power of social justice education by sharing the account, with permission, of a student who has only succeeded as a result of it. For the purposes of this narrative, we shall refer to the young man, whose journey we will be sharing, as "M."

THE EARLY YEARS

M was born in the city of Weymouth, Massachusetts, to Haitian immigrant parents in the early 1980s. His parents and their families were both politically active in their homeland and adamantly opposed the Duvalier regime, which came to power in the late 1950s, which ultimately led to them fleeing to the United States in search of political asylum and a better life. M's parents were also shrouded in secrecy. His father was a prominent Roman Catholic priest in the city of Boston, and his mother suffered from bipolar schizophrenia. M was their only child and throughout most of his childhood felt very proud to be Haitian American. He had a strong sense of pride in the culture, music, flag, language, and food. He was extremely proud of his large, close-knit extended family, which consisted of five uncles, two aunts, and numerous cousins. He was also proud of his responsibilities at home as a caretaker of his mother. Until the fourth grade.

It was during the fourth grade that M first encountered the notion that it was not okay to be himself. During this time period, there was a huge influx of Haitian refugees who were coming into the United States, and their presence was often unwelcome. They were sometimes referred to as "the boat people" or "Haitian bush boogies." M recalls that in addition to those insults, teachers and students would say to him, "You don't look Haitian, you don't sound Haitian, and you don't not smell Haitian. How can you be Haitian?" M did not know what a Haitian person was supposed to look, sound, or smell like, but he understood that the underlying message was that it was not okay to be Haitian, at least not at school. So he made a conscious decision to hide that aspect of his identity moving forward and claimed membership in what he calls the "fathered fatherless tribe."

As a black boy in an urban school classroom, M knew that if he simply stated that he was African American, instead of Haitian American, that no one would question his identity. He also understood that if he simply stated that he did not know or that he had no father, that would be enough to conceal the secret that his father was a well-known priest, because his teachers expected that boys who looked like him did not have or know their fathers. M also learned that it was not safe to talk about his responsibilities at home: cooking, cleaning, and making sure that bills were paid on time, in support of his mother, who was struggling with mental illness. Teachers often made disparaging comments about these circumstances such as "Your mother doesn't really love you," and "There must be something seriously wrong at home, because children your age aren't supposed to be dealing with that."

These experiences frustrated and confused M, who previously loved school. He was slowly coming to grips with the fact that he did not feel safe or welcomed at school. For the first time, he had to learn how to hide significant aspects of who he was. All of this transpired as M struggled to develop his social identity. His teachers failed to realize that M was dealing with trauma. M was the only child of a parent who was suffering from mental illness, and he had the extra burden of concealing the identity of his father. Instead of recognizing this and providing support and a safe space to process his life outside of school, his teachers, intentionally or not, contributed additional layers of trauma by making M feel unwelcome and creating an atmosphere where he felt like he needed to conceal his identity.

Data has shown that third and fourth grade reading and math scores have been linked to the school-to-prison pipeline (Reading Partners, 2013). It has been argued that urban students who are disengaged, distracted, and who perform poorly on third and fourth grade high-stakes assessments are highly likely to drop out and/or experience incarceration. While we are not taking a stance for or against that claim, we acknowledge that research in trauma-sensitive schools suggests that there is a strong correlation between trauma, disengagement, and poor performance in school and a correlation between the latter and dropout and incarceration rates (Citizens for Juvenile Justice, 2017; National Dropout Prevention Center, 2017).

This relates to M, as at this tender age he no longer felt safe in school and grew quite cynical on why he had to be there. He had no role models at school. The teachers did not look like him or hail from communities like his. The curriculum never reflected anyone who was from his background and was never connected to the world outside of school. M raised questions about this and was often sent to the principal's office for disturbing class and being disrespectful. Some teachers actually told him to "shut-up" or to put his head down and stop asking stupid questions. He felt like education was being done to him rather than being done with and for him.

As M coped with making sense of his identity and struggled to find examples of his community outside of school, he encountered equally disparaging and confusing messages on television. This was during the 1980s and 1990s before the age of the Internet, so M's only window to the world outside of school and/or his neighborhood was television. When he turned to TV to try to find examples and/or role models that he could emulate, he found that the shows that depicted families were always of middle-class white folk in suburban communities, in two-parent households. They coped with and struggled with issues that he considered nonissues, seemed to suffer no trauma, and had lifestyles that he could not relate to. It was like TV was reinforcing the societal message that he received at school—that he was invisible, that his community was invisible, and that he just didn't matter. In addition, it seemed to him as if he was being provided with three specific prototypes of what a socially acceptable brown man could be: a comedian like Eddie Murphy or Martin Lawrence, a star athlete like Michael Jordan, or a bad boy/tough guy like Tupac Shakur.

Through the process of elimination, he realized that although he thought he had a great sense of humor and had been often considered a class clown, he did not have the confidence or courage to be a good stand-up comedian. He also concluded that although he thought he had some amazing moves and skills on the basketball court, he was not a good enough athlete to become a professional. It was the bad boy/tough guy persona that resonated with him. On television and in his community, the bad boy/tough guys seemed to be well respected. They got to speak freely; no one bothered them, put them down, or got in the way. So M, as a scared elementary student, decided that this is who he would try to be.

During this time, the adults in school began telling him that he was nothing more than a disobedient troublemaker whose future would end in one of two pathways—being dead or being in jail. These messages reinforced his path. This began his reidentification as a behavior problem student. He was on a mission to prove to his peers that school was a waste of time and that teachers and administrators were liars who did not care for or believe in their students. He spiraled rapidly downward and ended up being expelled and forced to transfer from several schools at the threat of possible expulsion.

ENCOUNTERS WITH AUTHORITY

"People of color accounted for about 75 percent of those stopped by Boston police, 63 percent of them Black in a city where less than 25 percent of the population was Black."

—ACLU

Throughout middle school, M did not feel safe, welcomed, or respected at school, or in the community outside of school. One summer afternoon after playing basketball at a local park, M and his friends were sitting on the stoop of an apartment building on Bicknell Street in Boston, trash talking each other as teenage boys typically do. The boys argued about who was as smooth as Clyde Drexler and who looked silly. In the midst of their conversation, a friend, Darron, pointed out that there was a "Dtech Cruiser" at the top of the street, which was slang for a police detective cruiser or an unmarked police car. Darron suggested that before the cruiser came closer, they should all go inside the building and lay low until it left the area.

M disagreed, stating that they were doing nothing wrong. It was hot inside, and he thought it was okay for them to continue hanging out on the stoop. M's friends followed Darron's lead, laughing that he could stay outside if he wanted to, but that he'd learn his lesson. As the boys walked into the building, M stayed outside, resolute to prove them wrong.

Darron's father was a lieutenant in the Boston Police, and M thought the worst-case scenario was that if the police did bother them, Darron would simply state who his dad was and they'd be okay. Why then was Darron leading the charge to go indoors? Before he could finish his thought, he heard the cruiser's exhaust as it quickly raced down the street and abruptly stopped directly across from him. In what seemed like slow motion, he saw four burly white men in baseball caps, shorts, and lanyards that displayed their golden detective badges pour out of the vehicle, grab him, and pin him on top of the scorching hot hood of a hatchback Honda Civic that was parked directly in front of where he was.

As his face sizzled from the heat and he braced the pain of his arm being twisted behind his back, he heard the officers shouting, "Where are the guns and drugs?" and "Where did you steal this car from?" He tried to respond and wanted to, but the combination of pain from his twisted arm and shoulder, the pain from the heat of the car on his face, and the shock of what was happening prevented any words from escaping his lips. The car he was pinned on had unlocked doors and while continuing to shout at him, some officers began rummaging through the vehicle. He then felt them kicking his legs apart, loosening his belt, and pulling down his pants and underwear. They conducted a body cavity search right there on the street for all to see.

Just as quickly as it began, they yanked up his pants and underwear, rushed back into their cruiser and took off, never saying sorry or explaining their actions. Stunned, confused, and embarrassed, M sat down on the concrete sidewalk in a daze. His friends soon emerged from the building, some joking that he had now learned his lesson, and others saying unsavory things about the police, but he didn't say a word. He could not. He was shocked and upset—upset at the police, upset at his friends, upset that they watched and didn't do anything, then upset at himself for being mad at them, because he knew that there was nothing that they could do. He just sat there until he could muster the strength to silently get up and walk to the bus stop so that he could catch the next number 31 or 28 bus and go home.

M felt like the world was against him—that there was a conspiracy among school, television, and the police to make him feel worthless. They collectively had constructed a narrative about him and those who looked like him and were determined to make that narrative reality. He wrote a poem titled "You Ain't Nothing" to capture what that felt like, which has been included below:

You Ain't Nothing

Survival's a vicious game

Grab a tool, join a gang

Brown boy, you ain't nothing

In the hood you'll remain

Consumed by the anger and pain

Till your bloods pourn out and on concrete you lay slain

Brown boy, you ain't nothing

Join a team, hold heat, make a life in these streets

As a predator, super menace

Your worth is worthless

Drop-out

Life ain't for you

Drop-out

(Continued)

(Continued)

This world hated you before you were born

Drop-out

Brown boy, you ain't nothing

You weed smoking shadow dweller

Pariah of society

Be angry because we hate you

Fear us because we fear you

You'll never become anything

Because we don't want you to

And neither do you

Brown boy, you ain't nothing

By M

The Restoration

Shortly after writing that poem, M received a phone call that would forever change his life. His friend Darron was murdered over his white Jordan sneakers. M was stunned; he had known many others who were victims of street violence, but this was the first time that it happened to someone in his inner circle. He was shaken to his core since, among his friends, the assumption always was that Darron was the safest one because of what his father did for a living. Even Darron was not safe in the community. He was killed in front of his own home while his father, a lieutenant on the Boston Police force, was inside.

M's new resolve was to be safe. He purchased a gun on the street and carried it with him wherever he went until he was arrested one day while skipping school in downtown Boston.

While sitting in the back of the police cruiser, M heard a rush of the familiar words that adults hurled at him—failure, dead, jail. He felt guilt and despair like he had never felt before, and with tears in his eyes, he looked up at the officers in the front seats of the cruiser and said, "I'm sorry." The officers responded, half chuckling, "Too late for that kid. You're going away for a long time."

M was released from custody to his mother and was placed on strict school-to-home curfew and had to be home directly after school to answer the phone when his probation officer called to ensure that he was there. He was a freshman in high school and was, by chance, enrolled at a school that was like nothing he had ever experienced before. All of the teachers seemed deeply invested in him and wanted to develop a positive relationship with him. They were curious about his thoughts and ideas and believed in honoring the impact of their work on and in his life over their intentions. He tried hard to resist them at first, but they continued to prove that they were genuine.

This was the first school he had ever been to with teachers who looked like him and talked openly about the contributions that people who looked like him have made to society. They even welcomed his questions about why he had to study certain things, and if they didn't know, they would encourage him to work with them, so that they could figure it out together. They ensured that the work he was presented with always felt authentic, relevant, important, and connected to the world outside of school. It was here that M learned that it was okay to ask questions; it was here that he discovered that he had a voice and that he could use that voice to empower himself and others.

He learned at that school that school could be done differently in a way that matters and could treat young people with respect and dignity while making them feel safe and protected. It was there that he discovered that school should be a place to teach you how to cope, to think critically, and to examine all the things that didn't make sense.

A fire was lit inside of M there, and he developed a passion for helping other young people turn their lives around. He knew if other young people experienced school the way it was there, at Fenway High School in Boston, that their lives would be different too and that they'd finally get why education mattered. He went from being a straight F student with felony gun charges to graduating as an officer in student government. He started a school store, created a school newspaper, and even traveled alone to Holland to support a group of gypsy teens who were wrestling with issues of the intersection of traditionalism, youth culture, and voice through hip-hop.

M went on to Wheaton College in Norton, Massachusetts, where social justice and racial equity were his passions. He served in various elected student leadership positions, founded the "Tree House"—an all-men-of-color academic and mentoring housing program on campus—and spearheaded the Wheaton Improvement Association, which worked with the school administration to increase the diversity of the student body. This organization resulted in the hiring of nine African American professors on a campus that prior to then—for over a hundred years—had only one professor of color. While at Wheaton, M developed a passion for supporting young people, which led him to South Africa, where he supported the Southern African Reparations Social Movement as well as a youth empowerment social movement called Youth for Work. Upon returning to the states, M founded the New Hope Youth Coalition, a small NGO that, in partnership with the Boys and Girls Club of America, provided educational opportunities for Boston youth and supported libraries in schools in Johannesburg by sending them thousands of books.

M completed a master's in the art of education at Tufts University and took a job as a founding faculty member of the Lilla G. Frederick Pilot Middle School in Dorchester, which was located in a neighborhood where M spent a lot of time getting into trouble as a teen. He fell in love with teaching there, guided by the principles of valuing impact over intentions, learner visibility, and authentic relevance. He empowered students and families by sharing his journey and added that if he could make it, then they could and would too. He later became an administrator at this school because, in his words, "one classroom wasn't enough." He could keep kids safe in his classroom, but they experienced school differently when they were with his colleagues who did not have any knowledge of how school could be done differently.

His desire to pursue leadership in schools was to help teachers, so that students would be able to experience a systematic approach to being heard, seen, valued, and validated. That led to a short stint in the city of Randolph providing leadership for their alternative school program in hopes of finding and inspiring students who were deemed as throwaways, the way he once was.

M, who also goes by Mirko J. Chardin, the coauthor of this book, was then chosen to be the founding head of school at the Putnam Avenue Upper School in Cambridge, Massachusetts, where his hope has been to develop from the ground up a school community that would provide students with experiences similar to the ones that profoundly changed the course of his life trajectory while at Fenway High School. Mirko seeks to create a school that values impact over intentions, ensuring learner visibility and authentic relevance.

Throughout this text, you have experienced the power, the hope, and the possibility of education and how it has the power to transform lives. Mirko's story is one such example, but every student has the potential to be another example. In conclusion, Mirko leaves you with this:

"I believe in the notion of the *Going Beyond Access* framework. I believe in a socially just education not because of politics, guilt, or theory. I believe because a socially just education saved my life, forever changing the trajectory that I was on. A socially just education can and will do the same for any and all students, in particular our most vulnerable learners. Our calling is to drop our egos, commit to removing barriers, and treat our learners with the unequivocal respect and dignity they deserve."

APPENDIX A

Sociocultural theory (Rogoff, 2003) is used to explain how learning results directly from social interactions among the individual, society, and culture. Using this approach, educators are asked to look critically at the world and their position in it to examine their personal and cultural identities. They do so in an effort to understand the relationships between racial and ethnic identity and pedagogy and how schools can perpetuate inequality and how they can make their individual classrooms, if not the school, a site of equity and equality.

Bioecological Systems Theory (Bronfenbrenner, 1979) states that an individual's development is shaped throughout their lives by interactions and interpersonal relationships with people from various aspects within their immediate, intervening, and distant environments. Similarly, sociocultural theorists agree that higher-order cognitive development occurs during socialization. They contend that people internalize ideas, processes, and experiences. From both of these perspectives, educators explore how context influences cognitive and social development in an effort to understand how American society is stratified, for example, along racial/ethnic, social class, and gender lines.

Positionality is a perspective that must be disclosed; it identifies the frame of reference from which researchers, practitioners (teachers), and policy makers present their data, interpretations, and analysis (Van Langenhove & Harŕe, 1999). Positionality is a core principle of multiculturalism and is, in a similar way, a central tenet of critical race theory.

Taken together, these theoretical frameworks provide an opportunity for educators to become acutely aware that their expectations of students are affected by the way they have been socialized as individuals and prepared as teachers. This assignment, along with others, "ensures that teachers understand, embrace, and incorporate the perspectives of ethnically and socioeconomically diverse communities" (AACTE, 2018, p. 4).

UDL Progression Rubric

Based on the CAST UDL Guidelines (2018)

Katie Novak & Kristan Rodriguez

Provide multiple means of
Engagement

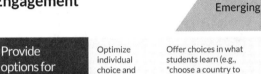

		Emerging	Proficient	Progressing Toward Expert Practice
Provide options for recruiting interest (7)	Optimize individual choice and autonomy (7.1)	Offer choices in what students learn (e.g., "choose a country to study" rather than "study France"), how students learn (e.g., use books, videos, and/or teacher instruction to build understanding), and how they express what they know (e.g., "you can create poster or write paragraph").	Encourage students to choose from multiple options to determine what they learn (guided by standards), how they learn, and how they express what they know. Encourage students to suggest additional options if they can still meet the standard.	Empower students to make choices or suggest alternatives for what they will learn, how they will learn, and how they will express what they know in authentic ways. Free them to self-monitor and reflect on their choices with teacher facilitation and feedback but not explicit direction.
	Optimize relevance, value, and authenticity (7.2)	Offer options that highlight what your learners deem relevant, valuable, and meaningful. For example, you may conduct a student survey and then make instructional decisions based on areas of interest.	Encourage students to share what is relevant, valuable and authentic to them and encourage them to suggest teaching and assessment options that would allow them to meet a defined standard, tying in their interests, culture, and personal strengths. This may be done in a weekly exit ticket, or class discussion, for example.	Empower students to make connections between the content, their own interests, and then push them to link their understanding to authentic real-world scenarios and authentic assessments so they can design their own learning experiences with coaching from the teacher. For example, instead of assigning a lab or giving students the choice of two labs, empower them to design their own lab based on the standard and their scientific interests.
	Minimize threats and distractions (7.3)	Offer options that reduce threats and negative distractions for everyone to create a safe space in which learning can occur. For example, have choices for seating, collaborative work, and clear PBIS expectations.	Collaborate with students to define classroom norms and PBIS expectations and encourage students to help to design the classroom so there are multiple options for seating, collaboration, etc..	Empower students to self-advocate and collaborate to identify threats and distractions and then devise create creative solutions that will allow them to excel. Student voice drives the environment.

CAST | **Until learning has no limits**™

Provide multiple means of
Engagement

		Emerging	Proficient	Progressing Toward Expert Practice
Provide options for sustaining effort and persistence (8)	Heighten salience of goals and objectives (8.1)	Build in "reminders" of both goals and their value. For example, write standards on the board and/or at the top of assessments and projects.	Encourage students to collaboratively discuss goals in light of students' own passions and interests and to choose from various options to reach the goals.	When given the learning standard, have students create personal goals for how they will learn the content, express the content, and challenge themselves throughout the process.
	Vary demands and resources to optimize challenge (8.2)	Provide options for students to learn content with clear degrees of difficulty. For example, "Explore one of the following resources to learn about the Civil War..." and there may be a rigorous primary source document and a video.	Provide multiple options for students to learn content with clear degrees of difficulty which will require them to reflect on the standard and their own strategy for learning. For example, "Choose two of the following six resources to learn about the Civil War..." and there may be rigorous primary source documents, summary documents, videos, and/or a podcasts from a professor.	Empower students to select their own content and/or own assessments, based on standards, and encourage them to collaborate to add to the multiple options offered to challenge themselves and identify appropriate resources that connect to their interests and passions.
	Foster collaboration and community (8.3)	Provide opportunities for students to learn how to work effectively with others. For example, create cooperative learning groups with clear goals, roles, and responsibilities.	Develop a classroom that values collaborative groupwork. Students construct their own groups and create their own group norms, responsibilities, etc. and students often seek out and work with diverse partners.	Create a classroom culture where students work together to define goals, create strategies, provide feedback to each other and push each other with mastery-oriented feedback while building integrative thinking.
	Increase mastery-oriented feedback (8.4)	Provide feedback that guides learners toward mastery rather than a fixed notion of performance or compliance. For example, provide feedback that encourages the use of specific supports and strategies in the face of challenge.	In addition to providing emerging feedback, empower students to provide mastery-oriented feedback to each other to support specific improvement and increased effort and persistence.	Implement proficient practice and also empower students to use mastery-oriented feedback independently to self-reflect, self-direct, and pursue personal growth in areas of challenge.

CAST | **Until learning has no limits**™

Provide multiple means of
Engagement

	Emerging	Proficient	Progressing Toward Expert Practice
Provide options for self-regulation (9)			
Promote expectations and beliefs that optimize motivation (9.1)	Teach students about the power of perseverance and use language and feedback that will allow all students to see themselves as capable learners.	Foster conversations with students to develop relationships and make authentic connections and use their personal passions and interests to help inspire them and push them toward success.	Create a classroom culture where students are empowered and able to support their own self-talk and support one another's positive attitudes toward learning.
Facilitate personal coping skills and strategies (9.2)	Offer reminders, models, and tools, to assist learners in managing and directing their emotional responses. For example, use stories or simulations to demonstrate coping skills. Offer options for stress release such as alternate seating, fidget tools, mindfulness breaks, etc.	Empower students to deal with difficult challenges by allowing them to choose from multiple strategies to regulate their learning (e.g., a relaxation corner, put on headphones, take a walk).	Encourage students to self-reflect, accurately interpret their feelings, and use appropriate coping strategies and skills to foster learning for themselves and their classmates.
Develop self-assessment and reflection (9.3)	Provide students with tools so they are reflecting on their learning through rubrics, self-assessment, etc.	Offer multiple models and scaffolds of different self-assessment techniques so students can identify and choose ones that are optimal. For example, these might include ways to collect, measure, and display data from their own behavior and academic performance for the purpose of monitoring growth.	Create a culture where students consistently reflect on the learning process and assessments so they become self-directed learners who grow over time.

CAST | **Until learning has no limits**™

Provide multiple means of
Representation

		Emerging	Proficient	Progressing Toward Expert Practice
Provide options for perception (1)	Offer ways of customizing the display of information (1.1)	Create resources and materials that address variability and meet the needs of more students (e.g., large size print, additional white space, visuals).	Create resources and materials that students can access electronically. Allow students to use their devices to interact with textual, visual and audio information so they can personalize, take notes, increase/decrease size/volume, etc.	Empower students to choose resources and materials that best meet their needs (e.g., watch a video OR explore a handout) so they can personalize their learning themselves without explicit direction from a teacher.
	Offer alternatives for auditory information (1.2)	Provide an embedded option for any information presented aurally. For example, use closed-captions when playing a video.	Provide multiple options for students to choose alternatives to learn content so they don't have to rely on auditory information (e.g., closed captions for video or the choice of reading a text).	Empower students to select auditory alternatives as well as provide them with a framework to locate additional, reputable resources to build their understanding (e.g., resources on how to determine if a website or author is credible).
	Offer alternatives for visual information (1.3)	Provide an embedded option for students so they don't have to rely on visual information. For example, reading aloud to the class while they read along.	Provide multiple options for students to choose alternatives to learn content so they don't have to rely on visual information (e.g., listen to audiobook instead of reading or choose to work with teacher for short presentation).	Empower students to select alternatives to visual information as well as provide them with a framework to locate additional, reputable resources to build their understanding (e.g., resources on how to determine if a website or author is credible).

UDL Progression Rubric | Page 4
Novak & Rodriguez | ©2018

CAST | Until learning has no limits™

Provide multiple means of
Representation

		Emerging	Proficient	Progressing Toward Expert Practice
Provide options for language, mathematical expressions, and symbols (2)	Clarify vocabulary and symbols (2.1)	Translate idioms, archaic expressions, culturally exclusive phrases, and slang. For example, explicitly teach vocabulary to students using definitions, visuals, explanations, and examples.	In addition to emerging practice, provide students with explicit instruction in context clues so they can independently learn words unfamiliar to them.	Empower students to use available resources to work collaboratively to determine authentic ways to use relevant vocabulary.
	Clarify syntax and structure (2.2)	Clarify unfamiliar syntax (in language or in math formulas) or underlying structure (in diagrams, graphs, illustrations, extended expositions or narratives). For example, highlight the transition words in an essay.	Provide students with resources that will allow they themselves to clarify syntax and structure (such as dictionaries, math reference sheets, thesaurus, etc.)	Empower students to preview material under study, highlight areas in need of clarification, and choose appropriate resources to build knowledge and understanding.
	Support decoding of text, mathematical notation, and symbols (2.3)	Provide direct instruction, prompts, and scaffolded materials for students who struggle to comprehend information. Or provide alternatives, such as visuals, to support this understanding.	Provide strategies and materials (e.g., math reference sheets, context clue strategies, and so forth) that lower barriers to understand and help students figure out notations, symbols, or problems.	Empower students to independently utilize learned strategies to decode text, mathematical notation, and symbols.
	Promote understanding across languages (2.4)	Provide alternative presentations of material, especially for key information or vocabulary. For example, make key information in the dominant language (e.g., English) also available in the first languages of learners with limited-English proficiency. Also, use images AND words, show opposites, etc.	Provide students with access to tools such as apps, websites, and dictionaries to translate material under study and to collaboratively build understanding.	Empower students to independently utilize options to translate material under study, collaborate to build understanding using tools, apps, etc.
	Illustrate through multiple media (2.5)	Present key concepts in one form of symbolic representation (e.g., an expository text or a math equation) with an alternative form (e.g., an illustration, diagram, video, etc.)	Present students with multiple options and symbolic representations to make meaning and allow them to choose options to build comprehension.	Empower students to choose effective resources from multiple options with multiple representations so not all students are required to learn from the same resources.

CAST | **Until learning has no limits**™

		Emerging	Proficient	Progressing Toward Expert Practice
Provide options for comprehension (3)	Activate or supply background knowledge (3.1)	Provide all students with background information on content using direct instruction with options for visuals, audio, etc.	Provide students with options that supply or activate relevant prior knowledge, or link to the prerequisite information elsewhere. For example, use advanced organizers (e.g., KWL methods, concept maps) and then encourage students to select resources that will allow them to build appropriate background knowledge.	Empower students to determine gaps in their own background knowledge and then select appropriate resources to build that knowledge in order to achieve the goals of a lesson. For example, begin with a diagnostic assessment and ask students to reflect and create a strategy for filling in gaps in learning.
	Highlight patterns, critical features, big ideas, and relationships (3.2)	Provide explicit cues or prompts to help students recognize the most important features in information. For example, teach students to use outlines, graphic organizers, highlighters, etc.	Provide students with options and multiple strategies to support recognition of the most important features in information. For example, allow them to use outlines, graphic organizer, highlighter, word cloud apps, and other organizing tools.	Empower students to self-reflect to determine the most effective strategies for highlighting critical information and independently select the strategies that allow them to support recognition of patterns, critical features, big ideas, and relationships.
	Guide information processing, visualization, and manipulation (3.3)	Provide all students with materials, strategies, and tools to support processing and visualization. Tools include manipulatives (i.e, counting cubes), glossaries, graphic organizers, and more.	Provide students with options of multiple materials, strategies, and tools to use to support processing and visualization, such as the option to make visual notes, use technology to locate images, and/or select and use manipulatives, etc.	Empower students to self-reflect and independently choose the most appropriate materials, strategies, and tools to guide information processing, visualization, and manipulation, searching for additional tools and strategies, if necessary.
	Maximize transfer and generalization (3.4)	Model explicit strategies students can use to transfer the information they have to other content areas and situations. For example, show how the knowledge could be used in another class or be used to make comparisons across content in the class (such as text to text comparisons).	Provide options for meaningful transfer, such as interdisciplinary projects, where students can make authentic connections and apply knowledge in meaningful ways in other content areas and in authentic situations.	Encourage students to apply knowledge and skills learned in class to enhance their understanding of content, design of their own authentic projects, and express their knowledge and understanding in authentic, real-world scenarios.

UDL Progression Rubric | Page 6
Novak & Rodriguez | ©2018

CAST | **Until learning has no limits**™

Provide multiple means of
Action & Expression

		Emerging	Proficient	Progressing Toward Expert Practice
Provide options for physical action (4)	Vary the methods for response and navigation (4.1)	Provide more than one option for the methods used for response and navigation within the same assignment. For example, some students may use iPads while others write by hand.	Provide multiple options for the methods used for response and navigation within the same assignment. For example, some students may use iPads, different writing utensils, keyboards, voice recognition software, etc.	Empower students to use their own devices to respond to and interact with materials for all assignments (e.g., options to use headphones, keyboards, manipulatives, joysticks, etc.).
	Optimize access to tools and assistive technologies (4.2)	Allow some students to use assistive technologies for navigation, interaction, and composition if required by an IEP or 504.	Provide multiple options for all students to use assistive technology like iPads, voice recognition, and 1:1 devices regardless of variability.	Empower students to assess the need for and choose technologies that work for them to provide additional, personalized options to express their knowledge and skills.
Provide options for expression and communication (5)	Use multiple media for communication (5.1)	Provide more than one way to answer on assessments so students can express their understanding without barriers. Taking a traditional test may be one option, but so, too, could be an oral presentation or writing an essay.	Provide students with multiple options to express their understanding--and let them suggest some ways of being assessed, so they understand that showing what they know is the point rather than how well they perform on a particular kind of test. Students may choose to express their understanding in text, audio, video, multimedia, live presentations, and many other ways.	Let students reflect on a standard or a set of competency or proficiency-based rubrics, and then independently create authentic and innovative products that allow them to demonstrate their mastery of the standard.
	Use multiple tools for construction and composition (5.2)	Provide the choice of more than one tool or strategy to help students express their knowledge. For example, allow students to compose a response using traditional pen and paper or allow them to create a multimedia presentation on their device.	Provide multiple tools and strategies to help students express their knowledge. For example, allow students to compose a response using traditional written methods, blogging software, or multimedia tools such as ThingLink or Emaze.	When provided with a task, or when independently creating an authentic product, students are empowered to self-reflect and select tools and materials that will support their learning and challenge them to strive for rigorous options to express knowledge and skills in accessible, engaging ways using, and then building upon, the tools they were exposed to in class.
	Build fluencies with graduated levels of support for practice and performance (5.3)	Implement a scaffolding model from teacher-directed to collaborative groups to independent work, slowly releasing responsibility to students. For example, in collaborative work, assign team members specific tasks and monitor their progress before moving to independent work or move from teacher-directed instruction to Socratic seminars.	Provide options for support and scaffolding throughout the learning process and encourage students to choose resources that allow them to build their own knowledge while working in collaborative groups and working independently. In collaborative groups, for example, encourage students to self-select roles; in class discussions, have students collaborate to design the rules and structures.	Empower students to create challenges that let them productively struggle to reach rigorous goals and use supports as tools to help them to make improvements rather than making things "easier." Encourage students to provide feedback and drive teacher instruction; encourage them to define roles and expectations for group work that include routine monitoring and reflection.

CAST | Until learning has no limits™

		Emerging	Proficient	Progressing Toward Expert Practice
Provide options for executive functions (6)	Guide appropriate goal-setting (6.1)	Provide clear goals to students so it's clear what they must do to meet or exceed expectations. For example, post standards on the board and on assignments, and articulate those standards and goals throughout the lesson.	Create conditions for learners to develop goal-setting skills. For example, provide students with standards on the board and on assignments, but also provide models or examples of the process and product of goal setting so all students can develop personalized goals while working toward standards.	Encourage students to create personalized learning plans that include goals that align to identified standards as well as action plans and strategies that optimize personal strengths while addressing individualized areas of challenge.
	Support planning and strategy develop-ment (6.2)	Facilitate the process of strategic planning. For example, provide all students with checklists for tasks, due dates, and planning templates to keep students organized.	Facilitate the process of strategic planning. For example, provide students not only with organizational tools but with scaffolds they need to create personalized strategies to meet their goals.	Empower students to self-reflect, self-assess, and create personalized action plans to achieve their identified goals. For example, encourage students to reflect on how much time and resources they need to perform selected tasks and then encourage them to make personal due dates and task lists to reach their goals.
	Facilitate managing information and resources (6.3)	Provide scaffolds and supports to act as organizational aids for students. For example, provide all students with templates for note-taking.	Provide exposure to multiple scaffolds, supports, and resources that act as organization aids, such as a variety of graphic organizers or different strategies for note-taking.	Empower students to self-reflect, self-assess, and independently choose the most appropriate supports and resources that will allow them to organize information and resources so they can achieve their identified goal(s).
	Enhance capacity for monitoring progress (6.4)	Provide formative feedback tools to students so they can monitor their own progress. For example, provide students with assessment checklists, scoring rubrics, and multiple examples of annotated student work/performance examples.	Provide multiple opportunities for students to receive feedback from the teacher, peers, and themselves using a variety of tools such as assessment checklists, scoring rubrics, and exemplars.	Empower students to use multiple resources, including teachers and peers, to consistently reflect on their performance, collect feedback, and revise their work to promote and highlight growth.

UDL Progression Rubric | Page 8
Novak & Rodriguez | ©2018

CAST | **Until learning has no limits**™

Source: CAST, 2018. www.cast.org. Reprinted with permission.

REFERENCES

AACTE. (2018). *Call for proposals: Sustaining and advancing the profession.* Washington, DC: AACTE.

Abelove, H. (1993). From Thoreau to queer politics, *Yale Journal of Criticism 6*(2), 17–27.

Abo-Zena, M. M. (2011). Faith from the fringes: Religious minorities in school. *Phi Delta Kappan, 93*(4), 15–19.

Allen, J. G., Harper, R. E., & Koschoreck, J. W. (2017). Social justice and school leadership preparation: Can we shift beliefs, values, and commitments? *International Journal of Educational Leadership Preparation, 12*(1).

Angelou, M. (1994). *The complete collected poems of Maya Angelou.* New York, NY: Random House.

Anyon, J. (1980). Social class and the hidden curriculum of work. *The Journal of Education, 162*(1), 67–92.

Baines, L. (2006). Does Horace Mann still matter? *Educational Horizons, 84*(4), 268–273.

Best, J. R., Miller, P. H., & Naglieri, J. A. (2011). Relations between executive function and academic achievement from age 5–17 in a large, representative national sample. *Learning and Individual Differences, 21,* 327–336.

Blair, C., & Raver, C. C. (2015). School readiness and self-regulation: A developmental psychobiological approach. *Annual Review of Psychology, 66,* 711–731.

Blake, C. (2015). *Teaching social justice in theory and practice.* Retrieved from https://education.cu-portland.edu/blog/classroom-resources/teaching-social-justice/

Brant, C. A. R. (2016a). How do I understand the term queer? Preservice teachers, LGBTQ knowledge, and LGBTQ self-efficacy. *The Educational Forum, 81*(1), 35–51.

Brant, C. A. R. (2016b). Teaching our teachers: Trans* and gender education in teacher preparation and professional development. In S. J. Miller (Eds), *Teaching, affirming, and recognizing trans and gender creative youth. Queer Studies and Education.* New York, NY: Palgrave Macmillan.

Brant, C. A. R., & Tyson, C. A. (2016). LGBTQ self-efficacy in the social studies. *Journal of Social Studies Research, 40*(3), 217–227.

Bronfenbrenner, U. (1979). *The ecology of human development: Experiments by nature and design.* Cambridge, MA: Harvard University Press.

Cabrera, N. L., Milem, J. F., Jaquette, O., & Marx, R. W. (2014). Missing the (student achievement) forest for all the (political) trees: Empiricism and the Mexican American studies controversy in Tucson. *American Educational Research Journal, 51*(6), 1084–1118.

CAST. (2018). *UDL guidelines.* Retrieved from http://udlguidelines.cast.org/

Castro, I. E., & Sujak, M. C. (2014). "Why can't we learn about this?" Sexual minority students navigate the official and hidden curricular spaces of high school. *Education and Urban Society, 46*(4), 450–473.

Cavanaugh, B. (2016). Trauma-informed classrooms and schools. *Beyond Behavior, 25*(2), 41–46.

Chan, M. (2018). "They are lifting us up." How Parkland students are using their moment to help minority anti-violence groups. *Time Magazine.* Retrieved from https://time.com/5201562/parkland-students-minority-groups/

Citizens for Juvenile Justice. (2017). *Shutting down the trauma to prison pipeline early: Appropriate care for child-welfare involved youth.* Retrieved from https://www.cfjj.org/trauma-to-prison

Cohen, A. D. (2015). Achieving academic control in two languages: Drawing on the psychology of language learning in considering the past, the present, and prospects for the future. *Studies in Second Language Learning and Teaching, 5*(2), 327–345.

Cohen, J., & Freiberg, J. A. (2013). School climate and bullying prevention. In T. Dary & T. Pickeral (Eds.), *School climate practices for implementation and sustainability. A school climate practice brief, Number 1*. New York, NY: National School Climate Center.

Cohen, G. L., & Steele, C. M. (2002). A barrier of mistrust: How negative stereotypes affect cross-race mentoring. In J. Aronson (Ed.), *Improving academic achievement: Impact of psychological factors on education* (pp. 303–327). San Diego, CA: Academic Press.

Cohen, G. L., Steele, C. M., & Ross, L. D. (1999). The mentor's dilemma: Providing critical feedback across the racial divide. *Personality and Social Psychology Bulletin, 25*(10), 1302–1318.

Conference on English Education Commission on Social Justice. (2009). *CEE position statement: Beliefs about social justice in English education*. CEE, Chicago, IL. Retrieved from www.ncte.org/cee/position/socialjustice

Costello, B., Wachtel, J., & Wachtel, T. (2009). *The restorative practices handbook: For teachers, disciplinarians and administrators*. International Institute for Restorative Practice.

Crosby, S. D. (2015). An ecological perspective on emerging trauma-informed teaching practices. *Children & Schools, 37*(4), 223–230.

DeAngeli, T. (2017). How to tackle tough topics in the classroom. *Monitor on Psychology, 48*(8), 60.

Diamond, A., & Lee, K. (2011). Interventions shown to aid executive function development in children 4–12 years old. *Science, 333*, 959–964.

Dykes, F. O., & Delport, J. L. (2017). Our voices count: The lived experiences of LGBTQ Marjory Stoneman Douglas High School educators and its impact on teacher education preparation programs. *Teaching Education, 29*(2), 135–146.

Emdin, C. (2016). *For white folks who teach in the hood . . . and the rest of y'all too: Reality pedagogy and urban education*. Boston, MA: Beacon Press.

Every Student Succeeds Act of 2015. (2020). S. 1177—114th Congress. Retrieved from https://www.govtrack.us /congress/bills/114/s1177

Facing History and Ourselves. (2020). *Confirmation and other biases: Facing Ferguson: News literacy in a digital age*. Retrieved from https://www.facinghistory.org/resource-library/facing-ferguson-news-literacy-digital-age /confirmation-and-other-biases

Feldman, J. (2018). *Grading for equity: What it is, why it matters, and how it can transform schools and classrooms*. Thousand Oaks, CA: Corwin.

Ferlazzo, L. (2017). *Author interview: "Culturally sustaining pedagogies."* Retrieved from http://blogs.edweek.org /teachers/classroom_qa_with_larry_ferlazzo/2017/07/author_interview_culturally_sustaining_pedagogies.html

Freire, P. (1972). *Pedagogy of the oppressed*. New York, NY: Herder and Herder.

Fritzgerald, T., & Novak, K. (2019). *Equity in our schools: A pretty little lie*. Think Inclusive. Retrieved from https://www .thinkinclusive.us/equity-in-our-schools/

Gay, G. (2010). *Culturally responsive teaching: Theory, research, and practice* (2nd ed.). New York, NY: Teachers College Press.

Gilligan, J. (1997). *Violence: Reflections on a national epidemic*. New York, NY: Vintage Books.

Gorski, P. (2019). *Guide for setting ground rules*. Retrieved from http://www.edchange.org/multicultural/activities /groundrules.html

Gorski, P. C., Davis, S. N., & Reiter, A. (2013). An examination of the (in)visibility of sexual orientation, heterosexism, homophobia and other LGBTQ concerns in U.S. multicultural teacher education coursework. *Journal of LGBTQ Youth, 10*, 224–248.

Greytak, E. A., & Kosciw, J. G. (2014). Predictors of US teachers' intervention in anti-lesbian, gay, bisexual, and transgender bullying and harassment. *Teaching Education, 25*(4), 410–426.

Hackman, D. A., & Farah, M. J. (2008). Socioeconomic status and the developing brain. *Trends in Cognitive Sciences*. *13*, 65–73.

Hammond, Z. (2015). *Culturally responsive teaching and the brain: promoting authentic engagement and rigor among culturally and linguistically diverse students*. Thousand Oaks, CA: Corwin.

Hart, E. L. (1989). *Literacy and the empowerment of lesbian and gay students*. Paper presented at the Annual Meeting of the Conference on College Composition and Communication, Seattle, WA.

Helmer, K. (2015). *Reading queerly in the high school classroom: Exploring a gay and lesbian literature course*. (Doctoral dissertation, University of Massachusetts, Amherst). Retrieved from https://scholarworks.umass.edu/dissertations_2/366/

Irvine, J., & Armento, B. (2001). *Culturally responsive teaching: Lesson planning for elementary and middle grades*. New York, NY: McGraw Hill.

Jacobson, L. A., & Mahone, E. M. (2012). Educational implications of executive dysfunction. In S. J. Hunter & E. P. Sparrow (Eds.), *Executive function and dysfunction: Identification, assessment, and treatment* (pp. 231–246). Cambridge, MA: Cambridge University Press.

Kabanoff, B. (1991). Equity, equality, power and conflict. *Academy of Management Review*, *16*(2), 416–441.

Kasky, C. [Cam Kasky]. (2018, March 10). Guys I just heard a crazy wild ridiculous bonkers rumor that amendments can be amended . . . [Tweet]. Retrieved from https://twitter.com/cameron_kasky/status/972562812772986881

Kean, M. E. (2017). *Conceptualizing gender, contextualizing curriculum: A case study of teacher education coursework*. Ann Arbor, MI: Michigan State University, ProQuest Dissertations Publishing.

Kena, G., Hussar, W., McFarland, J., de Brey, C., Musu-Gillette, L., Wang, X., Zhang, J., Rathbum, A., Wilkinson-Flicker, S., Diliberti, M., Barmer, A., Bullock Mann, F., & Dunlop Velez, F. (2016). *The condition of education 2016* (NCES 2016–144). Washington, DC: U.S. Department of Education, National Center for Education Statistics. Retrieved from nces.ed.gov/pubs2016/2016144.pdf.

Kleinfeld, J. (1975). Effective teachers of Eskimo and Indian students. *School Review*, 83, 301–344.

Kosciw, J. G., Greytak, E. A., Giga, N. M., Villenas, C., & Danischewski, D. J. (2016) The 2015 *National School Climate Survey: The experiences of lesbian, gay, bisexual, transgender, and queer youth in our nation's schools*. New York, NY: GLSEN.

Kozol, (1991). *Savage inequalities: Children in America's schools*. New York, NY: Crown Publishing.

Kuh, L. P., LeeKeenan, D., Given, H., & Beneke, M. R. (2016). Moving beyond anti-bias activities: Supporting the development of anti-bias practices. *Young Children*, *71*(1), 58–65.

Ladson-Billings, G. (1994). *The dreamkeepers: Successful teachers of African American children*. San Francisco, CA: Jossey-Bass Publishers.

Ladson-Billings, G. (2014) Culturally relevant pedagogy 2.0: a.k.a. the Remix. *Harvard Educational Review*, *84*(1), 74–84.

Lawrence-Lightfoot, S. (2005). Reflections on portraiture: A dialogue between art and science. *Qualitative Inquiry*, *11*(1), 3–15.

Lipkin, A. (2002). The challenges of gay topics in teacher education: Politics, content, and pedagogy. In R. Kissen (Ed.), *Getting ready for Benjamin: Preparing teachers for sexual diversity in the classroom*. New York, NY: Rowman & Littlefield.

Mares, B., & Danzinger, J. (2017). *The full vermonty: Vermont in the age of Trump*. Brattleboro, VT: Green Writers Press.

Massachusetts Department of Education. (2020). *DESE model feedback instruments & administration protocols*. Retrieved from http://www.doe.mass.edu/edeval/feedback/surveys.html

Mayworm, A. M., Sharkey, J. D., Hunnicutt, K. L., & Schiedel, K. C. (2016). Teacher consultation to enhance implementation of school-based restorative justice. *Journal of Educational & Psychological Consultation*, *26*(4), 385–412.

McClelland, M. M., Cameron, C. E., Duncan, R., Bowles, R. P., Acock, A. C., Miao, A., & Pratt, M. E. (2014). Predictors of early growth in academic achievement: The head-toes-knees-shoulders task. *Frontiers in Psychology, 5*, 599. Doi: 10.3389/fpsyg.2014.00599

McIntosh, P. (1988). *White privilege: Unpacking the invisible knapsack*. Retrieved from https://www.racialequitytools.org /resourcefiles/mcintosh.pdf

McRaith, M. (2018). *Empathy is a skill*. The Rowland Foundation. Retrieved from https://rowlandfoundation .wordpress.com/2018/03/30/empathy-is-a-skill/

Meyer, A., Rose, D., & Gordon, D. (2014). *Universal design for learning: Theory and practice*. Wakefield, MA: CAST Professional Publications.

Mid-Atlantic Equity Consortium (MAEC). (2020). *Equity audit*. Retrieved from https://maec.org/resource/equity -audit-materials/

Moll, L. C., Amanti, C., Neff, D., & Gonzalez, N. (1992). Funds of knowledge for teaching: Using a qualitative approach to connect homes and classrooms. *Theory Into Practice, 31*(2), 132–141.

Moore, L. (2003, April). Growing up Maya Angelou: The famed writer discusses her childhood, her writing and the importance of family. *Smithsonian Magazine*.

Nappa M., Palladino B., Menesini E., & Baiocco R. (2018). Teachers' reaction in homophobic bullying incidents: The role of self-efficacy and homophobic attitudes. *Sexuality Research & Social Policy: Journal of NSRC [serial online], 15*(2).

National Dropout Prevention Center. (2017). *Dropout prevention and trauma: Addressing a wide range of stressors that inhibit student success*. Retrieved from http://www.dropoutprevention.org/wp-content/uploads/2017/10/dropout-prevention -and-trauma-2017–10.pdf

Novak, K. (2019). *UDL flow chart*. Retrieved from https://www.novakeducation.com/wp-content/uploads/2019/01 /UDL_FlowChart_Rev1.pdf

Novak, K., & Rodriguez, K. (2018). *UDL progression rubric*. Retrieved from http://castpublishing.org/wp-content /uploads/2018/02/UDL_Progression_Rubric_FINAL_Web_REV1.pdf

O'Malley, M. P., & Capper, C. A. (2014). A measure of the quality of educational leadership programs for social justice: Integrating LGBTIQ identities into principal preparation. *Educational Administration Quarterly, 51*(2), 290.

Paris, D., & Alim, H. S. (2017). *Culturally sustaining pedagogies: Teaching and learning for justice in a changing world*. New York, NY: Teachers College Press.

Pascoe, C. J. (2011). *Dude, you're a fag: Masculinity and sexuality in high school, with a new preface*. Berkeley, CA: University of California Press.

Payne, E. C., & Smith, M. J. (2018) Refusing relevance: School administrator resistance to offering professional development addressing LGBTQ issues in schools. *Educational Administration Quarterly, 54*(2), 83–215.

Reading Partners. (2013). *Do prisons use third grade reading scores to predict the number of prison beds they'll need?* Retrieved from https://readingpartners.org/blog/do-prisons-use-third-grade-reading-scores-to-predict-the-number-of-prison -beds-theyll-need/

Roehlkepartain, E. C., & Syvertsen, A. K. (2014). Family strengths and resilience: Insights from a national study. *Reclaiming Children & Youth, 23*(2), 13–18. Retrieved from https://reclaimingjournal.com/

Rogoff, B. (2003). *The cultural nature of human development*. New York, NY: Oxford University Press.

Rosen, S. M., Boyle, J. R., Cariss, K., & Forchelli, G. A. (2014). Changing how we think, changing how we learn: Scaffolding executive function processes for students with learning disabilities. *Learning Disabilities: A Multidisciplinary Journal, 20*(4), 165–176.

Safta, C. G. (2017). Between flexibility and conventionalism. Elements of hidden curriculum with implications in managing conflicts in education. *Jus et Civitas, 68*(1), 95–101.

Sanjin, S. (2009). *How public schools destroy your children's lives and careers*. New York, NY: Bloomington.

School Reform Initiative (SRI). (2019). *Towards a general theory of SRI's intentional learning communities*. Retrieved from https://www.schoolreforminitiative.org/research/general-theory-of-intentional-learning-communities/

Sherwin, G., & Jennings, T. (2006). Feared, forgotten, or forbidden: Sexual orientation topics in secondary teacher preparation programs in the USA. *Teaching Education, 17*(3), 207–223.

Sims Bishop, R. (1990). Mirrors, windows, and sliding glass doors. *Perspectives, 1*(3), ix–xi.

Singleton, G., & Linton, C. (2006). *Courageous conversations about race: A field guide for achieving equity in schools*. Thousand Oaks, CA: Corwin.

Snapp, S. D., McGuire, J. K., Sinclair, K. O., Gabrion, K., & Russell, S. T. (2015). LGBTQ-inclusive curricula: Why supportive curricula matter. *Sex Education, 15*(6), 580–596.

Southern Poverty Law Center. (2020). *Teaching tolerance: A framework for anti-bias education*. Retrieved from https://www.tolerance.org/frameworks/social-justice-standards

Steck, A., & Perry, D. (2017). Secondary school leader perceptions about the inclusion of queer materials in the school course curricula. *The Curriculum Journal, 28*(3), 327–348.

Style, E. (1988). Curriculum as window and mirror. *Listening for All Voices*. Summit, NJ: Oak Knoll School monograph.

Swalwell, K. (2013). "With great power comes great responsibility": Privileged students' conceptions of justice-oriented citizenship. *Democracy and Education, 21*(1), Article 5.

Swanson, K., & Gettinger, M. (2016) Teachers' knowledge, attitudes, and supportive behaviors toward LGBT students: Relationship to Gay-Straight Alliances, antibullying policy, and teacher training. *Journal of LGBT Youth, 13*(4), 326–351.

Tatum, B. D. (2017). *Why are all the black kids sitting together in the cafeteria? And other conversations about race*. New York, NY: Basic Books.

Taylor, C. G., Meyer, E. J., Peter, T., Ristock, J., Short, D., & Campbell, C. (2016). Gaps between beliefs, perceptions, and practices: The Every Teacher Project on LGBTQ-inclusive education in Canadian schools. *Journal of LGBT Youth, 13*(1–2), 112–140.

Teaching Tolerance. (2013). *Problems with Christmas curriculum*. Retrieved from https://www.tolerance.org/magazine/problems-with-christmas-curriculum

TED Talk. (2013). Rita Pierson: Every kid needs a champion. [video]. Retrieved from http://www.ted.com/talks/rita_pierson_every_kid_needs_a_champion

Thein, A. H. (2013). Language arts teachers' resistance to teaching LGBT literature and issues. *Language Arts, 90*(3), 169–180.

Tyner, A. R. (2017). *The emergence of the school-to-prison pipeline*. American Bar Association. Retrieved from https://www.americanbar.org/groups/gpsolo/publications/gpsolo_ereport/2014/june_2014/the_emergence_of_the_school-to-prison_pipeline/

Van Langenhove, L., & Harré, R. (1999). Introducing positioning theory. In R. T. Harré & L. Van Langenhove (Eds.), *Positioning theory. Moral contexts of intentional action* (pp. 14–31). Oxford, England: Blackwell.

Way, N. (2011). *Deep secrets: Boys friendships and the crisis of connection*. Cambridge, MA: Harvard University Press.

Wiggins, G., & McTighe, J. (2011). *The Understanding by Design guide to creating high-quality units*. Alexandria, VA: ASCD.

Williford, A. P., Vick Whittaker, J. E., Vitiello, V. E., & Downer, J. T. (2013). Children's engagement within the preschool classroom and their development of self-regulation. *Early Education and Development, 24*, 162–187.

Wink, J. (2010). *Critical pedagogy: Notes from the real world* (4th ed.). New York, NY: Pearson.

Wright, B. (2018). *The brilliance of black boys: Cultivating school success in the early grades*. New York, NY: Teachers College Press.

INDEX

A SAGE Publishing Company

CORWIN HAS ONE MISSION: to enhance education through intentional professional learning.

We build long-term relationships with our authors, educators, clients, and associations who partner with us to develop and continuously improve the best evidence-based practices that establish and support lifelong learning.

Leadership That Makes an Impact

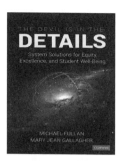

**MICHAEL FULLAN
& MARY JEAN
GALLAGHER**

With the goal of transforming
the culture of learning to
develop greater equity,
excellence, and student
well-being, this book will
help you liberate the system
and maintain focus.

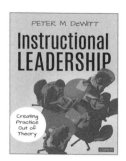

PETER M. DEWITT
This step-by-step
how-to guide presents
the six driving forces of
instructional leadership
within a multistage model for
implementation, delivering
lasting improvement through
small collaborative changes.

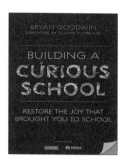

BRYAN GOODWIN
If you've ever wondered
anything, really—just out
of curiosity—then you have
what it takes to lead your
school to restored curiosity
and your students to
well-being and success.

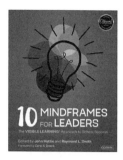

**JOHN HATTIE &
RAYMOND L. SMITH**

Based on the most current
Visible Learning® research with
contributions from education
thought leaders around the world,
this book includes practical ideas
for leaders to implement high-
impact strategies to strengthen
entire school cultures and
advocate for all students.

**DAVIS CAMPBELL &
MICHAEL FULLAN**

The model outlined in this
book develops a systems
approach to governing local
schools collaboratively to
become exemplars of highly
effective decision-making,
leadership, and action.

**MICHAEL FULLAN,
JOANNE QUINN, &
JOANNE MCEACHEN**

The comprehensive strategy
of deep learning incorporates
practical tools and processes
to engage educational
stakeholders in new
partnerships, mobilize whole-
system change, and transform
learning for all students.

**JOANNE QUINN,
JOANNE MCEACHEN,
MICHAEL FULLAN,
MAG GARDNER, &
MAX DRUMMY**

Dive into deep learning
with this hands-on guide to
creating learning experiences
that give purpose, unleash
student potential, and
transform not only learning,
but life itself.

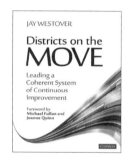

JAY WESTOVER
The transformative
framework outlined in this
book creates a districtwide
approach for changing
the culture of learning and
creating a coherent system of
continuous improvement.

To order your copies, visit **corwin.com/leadership**

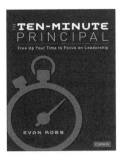